Slave Narratives of the underground railroad

Slave Narratives of the Underground Railroad

DOVER THRIFT EDITIONS

Edited by
Christine Rudisel
and
Bob Blaisdell

DOVER PUBLICATIONS
GARDEN CITY, NEW YORK

DOVER THRIFT EDITIONS

GENERAL EDITOR: MARY CAROLYN WALDREP
EDITOR OF THIS VOLUME: SUSAN L. RATTINER

Bibliographical Note

Slave Narratives of the Underground Railroad, first published by Dover Publications in 2014, is a new anthology, reprinted from standard sources. A new introductory Note has been specially prepared for this edition.

Library of Congress Cataloging-in-Publication Data

Slave narratives of the Underground Railroad / edited by Christine Rudisel and Bob Blaisdell.
   pages cm — (Dover thrift editions)
  Summary: "More than 100,000 people escaped slavery in the American South by following the Underground Railroad, a complex network of secret routes and safe houses. This inexpensive compilation of firsthand accounts offers authentic insights into the Civil War era and African-American history with compelling narratives by Frederick Douglass, Harriet Tubman, and lesser-known refugees"— Provided by publisher.
  Includes bibliographical references.
  ISBN-13: 978-0-486-78061-0 (paperback)
  ISBN-10: 0-486-78061-9 (paperback)
  1. Fugitive slaves—United States—Biography. 2. Underground Railroad—Sources. 3. Slaves—Southern States—Biography. 4. African Americans—Southern States—Biography. 5. Slavery—Southern States—History—19th century—Sources. 6. Slaves' writings, American. I. Rudisel, Christine. II. Blaisdell, Robert.
  E450.S585 2014
  973.7115092—dc23
  [B]
                                                                                    2014005072

Manufactured in the United States of America
78061912   2023
www.doverpublications.com

Contents

Alphabetically arranged by the last name of the primary subject; the author of the narrative, if *not* the subject, follows the title in brackets.

NOTE

No more driver's lash for me,
No more, no more,
No more driver's lash for me,
Many thousand gone.

— "No More Auction Block"

By the early 1840s, the act of African Americans fleeing slavery became known as the Underground Railroad. This term was after all only a metaphorical label that arrived with the advent of the real railroad that was transforming transportation over the vast continent. The Underground Railroad described not a public or private transportation system but the clandestine and illegalized impulse of slaves to flee from the American South by any means possible.[1] The term has become a way to organize our ideas about the political, legal, and physical challenges American slaves had to overcome to gain freedom in the nineteenth century, though slaves had been making escapes ever since they began arriving in the New World in the seventeenth century. Before the North or Canada became the symbolic "New Canaan," Spanish Florida welcomed runaway slaves. With the complete takeover of Florida by the United States after 1819, the path of freedom lay only northward. The most famous of escaped slaves, Frederick Douglass, recognized the slaves' quest for freedom not in terms of a system but of an individual soul's willingness to risk death to escape the legalized

---

1 "The Underground Railroad was neither underground nor a railroad but a multipronged attack on the system of chattel slavery carried out over a period of more than half a century," as John Michael Vlach defines it (in *Passages to Freedom: The Underground Railroad in History and Memory*. Edited by David W. Blight. Washington, D.C.: Smithsonian Books, 2004. 97).

immorality that America had imposed on nearly an eighth of its population. That is, the system of slavery was national, but the ways of escaping the system were personal, local, and intermittent—and, as Douglass pointed out, having helped others escape, the *number* of escapees (estimated at 70,000 to 100,000 from 1830 to 1860[2]) were only a drop in the bucket: "True, as a means of destroying slavery, [the Underground Railroad] was like an attempt to bail out the ocean with a teaspoon, but the thought that there was one less slave, and one more free-man…brought to my heart unspeakable joy."[3]

Yet to escape or to help someone escape slavery, which Harriet Jacobs called a "deep, and dark, and foul…pit of abominations,"[4] was a *criminal* offense. "While many sympathized with the slave in his chains," wrote the greatest historian of the Underground Railroad, William Still, "and freely wept over his destiny, or gave money to help buy his freedom, but few could be found who were willing to take the risk of going into the South, and standing face to face with Slavery, in order to conduct a panting slave to freedom. The undertaking was too fearful to think of in most cases. But there were instances when men and women too, moved by the love of freedom, would take their lives in their hands, beard the lion in his den, and nobly rescue the oppressed."[5] Those who acted on their belief in human liberty and in the words of the Declaration of Independence, "that all men are created equal," risked death, torture, return to slavery or prison. A slave who escaped was legally guilty of theft: stealing someone else's property.

There is no end to the outrage we can feel that the Founding Fathers of our country accepted slavery while demanding national liberty from Great Britain in the American Revolution in 1776 and then even embraced it in the disgusting compromises made in composing the Constitution in 1787. The famed British author Samuel

---

2 "Modern estimates of the number of fugitives assisted by the underground between 1830 and 1860 range from 70,000 to 100,000, of whom perhaps one-third or one-quarter were delivered to Canada," writes Fergus M. Bordewich in his *Bound for Canaan: The Underground Railroad and the War for the Soul of America.* New York: HarperCollins, 2005. 436.

3 Frederick Douglass. *The Life and Times of Frederick Douglass: Written by Himself.* Hartford, Connecticut: Park Publishing, 1882. 329.

4 Harriet Jacobs. *Incidents in the Life of a Slave Girl.* Mineola, New York: Dover Publications, 2001. 3. [Originally published in Boston in 1861.]

5 See William Still's account of Matilda Mahoney below, page 160.

Johnson mocked the Americans' demands for freedom while they continued enslaving hundreds of thousands of individuals for the crime of having dark skin and African ancestors: "How is it that we hear the loudest *yelps* for liberty among the drivers of negroes?"[6] Powerful American political and religious leaders vigorously justified slavery's necessity, further helping Americans to accustom themselves to the injustices of the system and to their contradictory impulses. When moral objections arose, these same leaders had no compunction or second thoughts about asserting slavery's *goodness*.

★

In this anthology of American history, we admire not the upholders of the laws but the "criminals": the courageous slaves who attempted escape and all those heroic individuals who helped them along. We respect the illegal, freedom-seeking actions of fugitives who risked capture and brutal punishments, such as whippings, branding, and the amputation of limbs, and the work of their abettors, men and women who risked fines, imprisonment, and violent, if not fatal, retaliation for their efforts. Slaves who decided to run usually believed that anything, even death, was an improvement over being perceived as chattel in a system that was, according to runaway Moses Wood, "no more justifiable than murder."[7] Fugitive slaves William and Ellen Craft were "willing to make any sacrifice, or to endure any amount of suffering"[8] to be free. Abolitionists remained true to their principles, regularly frustrating slave-owners, hampering slave-catchers, and imperiling themselves. William Still, a free African American who helped hundreds of fugitives through his work with the Vigilance Committee of Philadelphia, was so fearful of slaveholder vengeance that he hid the records of everyone he assisted and withheld names when he introduced abettors to the fugitives they were helping.

Seth Concklin, a brave Quaker abolitionist, lost his life for attempting to usher the family of William Still's brother to freedom. Concklin's chained, beaten, and lifeless body was found in the Ohio River. Levi

---

6 Samuel Johnson, "Taxation No Tyranny: An Answer to the Resolutions and Address of the American Congress" (London: T. Cadell, 1775).

7 See "Lew Jones, Oscar Payne, Mose Wood, Dave Diggs, Jack, Hen, and Bill Dade, and Joe Ball: Arrival from the Old Dominion: Nine Very Fine 'Articles'" below, page 150.

8 See William Still's account of William and Ellen Craft below, page 39.

Coffin and his wife, Quakers who fed, hid, clothed, and transported thousands of fugitives, were repeatedly threatened by slave-hunters and their sympathizers. In his *Reminiscences*, Coffin tells us, "These men often threatened to kill me, and at various times offered a reward for my head. I often received anonymous letters warning me that my store, pork-house, and dwelling would be burned to the ground, and one letter...informed me that a body of armed men were then on their way...to destroy the town."[9] He and his wife continued their anti-slavery efforts, believing they had God's approval and that "the work was its own reward."[10] Slave-owners offered $40,000 for the head of fugitive slave and Underground Railroad conductor Harriet Tubman, who led over three hundred fugitives to freedom. Wary of discovery and danger, Tubman threatened to shoot any passenger who considered turning back: "Then the revolver carried by this bold and daring pioneer, would come out, while pointing it at their heads she would say, 'Dead niggers tell no tales; you go on or die!'"[11] Similarly, fugitive slave and Underground Railroad conductor William Wells Brown was determined to do everything in his power "for the emancipation of his brethren yet in chains." He used his job on a steamboat to transport as many as five fugitives at a time over Lake Erie to Canada. Brown, too, embraced his criminal activity, for he understood what it meant to "walk, talk, eat and sleep as a man, and no one to stand over [him] with the blood-clotted cowhide."[12]

As the abolitionists of the North finally began making their voices heard in the 1830s—that is, explaining to their fellow Christians the revelation that slavery was wicked—they were wonderfully naïve that the slave-interests would agree. The abolitionists, consulting their consciences and their bibles, wondered how could anyone disagree that slaves were people, that slavery was evil, that slavery made slaveholders cruel, that an economy based on exploitation of human beings was wrong? But preachers North and South made believe that invoking God in slavery's name made one's actions godly, and slaveholders

---

9 Levi Coffin. *Reminiscences of Levi Coffin, the Reputed President of the Underground Railroad; Being a Brief History of the Labors of a Lifetime in Behalf of the Slave, with the Stories of Numerous Fugitives, Who Gained Their Freedom Through His Instrumentality, and Many Other Incidents*. Second edition. Cincinnati: Robert Clarke and Company, 1880. 116.

10 Coffin 117.

11 See Sarah Bradford's account of Harriet Tubman below, page 187.

12 See William Wells Brown's narrative below, page 14.

insisted they were doing a favor to those creatures they held in bondage! Although able to justify the system and their behavior, not a single one of slavery's advocates, even those most ardent in their belief of its divine justice, ever submitted himself to enslavement. We see, however, in countless instances (and a few in this anthology) the slaveholder's willingness to enslave his own children.

It is hard to think about cotton and Eli Whitney without wishing that his invention of the cotton gin had awaited a later day, as this advancement increased the number of enslaved men and women by more than 200 percent between 1790 and 1830.[13] In spite of the conscience of the majority of white Americans awakening to the immorality of slavery, politicians and slaveholders across the South and in Washington, D.C., worked like demons to insure that the ultimate exploitation of human beings could continue and spread. So dangerous was America's moral awakening that its politicians outlawed even the questioning of slavery's justice or the quoting of "all men are created equal" or the reading of literature that suggested the humanity of slaves. And there was absolute silence regarding the sexual abuse and exploitation of female slaves by their family-loving, God-fearing owners. The last straw for abolitionists was the Fugitive Slave Act of 1850, an outrageous law instituted by Congress requiring that any and all Americans actively participate in capturing fugitive slaves.[14] Although abolitionists countered with local laws to undermine the federal law, their anti-slavery activity was still considered criminal, and the escaped slaves they had assisted were devastated to learn they had not truly found freedom in the Northern states. Canada proved to be the closest refuge that ensured freedom and safety from recapture for escaped slaves. "The Underground Railroad was not the end of the journey from slavery to freedom,"

---

13 "From the 1830s until the onset of the Civil War, enslaved humans constituted the nation's second largest form of capital investment, exceeded only by investment in land itself. After 1810, when Eli Whitney's gin had opened vast new opportunities for planters to adapt slave labor to an important new commodity, cotton quickly replaced rice and tobacco as the South's most lucrative product.... In 1790 the nation's enslaved had numbered 600,000. By 1830 they counted for close to 2,000,000," writes James Brewer Stewart in "From Moral Suasion to Political Confrontation: American Abolitionists and the Problem of Resistance, 1831–1861" in *Passages to Freedom: The Underground Railroad in History and Memory*. Edited by David W. Blight. Washington, D.C.: Smithsonian Books, 2004. 71.

14 See the Appendix for the full text of this law.

writes Fergus Bordewich, "but the beginning. Paradoxically, it was in Canada that blacks became real Americans."[15]

★

> *Oh, de land I am bound for, Sweet Canaan's happy land,*
> *I am bound for, Sweet Canaan's happy land.*
> *... Oh, my brother, did you come for to help me?*
> *Pray, give me your right hand, your right hand.*
>
> —"SWEET CANAAN"

In Philadelphia, William Still, the son of slaves, believed in the power of narratives to create a sense of individual lives. He risked his life and position in giving refuge, encouragement, and material aid to escaping slaves. About half of the narratives we have included in this collection are ones he collected. As the secretary and chairman of the Vigilance Committee of Philadelphia and on the lookout for escaped slaves in need of help, he became fascinated by their astounding and terrifying stories. As a literate person, as a person of responsibility, he saw his job as helping the slaves get away and in preserving their stories not only for the world but for the escapees themselves as well (many of whom were illiterate). But the world would have to wait for the stories that testified to the men and women's courage and daring. The Fugitive Slave Act of 1850 meant Still was a serial criminal, and his stories of human beings and what they lived and suffered through were evidence of *his* hundreds of crimes. He collected and hid his stories of true crime for the days when slavery—and not truth—was illegal.[16]

Seven years after the end of the devastating Civil War, brought on by the South's determination to continue its reign of slavery by

---

15 Fergus M. Bordewich. *Bound for Canaan: The Underground Railroad and the War for the Soul of America.* New York: HarperCollins, 2005. 244.

16 "In publishing the collective testimony of individuals who would probably not otherwise have had the opportunity to contribute to the historical record," writes Ian Frederick Finseth, "Still provided a major corrective to the distorted image of African-Americans prevalent in American literary and popular culture. His compendium is a work not only of history, but of counter-history, one which challenges the already emergent story line of faded Southern glory and black incapacity for freedom—a work which revises the revisionists, so to speak." (William Still. *The Underground Railroad: Authentic Narratives and First-Hand Accounts.* Edited by Ian Frederick Finseth. Mineola, New York: Dover Publications, 2007. vii–viii.)

seceding from the United States, Still published hundreds of the stories. They are an assortment of amazing tales and matter-of-fact accounts. Some of them remain in the question and answer format in which he recorded them on the spot, and others are summaries of hasty stories he reconstituted in the peace and quiet of recollection. We have included some of the most famous and others deserving renewed attention that are revealing of particular strategies or the extraordinary characters of particular individuals. We have supplemented Still's work with excerpts from other great narratives recorded in autobiographies or memoirs of slaves and workers on the Underground Railroad, among them those by Frederick Douglass, Sojourner Truth, Harriet Tubman, and Levi Coffin.

In narrative after narrative, we read of human beings owning themselves, loving the idea of freedom more than fearing death. Unfortunately, the Underground Railroad was a path that few could even attempt to take. It was so difficult that we know more failed than succeeded and that even having succeeded, life in the North or Canada was challenging too, not least of all for the haunting thoughts of friends and family left behind. Harriet Jacobs, one of the most affecting narrators, describes her joy upon reaching the North: "The next morning I was on deck as soon as the day dawned. I called Fanny to see the sunrise, for the first time in our lives, on free soil; for such I *then* believed it to be. We watched the reddening sky, and saw the great orb come up slowly out of the water, as it seemed. Soon the waves began to sparkle, and every thing caught the beautiful glow. Before us lay the city of strangers. We looked at each other, and the eyes of both were moistened with tears. We had escaped from slavery, and we supposed ourselves to be safe from the hunters. But we were alone in the world, and we had left dear ties behind us; ties cruelly sundered by the demon Slavery."[17]

All of the subjects of the narratives are truly exceptional. Opportunity to escape was limited, and these were some of the fortunate few. Being sold "Down South," one of the threats slaves in the border states knew, was terrifying because Down South was further into the pit of Hell, where even the ability to contemplate the idea of the land of "Canaan" diminished. While we include several stories of

---

17 See Harriet Jacobs' account below, page 134.

women, the percentage of women who escaped, connected as they often were to children, was much less than that of men.[18]

We have retitled some of Still's selections to emphasize the names of the escaping slaves rather than Still's somewhat haphazard naming of the state from which the slaves escaped or the year of their escape and have arranged the narratives alphabetically. We have retained the spellings and punctuation of the original sources.

—CR/BB

18 "Eighty percent of these fugitives were young males in their teens and twenties who generally absconded alone," writes David Blight. "Indeed, in the later period, 95 percent fled alone. Young slave women were much less likely to run away because of their family and child-rearing responsibilities. Entire families with children did attempt flight to freedom, but such instances were rare." (*Passages to Freedom: The Underground Railroad in History and Memory*. Edited by David W. Blight. Washington, D.C.: Smithsonian Books, 2004. 243.)

HENRY BOX BROWN

Arrived by Adams' Express

[William Still]

Henry Box Brown escaped from his owner by having Samuel A. Smith ship him to a member of Philadelphia's Vigilance Committee in a box that was nailed shut and secured with hickory hoops. Brown arrived safely, but Smith was arrested and imprisoned when he attempted to help two other slaves escape in the same manner.

ALTHOUGH THE NAME of Henry Box Brown has been echoed over the land for a number of years, and the simple facts connected with his marvelous escape from slavery in a box published widely through the medium of anti-slavery papers, nevertheless it is not unreasonable to suppose that very little is generally known in relation to this case.

Briefly, the facts are these, which doubtless have never before been fully published—

Brown was a man of invention as well as a hero. In point of interest, however, his case is no more remarkable than many others. Indeed, neither before nor after escaping did he suffer one-half what many others have experienced. He was decidedly an unhappy piece of property in the city of Richmond, Va. In the condition of a slave he felt that it would be impossible for him to remain. Full well did he know, however, that it was no holiday task to escape the vigilance of Virginia slave-hunters, or the wrath of an enraged master for committing the unpardonable sin of attempting to escape to a land of liberty. So Brown counted well the cost before venturing upon this hazardous undertaking. Ordinary modes of travel he concluded might prove disastrous to his hopes; he, therefore, hit upon a new invention altogether, which was to have himself boxed up and forwarded to Philadelphia direct by express. The size of the box and how it was to be made to fit him most comfortably, was of his own ordering. Two feet eight inches deep, two feet wide, and three feet long were the exact dimensions of the box, lined with baize. His resources with regard to food and water consisted of the following: One bladder of water and a few small biscuits. His mechanical implement to meet the death-struggle for fresh air, all told, was one large gimlet. Satisfied that it would be far better to peril his life for freedom in this way than to remain under the galling yoke of Slavery, he entered his box, which was safely nailed up and hooped with five hickory hoops, and was then addressed by his next friend, James A. Smith, a shoe dealer, to Wm. H. Johnson, Arch street, Philadelphia, marked, "This side up with care." In this condition he was sent to Adams' Express office in a dray, and thence by overland express to Philadelphia. It was twenty-six hours from the time he left Richmond until his arrival in the City of Brotherly Love. The notice, "This side up, &c.," did not avail with the different expressmen, who hesitated not to handle the box in the usual rough manner common to this class of men. For a while they actually had the box upside down, and had him on his head for miles. A few days before he was expected, certain intimation was conveyed to a member of the Vigilance Committee that a box might be expected by the three o'clock morning train from the South, which might contain a man. One of the most serious walks he ever took and they had not been a few to meet and accompany passengers, he took at half past two o'clock that morning to the depot. Not once, but for more than a score of times, he fancied the slave would be dead. He anxiously looked while the freight was being unloaded from the cars, to see if he could recognize a box that might contain a man; one alone had that appearance, and he confessed it really seemed as if there was the scent of death about it. But on inquiry, he soon learned that it was not the one he was looking after, and he was free to say he experienced a marked sense of relief. That same afternoon, however, he received from Richmond a telegram, which read thus, "Your case of goods is shipped and will arrive to-morrow morning."

At this exciting juncture of affairs, Mr. McKim, who had been engineering this important undertaking, deemed it expedient to change the programme slightly in one particular at least to insure greater safety. Instead of having a member of the Committee go again to the depot for the box, which might excite suspicion, it was decided that it would be safest to have the express bring it direct to the Anti-Slavery Office.

But all apprehension of danger did not now disappear, for there was no room to suppose that Adams' Express office had any sympathy with the abolitionist or the fugitive, consequently for Mr. McKim to appear personally at the express office to give directions with reference to the coming of a box from Richmond which would be directed to Arch street, and yet not intended for that street, but for the Anti-Slavery office at 107 North Fifth street, it needed of course no great discernment to foresee that a step of this kind was wholly impracticable and that a more indirect and covert method would have to be adopted. In this dreadful crisis Mr. McKim, with his usual good judgment and remarkably quick, strategical mind, especially in matters pertaining to the U. G. R. R., hit upon the following plan, namely, to go to his friend, E. M. Davis,[1] who was then extensively engaged in mercantile business, and relate the circumstances. Having daily intercourse with said Adams' Express office, and being well acquainted with the firm and some of the drivers, Mr. Davis could, as Mr. McKim thought, talk about "boxes, freight, etc.," from any part of the country without risk. Mr. Davis heard Mr. McKim's plan and instantly approved of it, and was heartily at his service.

"Dan, an Irishman, one of Adams' Express drivers, is just the fellow to go to the depot after the box," said Davis. "He drinks a little too much whiskey sometimes, but he will do anything I ask him to do, promptly and obligingly. I'll trust Dan, for I believe he is the very man." The difficulty which Mr. McKim had been so anxious to overcome was thus pretty well settled. It was agreed that Dan should go after the box next morning before daylight and bring it to the Anti-Slavery office direct, and to make it all the more agreeable for Dan to get up out of his warm bed and go on this errand before day, it was decided that he should have a five dollar gold piece for himself. Thus these preliminaries having been satisfactorily arranged, it only remained for Mr. Davis to see Dan and give him instructions accordingly, etc.

Next morning, according to arrangement, the box was at the Anti-Slavery office in due time. The witnesses present to behold the

---

1 E. M. Davis was a member of the Executive Committee of the Pennsylvania Anti-Slavery Society and a long-tried Abolitionist, son-in-law of James and Lucretia Mott. [Note by William Still.]

resurrection were J. M. McKim, Professor C. D. Cleveland, Lewis Thompson, and the writer.

Mr. McKim was deeply interested; but having been long identified with the Anti-Slavery cause as one of its oldest and ablest advocates in the darkest days of slavery and mobs, and always found by the side of the fugitive to counsel and succor, he was on this occasion perfectly composed.

Professor Cleveland, however, was greatly moved. His zeal and earnestness in the cause of freedom, especially in rendering aid to passengers, knew no limit. Ordinarily he could not too often visit these travelers, shake them too warmly by the hand, or impart to them too freely of his substance to aid them on their journey. But now his emotion was overpowering.

Mr. Thompson, of the firm of Merrihew & Thompson—about the only printers in the city who for many years dared to print such incendiary documents as anti-slavery papers and pamphlets—one of the truest friends of the slave, was composed and prepared to witness the scene.

All was quiet. The door had been safely locked. The proceedings commenced. Mr. McKim rapped quietly on the lid of the box and called out, "All right!" Instantly came the answer from within. "All right, sir!"

The witnesses will never forget that moment. Saw and hatchet quickly had the five hickory hoops cut and the lid off, and the marvellous resurrection of Brown ensued. Rising up in his box, he reached out his hand, saying, "How do you do, gentlemen?" The little assemblage hardly knew what to think or do at the moment. He was about as wet as if he had come up out of the Delaware. Very soon he remarked that, before leaving Richmond he had selected for his arrival-hymn (if he lived) the Psalm beginning with these words: *"I waited patiently for the Lord, and He heard my prayer."* And most touchingly did he sing the psalm, much to his own relief, as well as to the delight of his small audience.

He was then christened Henry Box Brown, and soon afterwards was sent to the hospitable residence of James Mott and E. M. Davis, on Ninth street, where, it is needless to say, he met a most cordial reception from Mrs. Lucretia Mott and her household. Clothing and creature comforts were furnished in abundance, and delight and joy filled all hearts in that stronghold of philanthropy.

As he had been so long doubled up in the box he needed to promenade considerably in the fresh air, so James Mott put one of his broad-brim hats on his head and tendered him the hospitalities of his yard as well as his house, and while Brown promenaded the yard flushed with victory, great was the joy of his friends.

After his visit at Mr. Mott's, he spent two days with the writer, and then took his departure for Boston, evidently feeling quite conscious of the wonderful feat he had performed, and at the same time it may be safely said that those who witnessed this strange resurrection were not only elated at his success, but were made to sympathize more deeply than ever before with the slave. Also the noble-hearted Smith who boxed him up was made to rejoice over Brown's victory, and was thereby encouraged to render similar service to two other young bondmen, who appealed to him for deliverance. But, unfortunately, in this attempt the undertaking proved a failure. Two boxes containing the young men alluded to above, after having been duly expressed and some distance on the road, were, through the agency of the telegraph, betrayed, and the heroic young fugitives were captured in their boxes and dragged back to hopeless bondage. Consequently, through this deplorable failure, Samuel A. Smith was arrested, imprisoned, and was called upon to suffer severely, as may be seen from the subjoined correspondence, taken from the *New York Tribune* soon after his release from the penitentiary.

THE DELIVERER OF BOX BROWN—MEETING OF THE COLORED CITIZENS OF PHILADELPHIA

[Correspondence of the N.Y. Tribune.]

PHILADELPHIA, SATURDAY, JULY 5, 1856.

SAMUEL A. SMITH, who boxed up Henry Box Brown in Richmond, Va., and forwarded him by overland express to Philadelphia, and who was arrested and convicted, eight years ago, for boxing up two other slaves, also directed to Philadelphia, having served out his imprisonment in the Penitentiary, was released on the 18th ultimo, and arrived in this city on the 21st.

Though he lost all his property; though he was refused witnesses on his trial (no officer could be found, who would serve a summons on a witness); though for five long months, in hot weather, he was kept heavily chained in a cell four by eight feet in dimensions; though he received five dreadful stabs, aimed at his heart, by a bribed assassin, nevertheless he still rejoices in the motives which prompted him to "undo the heavy burdens, and let the oppressed go free." Having resided nearly all his life in the South, where he had traveled and seen much of the "peculiar institution," and had witnessed the most horrid enormities inflicted upon the slave, whose cries were ever ringing in his ears, and for whom he had the warmest sympathy, Mr. Smith could not refrain from believing that the black man, as well as the white, had God-given rights. Consequently, he was not accustomed to shed tears when a poor creature escaped from his "kind master;" nor was he willing to turn a deaf ear to his appeals and groans, when he knew he was thirsting for freedom. From 1828 up to the day he was incarcerated, many had sought his aid and counsel, nor had they sought in vain. In various places he operated with success. In Richmond, however, it seemed expedient to invent a new plan for certain emergencies, hence the Box and Express plan was devised, at the instance of a few heroic slaves, who had manifested their willingness to die in a box, on the road to liberty, rather than continue longer under the yoke. But these heroes fell into the power of their enemies. Mr. Smith had not been long in the Penitentiary before he had fully gained the esteem and confidence of the Superintendent and other officers. Finding him to be humane and generous-hearted—showing kindness toward all, especially in buying bread, &c., for the starving prisoners, and by a timely note of warning, which had saved the life of one of the keepers, for whose destruction a bold plot had been arranged—the officers felt disposed to show him such favors as the law would allow. But their good intentions were soon frustrated. The Inquisition (commonly called the Legislature), being in session in Richmond, hearing that the Superintendent had been speaking well of Smith, and circulating a petition for his pardon, indignantly demanded to know if the rumor was well founded. Two weeks were spent by the Inquisition, and many witnesses were placed upon oath, to solemnly testify in the matter. One of the keepers swore that his life had been saved by Smith. Col. Morgan, the Superintendent, frequently testified in writing and verbally to Smith's good deportment; acknowledging that he had circulated petitions, &c.; and took the position, that he sincerely believed, that it would be to the interest of the institution to pardon him; calling the attention of the Inquisition, at the same time, to the fact, that not unfrequently pardons had been granted to criminals, under sentence of death, for the most cold-blooded murder, to say nothing of other gross crimes. The effort for pardon was soon abandoned, for the following reason given by the Governor: "I can't, and I won't pardon him!"

In view of the unparalleled injustice which Mr. S. had suffered, as well as on account of the aid he had rendered to the slaves, on his arrival in this city the colored citizens of Philadelphia felt that he was entitled to sympathy and aid, and straightway invited him to remain a few days, until arrangements could be made for a mass meeting to receive him. Accordingly, on last Monday evening, a mass meeting convened in the Israel church, and the Rev. Wm. T. Catto was called to the chair, and Wm. Still was appointed secretary. The chairman briefly stated the object of the meeting. Having lived in the South, he claimed to know something of the workings of the oppressive system of slavery generally, and declared that, notwithstanding the many exposures of the evil which came under his own observation, the most vivid descriptions fell far short of the realities his own eyes had witnessed. He then introduced Mr. Smith, who arose and in a plain manner briefly told his story, assuring the audience that he had always hated slavery, and had taken great pleasure in helping many out of it, and though he had suffered much physically and pecuniarily for the cause's sake, yet he murmured not, but rejoiced in what he had done. After taking his seat, addresses were made by the Rev. S. Smith, Messrs. Kinnard, Brunner, Bradway, and others. The following preamble and resolutions were adopted—

WHEREAS, We, the colored citizens of Philadelphia, have among us Samuel A. Smith, who was incarcerated over seven years in the Richmond Penitentiary, for doing an act that was honorable to his feelings and his sense of justice and humanity, therefore,

Resolved, That we welcome him to this city as a martyr to the cause of Freedom.

Resolved, That we heartily tender him our gratitude for the good he has done to our suffering race.

Resolved, That we sympathize with him in his losses and sufferings in the cause of the poor, down-trodden slave.

W.S.

During his stay in Philadelphia, on this occasion, he stopped for about a fortnight with the writer, and it was most gratifying to learn from him that he was no new worker on the U. G. R. R. But that he had long hated slavery thoroughly, and although surrounded with perils on every side, he had not failed to help a poor slave whenever the opportunity was presented.

Pecuniary aid, to some extent, was rendered him in this city, for which he was grateful, and after being united in marriage, by Wm.

H. Furness, D.D., to a lady who had remained faithful to him through all his sore trials and sufferings, he took his departure for Western New York, with a good conscience and an unshaken faith in the belief that in aiding his fellow-man to freedom he had but simply obeyed the word of Him who taught man to do unto others as he would be done by.

SOURCE: William Still. *The Underground Rail Road: A Record of Facts, Authentic Narratives, Letters &c., Narrating the Hardships, Hair-breadth Escapes and Death Struggles of the Slaves in Their Efforts for Freedom, as Related by Themselves and Others, or Witnessed by the Author; Together with Sketches of Some of the Largest Stockholders, and Most Liberal Aiders and Advisers of the Road.* Philadelphia: Porter and Coates, 1872.

WILLIAM WELLS BROWN

Narrative of William Wells Brown, a Fugitive Slave (excerpts)

Brown escaped from slavery while working on his owner's boat as a steward. When the boat arrived in Ohio, Brown fled the ship, hid in the woods, and traveled North by night. When the weather and his health forced him to trust someone other than himself, he allowed a Quaker named Wells Brown to help him. Brown's immense gratitude for the care he received from this man is clear. In the dedication to his autobiography, he states: "I came to your door, a weary fugitive. ... I was a stranger, and you took me in ... Even a name by which to be known among men, slavery had denied me. You bestowed upon me your own. Base indeed should I be, if I ever forget what I owe you, or do anything to disgrace that honored name!"[1] Fed, clothed, returned to health, and given money, Brown left the abode of his "first white friend" and continued his journey northward (see below, p. 15). His job on a Lake Erie steamboat marked the beginning of his work as a conductor for the Underground Railroad, for it was during this time that Brown transported scores of fugitives to Canada. His struggle against slavery continued for years and influenced his development as an abolitionist lecturer, writer, and historian.

1 William Wells Brown. *Narrative of William Wells Brown, a Fugitive Slave.* Boston: The Anti-Slavery Office, 1847. iii.

CHAPTER XII

CAPTAIN PRICE purchased me in the month of October, and I remained with him until December, when the family made a voyage to New Orleans, in a boat owned by himself, and named the "Chester." I served on board, as one of the stewards. On arriving at New Orleans, about the middle of the month, the boat took in freight for Cincinnati; and it was decided that the family should go up the river in her, and what was of more interest to me, I was to accompany them.

The long looked for opportunity to make my escape from slavery was near at hand.

Captain Price had some fears as to the propriety of taking me near a free State, or a place where it was likely I could run away, with a prospect of liberty. He asked me if I had ever been in a free State. "Oh yes," said I, "I have been in Ohio; my master carried me into that State once, but I never liked a free State."

It was soon decided that it would be safe to take me with them, and what made it more safe, Eliza was on the boat with us, and Mrs. Price, to try me, asked if I thought as much as ever of Eliza [a fellow slave, to whom the Prices had meant to attach Wells]. I told her that Eliza was very dear to me indeed, and that nothing but death should part us. It was the same as if we were married. This had the desired effect. The boat left New Orleans, and proceeded up the river.

I had at different times obtained little sums of money, which I had reserved for a "rainy day." I procured some cotton cloth, and made me a bag to carry provisions in. The trials of the past were all lost in hopes for the future. The love of liberty, that had been burning in my bosom for years, and had been well nigh extinguished, was now resuscitated. At night, when all around was peaceful, I would walk the decks, meditating upon my happy prospects.

I should have stated, that before leaving St. Louis, I went to an old man named Frank, a slave, owned by a Mr. Sarpee. This old man was very distinguished (not only among the slave population, but also the whites) as a fortune-teller. He was about seventy years of age, something over six feet high, and very slender. Indeed, he was so small around his body that it looked as though it was not strong enough to hold up his head.

Uncle Frank was a very great favorite with the young ladies, who would go to him in great numbers to get their fortunes told. And it was generally believed that he could really penetrate into the mysteries of futurity. Whether true or not, he had the name, and that is about half of what one needs in this gullible age. I found Uncle Frank seated in the chimney corner, about ten o'clock at night. As soon as I entered, the old man left his seat. I watched his movement as well as I could by the dim light of the fire. He soon lit a lamp, and coming up, looked me full in the face, saying, "Well, my son, you have come to get uncle to tell your fortune, have you?" "Yes," said I. But how the old man should know what I had come for, I could not tell. However, I paid the fee of twenty-five cents, and he commenced by looking into a gourd, filled with water. Whether the old man was a prophet, or the son of a prophet, I cannot say; but there is one thing certain, many of his predictions were verified.

I am no believer in soothsaying; yet I am sometimes at a loss to know how Uncle Frank could tell so accurately what would occur in the future. Among the many things he told was one which was enough to pay me for all the trouble of hunting him up. It was that I should be free! He further said, that in trying to get my liberty, I would meet with many severe trials. I thought to myself, any fool could tell me that!

The first place in which we landed in a free State was Cairo, a small village at the mouth of the Ohio river. We remained here but a few hours, when we proceeded to Louisville. After unloading some of the cargo, the boat started on her upward trip. The next day was the first of January. I had looked forward to New Year's day as the commencement of a new era in the history of my life. I had decided upon leaving the peculiar institution that day.

During the last night that I served in slavery, I did not close my eyes a single moment. When not thinking of the future, my mind dwelt on the past. The love of a dear mother, a dear sister, and three dear brothers, yet living, caused me to shed many tears. If I could only have been assured of their being dead, I should have felt satisfied; but I imagined I saw my dear mother in the cotton-field, followed by a merciless taskmaster, and no one to speak a consoling word to her! I beheld my dear sister in the hands of a slave-driver, and compelled to submit to his cruelty! None but one placed in such a situation can for a moment imagine the intense agony to which these reflections subjected me.

CHAPTER XIII

At last the time for action arrived. The boat landed at a point which appeared to me the place of all others to start from. I found that it would be impossible to carry anything with me, but what was upon my person. I had some provisions, and a single suit of clothes, about half worn. When the boat was discharging her cargo, and the passengers engaged carrying their baggage on and off shore, I improved the opportunity to convey myself with my little effects on land. Taking up a trunk, I went up the wharf, and was soon out of the crowd. I made directly for the woods, where I remained until night, knowing well that I could not travel, even in the State of Ohio, during the day, without danger of being arrested.

I had long since made up my mind that I would not trust myself in the hands of any man, white or colored. The slave is brought up to look upon every white man as an enemy to him and his race; and twenty-one years in slavery had taught me that there were traitors, even among colored people. After dark, I emerged from the woods into a narrow path, which led me into the main travelled road. But I knew not which way to go. I did not know North from South, East from West. I looked in vain for the North Star; a heavy cloud hid it from my view. I walked up and down the road until near midnight, when the clouds disappeared, and I welcomed the sight of my friend,—truly the slave's friend,—the North Star!

As soon as I saw it, I knew my course, and before daylight I travelled twenty or twenty-five miles. It being in the winter, I suffered intensely from the cold; being without an overcoat, and my other clothes rather thin for the season. I was provided with a tinderbox, so that I could make up a fire when necessary. And but for this, I should certainly have frozen to death; for I was determined not to go to any house for shelter. I knew of a man belonging to Gen. Ashly, of St. Louis, who had run away near Cincinnati, on the way to Washington, but had been caught and carried back into slavery; and I felt that a similar fate awaited me, should I be seen by any one. I travelled at night, and lay by during the day.

On the fourth day, my provisions gave out, and then what to do I could not tell. Have something to eat, I must; but how to get it was the question! On the first night after my food was gone, I went to a barn on the road-side, and there found some ears of corn. I took ten or twelve of them, and kept on my journey. During the next day, while in the woods, I roasted my corn and feasted upon it, thanking God that I was so well provided for.

My escape to a land of freedom now appeared certain, and the prospects of the future occupied a great part of my thoughts. What should be my occupation, was a subject of much anxiety to me; and the next thing what should be my name? I have before stated that my old master, Dr. Young, had no children of his own, but had with him a nephew, the son of his brother, Benjamin Young. When this boy was brought to Doctor Young, his name being William, the same as mine, my mother was ordered to change mine to something else. This, at the time, I thought to be one of the most cruel acts that could be committed upon my rights; and I received several very severe whippings for telling people that my name was William, after orders were given to change it. Though young, I was old enough to place a high appreciation upon my name. It was decided, however, to call me "Sandford," and this name I was known by, not only upon my master's plantation, but up to the time that I made my escape. I was sold under the name of Sandford.

But as soon as the subject came to my mind, I resolved on adopting my old name of William, and let Sandford go by the board, for I always hated it. Not because there was anything peculiar in the name; but because it had been forced upon me. It is sometimes common at the south, for slaves to take the name of their masters. Some have a legitimate right to do so. But I always detested the idea of being called by the name of either of my masters. And as for my father, I would rather have adopted the name of "Friday," and been known as the servant of some Robinson Crusoe, than to have taken his name. So I was not only hunting for my liberty, but also hunting for a name; though I regarded the latter as of little consequence, if I could but gain the former. Travelling along the road, I would sometimes speak to myself, sounding my name over, by way of getting used to it, before I should arrive among civilized human beings. On the fifth or sixth day, it rained very fast, and it froze about as fast as it fell, so that my clothes were one glare of ice. I travelled on at night until I became so chilled and benumbed—the wind blowing into my face—that I found it impossible to go any further, and accordingly took shelter in a barn, where I was obliged to walk about to keep from freezing.

I have ever looked upon that night as the most eventful part of my escape from slavery. Nothing but the providence of God, and that old barn, saved me from freezing to death. I received a very severe cold, which settled upon my lungs, and from time to time my feet had been frost-bitten, so that it was with difficulty I could walk. In this situation I travelled two days, when I found that I must seek shelter somewhere, or die.

The thought of death was nothing frightful to me, compared with that of being caught, and again carried back into slavery. Nothing but the prospect of enjoying liberty could have induced me to undergo such trials, for

> *"Behind I left the whips and chains,*
> *Before me were sweet Freedom's plains!"*

This, and this alone, cheered me onward. But I at last resolved to seek protection from the inclemency of the weather, and therefore I secured myself behind some logs and brush, intending to wait there until some one should pass by; for I thought it probable that I might see some colored person, or, if not, some one who was not a slaveholder; for I had an idea that I should know a slaveholder as far as I could see him.

CHAPTER XIV

The first person that passed was a man in a buggy-wagon. He looked too genteel for me to hail him. Very soon, another passed by on horse-back. I attempted speaking to him, but fear made my voice fail me. As he passed, I left my hiding-place, and was approaching the road, when I observed an old man walking towards me, leading a white horse. He had on a broad-brimmed hat and a very long coat, and was evidently walking for exercise. As soon as I saw him, and observed his dress, I thought to myself, "You are the man that I have been looking for!" Nor was I mistaken. He was the very man!

On approaching me, he asked me, "if I was not a slave." I looked at him some time, and then asked him "if he knew of any one who would help me, as I was sick." He answered that he would; but again asked, if I was not a slave. I told him I was. He then said that I was in a very pro-slavery neighborhood, and if I would wait until he went home, he would get a covered wagon for me. I promised to remain. He mounted his horse, and was soon out of sight.

After he was gone, I meditated whether to wait or not; being apprehensive that he had gone for some one to arrest me. But I finally concluded to remain until he should return; removing some few rods to watch his movements. After a suspense of an hour and a half or more, he returned with a two horse covered-wagon, such as are usually seen under the shed of a Quaker meeting-house on Sundays and Thursdays; for the old man proved to be a Quaker of the George Fox stamp.

He took me to his house, but it was some time before I could be induced to enter it; not until the old lady came out, did I venture into the house. I thought I saw something in the old lady's cap that told me I was not only safe, but welcome, in her house. I was not, however, prepared to receive their hospitalities. The only fault I found with them was their being too kind. I had never had a white man to treat me as an equal, and the idea of a white lady waiting on me at the table was still worse! Though the table was loaded with the good things of this life, I could not eat. I thought if I could only be allowed the privilege of eating in the kitchen, I should be more than satisfied!

Finding that I could not eat, the old lady, who was a "Thompsonian," made me a cup of "composition," or "number six;" but it was so strong and hot, that I called it "number seven!" However, I soon found myself at home in this family. On different occasions, when telling these facts, I have been asked how I felt upon finding myself regarded as a man by a white family; especially just having run away from one. I cannot say that I have ever answered the question yet.

The fact that I was in all probability a freeman, sounded in my ears like a charm. I am satisfied that none but a slave could place such an appreciation upon liberty as I did at that time. I wanted to see mother and sister, that I might tell them "I was free!" I wanted to see my fellow slaves in St. Louis, and let them know that the chains were no longer upon my limbs. I wanted to see Captain Price, and let him learn from my own lips that I was no more a chattel, but a man! I was anxious, too, thus to inform Mrs. Price that she must get another coachman. And I wanted to see Eliza more than I did either Mr. or Mrs. Price!

The fact that I was a freeman—could walk, talk, eat and sleep as a man, and no one to stand over me with the blood-clotted cowhide— all this made me feel that I was not myself.

The kind friend that had taken me in was named Wells Brown. He was a devoted friend of the slave; but was very old, and not in the enjoyment of good health. After being by the fire awhile, I found that my feet had been very much frozen. I was seized with a fever which threatened to confine me to my bed. But my Thompsonian friends soon raised me, treating me as kindly as if I had been one of their own children. I remained with them twelve or fifteen days, during which time they made me some clothing, and the old gentleman purchased me a pair of boots.

I found that I was about fifty or sixty miles from Dayton, in the State of Ohio, and between one and two hundred miles from Cleveland, on Lake Erie, a place I was desirous of reaching on my way to Canada. This I know will sound strangely to the ears of people in foreign lands, but it is nevertheless true. An American citizen was fleeing from a Democratic, Republican, Christian government, to receive protection under the monarchy of Great Britain. While the people of the United States boast of their freedom, they at the same time keep three millions of their own citizens in chains; and while I am seated here in sight of Bunker Hill Monument, writing this narrative, I am a slave, and no law, not even in Massachusetts, can protect me from the hands of the slaveholder!

Before leaving this good Quaker friend, he inquired what my name was besides William. I told him that I had no other name. "Well," said he, "thee must have another name. Since thee has got out of slavery, thee has become a man, and men always have two names."

I told him that he was the first man to extend the hand of friendship to me, and I would give him the privilege of naming me.

"If I name thee," said he, "I shall call thee Wells Brown, after myself."

"But," said I, "I am not willing to lose my name of William. As it was taken from me once against my will, I am not willing to part with it again upon any terms."

"Then," said he, "I will call thee William Wells Brown."

"So be it," said I; and I have been known by that name ever since I left the house of my first white friend, Wells Brown.

After giving me some little change, I again started for Canada. In four days I reached a public house, and went in to warm myself. I there learned that some fugitive slaves had just passed through the place. The men in the bar-room were talking about it, and I thought that it must have been myself they referred to, and I was therefore afraid to start, fearing they would seize me; but I finally mustered courage enough, and took my leave. As soon as I was out of sight, I went into the woods, and remained there until night, when I again regained the road, and travelled on until the next day.

Not having had any food for nearly two days, I was faint with hunger, and was in a dilemma what to do, as the little cash supplied me by my adopted father, and which had contributed to my comfort, was now all gone. I however concluded to go to a farm-house, and ask for something to eat. On approaching the door of the first one presenting itself, I knocked, and was soon met by a man who asked me what I wanted. I told him that I would like something to eat. He asked where I was from, and where I was going. I replied that I had come some way, and was going to Cleveland.

After hesitating a moment or two, he told me that he could give me nothing to eat, adding, "that if I would work, I could get something to eat."

I felt bad, being thus refused something to sustain nature, but did not dare tell him that I was a slave.

Just as I was leaving the door, with a heavy heart, a woman, who proved to be the wife of this gentleman, came to the door, and asked her husband what I wanted? He did not seem inclined to inform her. She therefore asked me herself. I told her that I had asked for something to eat. After a few other questions, she told me to come in, and that she would give me something to eat.

I walked up to the door, but the husband remained in the passage, as if unwilling to let me enter.

She asked him two or three times to get out of the way, and let me in. But as he did not move, she pushed him on one side, bidding me walk in! I was never before so glad to see a woman push a man aside! Ever since that act, I have been in favor of "woman's rights!"

After giving me as much food as I could eat, she presented me with ten cents, all the money then at her disposal, accompanied with a note to a friend, a few miles further on the road. Thanking this angel of mercy from an overflowing heart, I pushed on my way, and in three days arrived at Cleveland, Ohio.

Being an entire stranger in this place, it was difficult for me to find where to stop. I had no money, and the lake being frozen, I saw that I must remain until the opening of navigation, or go to Canada by way of Buffalo. But believing myself to be somewhat out of danger, I secured an engagement at the Mansion House, as a table waiter, in payment for my board. The proprietor, however, whose name was E. M. Segur, in a short time, hired me for twelve dollars per month; on which terms I remained until spring, when I found good employment on board a lake steamboat.

I purchased some books, and at leisure moments perused them with considerable advantage to myself. While at Cleveland, I saw, for the first time, an anti-slavery newspaper. It was the *Genius of Universal Emancipation*, published by Benjamin Lundy, and though I had no home, I subscribed for the paper. It was my great desire, being out of slavery myself, to do what I could for the emancipation of my brethren yet in chains, and while on Lake Erie, I found many opportunities of "helping their cause along."

It is well known, that a great number of fugitives make their escape to Canada, by way of Cleveland; and while on the lake, I always made arrangement to carry them on the boat to Buffalo or Detroit, and thus effect their escape to the "promised land." The friends of the slave, knowing that I would transport them without charge, never failed to have a delegation when the boat arrived at Cleveland. I have sometimes had four or five on board, at one time.

In the year 1842, I conveyed, from the first of May to the first of December, sixty-nine fugitives over Lake Erie to Canada. In 1843, I visited Malden, in Upper Canada, and counted seventeen, in that small village, who owed their escape to my humble efforts.

Soon after coming North, I subscribed for the *Liberator*, edited by that champion of freedom, William Lloyd Garrison. I labored a season to promote the temperance cause among the colored people, but for the last three years, have been pleading for the victims of American slavery.

SOURCE: William Wells Brown. *Narrative of William Wells Brown, a Fugitive Slave*. Boston: The Anti-Slavery Office, 1847.

JAMES HAMBLETON CHRISTIAN

Ex-President Tyler's Household Loses an Aristocratic "Article"

[William Still]

James Hambleton Christian was the slave of former President John Tyler. Christian was treated well by his owners, but his status as a slave prevented him from marrying the woman he loved. The "luxuries" he abandoned when he escaped "were nothing to be compared with the blessings of liberty and a free wife in Canada."

JAMES HAMBLETON CHRISTIAN is a remarkable specimen of the "well fed, &c." In talking with him relative to his life as a slave, he said very promptly, "I have always been treated well; if I only have half as good times in the North as I have had in the South, I shall be perfectly satisfied. Any time I desired spending money, five or ten dollars were no object." At times, James had borrowed of his master, one, two, and three hundred dollars, to loan out to some of his friends. With regard to apparel and jewelry, he had worn the best, as an every-day adornment. With regard to food also, he had fared as well as heart could wish, with abundance of leisure time at his command. His deportment was certainly very refined and gentlemanly. About fifty per cent of Anglo-Saxon blood was visible in his features and his hair, which gave him no inconsiderable claim to sympathy and care. He had been to William and Mary's College in his younger days, to wait on young master James B. C., where, through the kindness of some of the students he had picked up a trifling amount of book learning. To be brief, this man was born the slave of old Major Christian, on the Glen Plantation, Charles City county, Va. The Christians were wealthy and owned many slaves, and belonged in reality to the F. F. Vs.[1] On the death of the old Major, James fell into the hands of his son, Judge Christian, who was executor to his father's estate. Subsequently he fell into the hands of one of the Judge's sisters, Mrs. John Tyler (wife of Ex-President Tyler), and then he became a member of the President's domestic household, was at the White House, under the President, from 1841 to 1845. Though but very young at that time, James was only fit for training in the arts, science, and mystery of waiting, in which profession, much pains were taken to qualify him completely for his calling. After a lapse of time, his mistress died. According to her request, after this event, James and his old mother were handed over to her nephew, William H. Christian, Esq., a merchant of Richmond. From this gentleman, James had the folly to flee. Passing hurriedly over interesting details, received from him respecting his remarkable history, two or three more incidents too good to omit must suffice.

"How did you like Mr. Tyler?" said an inquisitive member of the Vigilance Committee. "I didn't like Mr. Tyler much," was the reply. "Why?" again inquired the member of the Committee. "Because Mr. Tyler was a poor man. I never did like poor people. I didn't like his marrying into our family, who were considered very far Tyler's superiors." "On the plantation," he said, "Tyler was a very cross man, and treated the servants very cruelly; but the house servants were treated much better, owing to their having belonged to his wife, who protected them from persecution, as they had been favorite servants in her father's family." James estimated that "Tyler got about thirty-five thousand dollars and twenty-nine slaves, young and old, by his wife."

---

1 First Families of Virginia.

What prompted James to leave such pleasant quarters? It was this: He had become enamored of a young and respectable free girl in Richmond, with whom he could not be united in marriage solely because he was a slave, and did not own himself. The frequent sad separations of such married couples (where one or the other was a slave) could not be overlooked; consequently, the poor fellow concluded that he would stand a better chance of gaining his object in Canada than by remaining in Virginia. So he began to feel that he might himself be sold some day, and thus the resolution came home to him very forcibly to make tracks for Canada.

In speaking of the good treatment he had always met with, a member of the Committee remarked, "You must be akin to some one of your master's family?" To which he replied, "I am Christian's son." Unquestionably this passenger was one of that happy class so commonly referred to by apologists for the "Patriarchal Institution." The Committee, feeling a deep interest in his story, and desiring great success to him in his Underground efforts to get rid of slavery, and at the same time possess himself of his affianced, made him heartily welcome, feeling assured that the struggles and hardships he had submitted to in escaping, as well as the luxuries he was leaving behind, were nothing to be compared with the blessings of liberty and a free wife in Canada.

SOURCE: William Still, 1872 (see the Bibliography on p. 203 for complete information).

THEOPHILUS COLLINS

Arrival from Delaware, 1858: A Desperate, Bloody Struggle—
Gun, Knife and Fire Shovel, Used by an Infuriated Master

[William Still]

William Still again reveals his interest in recording "extraordinary revelations" about life under slavery. The details Still recorded below were refutations of any illusions about slavery's benignity or doubts about the cruelty wielded by slaveholders. In the case of Theophilus Collins, we hear the tale of a slave's brave and near-fatal resistance to a slaveholder's violent attack.

Judged from their outward appearance, as well as from the fact that they were from the neighboring State of Delaware, no extraordinary revelations were looked for from the above-named party. It was found, however, that one of their number, at least, had a sad tale of outrage and cruelty to relate. The facts stated are as follows:

Theophilus is twenty-four years of age, dark, height and stature hardly medium, with faculties only about average compared with ordinary fugitives from Delaware and Maryland. His appearance is in no way remarkable. His bearing is subdued and modest; yet he is not lacking in earnestness. Says Theophilus, "I was in servitude under a man named Houston, near Lewes, Delaware; he was a very mean man, he didn't allow you enough to eat, nor enough clothes to wear. He never allowed a drop of tea, or coffee, or sugar, and if you didn't eat your breakfast before day he wouldn't allow you any, but would drive you out without any. He had a wife; she was mean, too, meaner than he was. Four years ago last Fall my master cut my entrails out for going to meeting at Daniel Wesley's church one Sabbath night. Before day, Monday morning, he called me up to whip me; called me into his dining-room, locked the doors, then ordered me to pull off my shirt. I told him no, sir, I wouldn't; right away he went and got the cowhide, and gave me about twenty over my head with the butt. He tore my shirt off, after I would not pull it off; he ordered me to cross my hands. I didn't do that. After I wouldn't do that he went and got his gun and broke the breech of that over my head. He then seized up the fire-tongs and struck me over the head ever so often. The next thing he took was the parlor shovel and he beat on me with that till he broke the handle; then he took the blade and stove it at my head with all his might. I told him that I was bound to come out of that room. He run up to the door and drawed his knife and told me if I ventured to the door he would stab me. I never made it any better or worse, but aimed straight for the door; but before I reached it he stabbed me, drawing the knife (a common pocket knife) as hard as he could rip across my stomach; right away he began stabbing me about my head" (marks were plainly to be seen). After a desperate struggle, Theophilus succeeded in getting out of the building.

"I started," said he, "at once for Georgetown, carrying a part of my entrails in my hands for the whole journey, sixteen miles. I went to my young masters, and they took me to an old colored woman, called

Judah Smith, and for five days and nights I was under treatment of Dr. Henry Moore, Dr. Charles Henry Richards, and Dr. William Newall; all these attended me. I was not expected to live for a long time, but the Doctors cured me at last." ...

Source: William Still, 1872 (see the Bibliography on p. 203 for complete information).

SETH CONCKLIN

An Abolitionist in the Underground

[William Still]

Still tells two intertwined narratives here: the amazing discovery of his long-lost brother Peter, who had been kidnapped into slavery, and of Seth Concklin, a white abolitionist who in 1851 sacrificed his life in his attempt to help Peter Still's enslaved wife and children escape from Alabama.

In the long list of names who have suffered and died in the cause of freedom, not one, perhaps, could be found whose efforts to redeem a poor family of slaves were more Christ-like than Seth Concklin's, whose noble and daring spirit has been so long completely shrouded in mystery. Except John Brown, it is a question, whether his rival could be found with respect to boldness, disinterestedness and willingness to be sacrificed for the deliverance of the oppressed.

By chance one day he came across a copy of the Pennsylvania *Freeman*, containing the story of Peter Still, "The Kidnapped and the Ransomed,"—how he had been torn away from his mother, when a little boy six years old; how, for forty years and more, he had been compelled to serve under the yoke, totally destitute as to any knowledge of his parents' whereabouts; how the intense love of liberty and desire to get back to his mother had unceasingly absorbed his mind through all those years of bondage; how, amid the most appalling discouragements, prompted alone by his undying determination to be free and be reunited with those from whom he had been sold away, he contrived to buy himself; how, by extreme economy, from doing over-work, he saved up five hundred dollars, the amount of money required for his ransom, which, with his freedom, be, from necessity, placed unreservedly in the confidential keeping of a Jew, named Joseph Friedman, whom he had known for a long time and could venture to trust,——how he had further toiled to save up money to defray his expenses on an expedition in search of his mother and kindred; how, when this end was accomplished, with an earnest purpose he took his carpet-bag in his hand, and his heart throbbing for his old home and people, he turned his mind very privately towards Philadelphia, where he hoped, by having notices read in the colored churches to the effect that "forty-one or forty-two years before two little boys[1] were kidnapped and carried South"—that the memory of some of the older members might recall the circumstances, and in this way he would be aided in his ardent efforts to become restored to them.

And, furthermore, Seth Concklin had read how, on arriving in Philadelphia, after traveling sixteen hundred miles, that almost the first man whom Peter Still sought advice from was his own unknown brother (whom he had never seen or heard of), who made the discovery that he was the long-lost boy, whose history and fate had been enveloped in sadness so long, and for whom his mother had shed so many tears and offered so many prayers, during the long years of their separation; and, finally, how this self-ransomed and restored captive, notwithstanding his great success, was destined to suffer the keenest pangs of sorrow for his wife and children, whom he had left in Alabama bondage.

Seth Concklin was naturally too singularly sympathetic and humane not to feel now for Peter, and especially for his wife and children left in bonds as bound with them. Hence, as Seth was a man who seemed wholly insensible to fear, and to know no other law of humanity and right, than whenever the claims of the suffering and the wronged appealed to him, to respond unreservedly, whether those thus injured were amongst his nearest kin or the greatest strangers,——it mattered not to what race or clime they might belong,——he, in the

---

[1] Sons of Levin and Sidney—he was too young to remember the last names of his parents.

spirit of the good Samaritan, owning all such as his neighbors, volunteered his services, without pay or reward, to go and rescue the wife and three children of Peter Still.

The magnitude of this offer can hardly be appreciated. It was literally laying his life on the altar of freedom for the despised and oppressed whom he had never seen, whose kinsfolk even he was not acquainted with. At this juncture even Peter was not prepared to accept this proposal. He wanted to secure the freedom of his wife and children as earnestly as he had ever desired to see his mother, yet he could not, at first, hearken to the idea of having them rescued in the way suggested by Concklin, fearing a failure.

To J. M. McKim and the writer, the bold scheme for the deliverance of Peter's family was alone confided. It was never submitted to the Vigilance Committee, for the reason, that it was not considered a matter belonging thereto. On first reflection, the very idea of such an undertaking seemed perfectly appalling. Frankly was he told of the great dangers and difficulties to be encountered through hundreds of miles of slave territory. Seth was told of those who, in attempting to aid slaves to escape, had fallen victims to the relentless Slave Power, and had either lost their lives, or been incarcerated for long years in penitentiaries, where no friendly aid could be afforded them; in short, he was plainly told, that without a very great chance, the undertaking would cost him his life. The occasion of this interview and conversation, the seriousness of Concklin and the utter failure in presenting the various obstacles to his plan, to create the slightest apparent misgiving in his mind, or to produce the slightest sense of fear or hesitancy, can never be effaced from the memory of the writer. The plan was, however, allowed to rest for a time.

In the meanwhile, Peter's mind was continually vacillating between Alabama, with his wife and children, and his newfound relatives in the North. Said a brother, "If you cannot get your family, what will you do? Will you come North and live with your relatives?" "I would as soon go out of the world, as not to go back and do all I can for them," was the prompt reply of Peter.

The problem of buying them was seriously considered, but here obstacles quite formidable lay in the way. Alabama laws utterly denied the right of a slave to buy himself, much less his wife and children. The right of slave masters to free their slaves, either by sale or emancipation, was positively prohibited by law. With these reflections weighing upon his mind, having stayed away from his wife as long as he could content himself to do, he took his carpet-bag in his hand, and turned his face toward Alabama, to embrace his family in the prison-house of bondage.

His approach home could only be made stealthily, not daring to breathe to a living soul, save his own family, his nominal Jew master, and one other friend—a slave—where he had been, the prize he had found, or anything in relation to his travels. To his wife and children his return was unspeakably joyous. The situation of his family concerned him with tenfold more weight than ever before.

As the time drew near to make the offer to his wife's master to purchase her with his children, his heart failed him through fear of awakening the ire of slaveholders against him, as he knew that the law and public sentiment were alike deadly opposed to the spirit of freedom in the slave. Indeed, as innocent as a step in this direction might appear, in those days a man would have stood about as good a chance for his life in entering a lair of hungry hyenas, as a slave or free colored man would, in talking about freedom.

He concluded, therefore, to say nothing about buying. The plan proposed by Seth Concklin was told to Vina, his wife; also what he had heard from his brother about the Underground Rail Road,— how, that many who could not get their freedom in any other way, by being aided a little, were daily camping to Canada. Although the wife and children had never tasted the pleasures of freedom for a single hour in their lives, they hated slavery heartily, and being about to be far separated from husband and father, they were ready to assent to any proposition that looked like deliverance.

Peter proposed to Vina, that she should give him certain small articles, consisting of a cape, etc., which he would carry with him as memorials, and, in case Concklin or any one else should ever come for her from him, as an unmistakable sign that all was right, he would send back, by whoever was to befriend them, the cape, so that she and the children might not doubt but have faith in the man, when he gave her the sign, (cape).

Again Peter returned to Philadelphia, and was now willing to accept the offer of Concklin. Ere long, the opportunity of an interview was had, and Peter gave Seth a very full description of the country and of his family, and made known to him, that he had very carefully gone over with his wife and children the matter of their freedom. This interview interested Concklin most deeply. If his own wife and children had been in bondage, scarcely could he have manifested greater sympathy for them.

For the hazardous work before him he was at once prepared to make a start. True he had two sisters in Philadelphia for whom he had always cherished the warmest affection, but he conferred not with them on this momentous mission. For full well did he know that it was not in human nature for them to acquiesce in this perilous undertaking, though one of these sisters, Mrs. Supplee, was a most faithful abolitionist.

Having once laid his hand to the plough he was not the man to look back,—not even to bid his sisters good-bye, but he actually left them as though he expected to be home to his dinner as usual. What had become of him during those many weeks of his perilous labors in Alabama to rescue this family was to none a greater mystery than to his sisters. On leaving home he simply took two or three small articles in the way of apparel with one hundred dollars to defray his expenses for a time; this sum he considered ample to start with. Of course he had very safely concealed about him Vina's cape and one or two other articles which he was to use for his identification in meeting her and the children on the plantation.

His first thought was, on reaching his destination, after becoming acquainted with the family, being familiar with Southern manners, to have them all prepared at a given hour for the starting of the steamboat for Cincinnati, and to join him at the wharf, when he would boldly assume the part of a slaveholder, and the family naturally that of slaves, and in this way he hoped to reach Cincinnati direct, before their owner had fairly discovered their escape.

But alas for Southern irregularity, two or three days' delay after being advertised to start, was no uncommon circumstance with steamers; hence this plan was abandoned. What this heroic man endured from severe struggles and unyielding exertions, in traveling thousands of miles on water and on foot, hungry and fatigued, sowing his living freight for seven days and seven nights in a skiff, is hardly to be paralleled in the annals of the Underground Rail Road. The following interesting letters penned by the hand of Concklin convey minutely his last struggles and characteristically represent the singleness of heart which impelled him to sacrifice his life for the slave—

EASTPORT, Miss., Feb. 3, 1851.

TO WM. STILL:—Our friends in Cincinnati have failed finding anybody to assist me on my return. Searching the country opposite Paducah, I find that the whole country fifty miles round is inhabited only by

Christian wolves. It is customary, when a strange negro is seen, for any white man to seize the negro and convey such negro through and out of the State of Illinois to Paducah, Ky., and lodge such stranger in Paducah jail, and there claim such reward as may be offered by the master.

There is no regularity by the steamboats on the Tennessee River. I was four days getting to Florence from Paducah. Sometimes they are four days starting, from the time appointed, which alone puts to rest the plan for returning by steamboat. The distance from the mouth of the river to Florence, is from between three hundred and five to three hundred and forty-five miles by the river; by land, two hundred and fifty, or more.

I arrived at the shoe-shop on the plantation, one o'clock, Tuesday, 28th. William and two boys were making shoes. I immediately gave the first signal, anxiously waiting thirty minutes for an opportunity to give the second and main signal, during which time I was very sociable. It was rainy and muddy—my pants were rolled up to the knees. I was in the character of a man seeking employment in this country. End of thirty minutes gave the second signal.

William appeared unmoved; soon sent out the boys; instantly sociable; Peter and Levin at the Island; one of the young masters with them; not safe to undertake to see them till Saturday night, when they would be at home: appointed a place to see Vina, in an open field, that night; they to bring me something to eat; our interview only four minutes; I left; appeared by night; dark and cloudy; at ten o'clock appeared William; exchanged signals; led me a few rods to where stood Vina; gave her the signal sent by Peter; our interview ten minutes; she did not call me "master," nor did she say "sir," by which I knew she had confidence in me.

Our situation being dangerous, we decided that I meet Peter and Levin on the bank of the river early dawn of day, Sunday, to establish the laws. During our interview, William prostrated on his knees, and face to the ground; arms sprawling; head cocked back, watching for wolves, by which position a man can see better in the dark. No house to go to safely, traveled round till morning, eating hoe cake which William had given me for supper; next day going around to get employment. I thought of William, who is a Christian preacher, and of the Christian preachers in Pennsylvania. One watching for wolves by night, to rescue Vina and her three children from Christian licentiousness; the other standing erect in open day, seeking the praise of men.

During the four days waiting for the important Sunday morning, I thoroughly surveyed the rocks and shoals of the river from Florence seven miles up, where will be my place of departure. General notice was taken of me as being a stranger, lurking around. Fortunately there are several small grist mills within ten miles around. No taverns here, as in the North; any planter's house entertains travelers occasionally.

One night I stayed at a medical gentleman's, who is not a large planter; another night at an ex-magistrate's house in South Florence—a Virginian by birth—one of the late census takers; told me that many more persons cannot read and write than is reported; one fact, amongst many others, that many persons who do not know the letters of the alphabet, have learned to write their own names; such are generally reported readers and writers.

It being customary for a stranger not to leave the house early in the morning where he has lodged, I was under the necessity of staying out all night Saturday, to be able to meet Peter and Levin, which was accomplished in due time. When we approached, I gave my signal first; immediately they gave theirs. I talked freely. Levin's voice, at first, evidently trembled. No wonder, for my presence universally attracted attention by the lords of the land. Our interview was less than one hour; the laws were written. I to go to Cincinnati to get a rowing boat and provisions; a first class clipper boat to go with speed. To depart from the place where the laws were written, on Saturday night of the first of March. I to meet one of them at the same place Thursday night, previous to the fourth Saturday from the night previous to the Sunday when the laws were written. We to go down the Tennessee river to some place up the Ohio, not yet decided on, in our row boat. Peter and Levin are good oarsmen. So am I. Telegraph station at Tuscumbia, twelve miles from the plantation, also at Paducah.

Came from Florence to here Sunday night by steamboat. Eastport is in Mississippi. Waiting here for a steamboat to go down; paying one dollar a day for board. Like other taverns here, the wretchedness is indescribable; no pen, ink, paper or newspaper to be had; only one room for everybody, except the gambling rooms. It is difficult for me to write. Vina intends to get a pass for Catharine and herself for the first Sunday in March.

The bank of the river where I met Peter and Levin is two miles from the plantation. I have avoided saying I am from Philadelphia. Also avoided talking about negroes. I never talked so much about milling before. I consider most of the trouble over, till I arrive in a free State with my crew, the first week in March; then will I have to be wiser than Christian serpents, and more cautious than doves. I do not consider it safe to keep this letter in my possession, yet I dare not put it in the post-office here; there is so little business in these post-offices that notice might be taken.

I am evidently watched; everybody knows me to be a miller. I may write again when I get to Cincinnati, if I should have time. The ex-magistrate, with whom I stayed in South Florence, held three hours' talk with me, exclusive of our morning talk. Is a man of good general information; he was exceedingly inquisitive. "I am from Cincinnati, formerly from the State of New York." I had no opportunity to get anything to eat from seven o'clock Tuesday morning till six o'clock Wednesday evening, except the hoe cake, and no sleep.

Florence is the head of navigation for small steamboats. Seven miles, all the way up to my place of departure, is swift water, and rocky. Eight hundred miles to Cincinnati. I found all things here as Peter told me, except the distance of the river. South Florence contains twenty white families, three warehouses of considerable business, a post-office, but no school. McKiernon is here waiting for a steamboat to go to New Orleans, so we are in company.

PRINCETON, GIBSON COUNTY, INDIANA, Feb. 18, 1851.

To WM. STILL:—The plan is to go to Canada, on the Wabash, opposite Detroit. There are four routes to Canada. One through Illinois, commencing above and below Alton; one through to North Indiana, and the Cincinnati route, being the largest route in the United States.

I intended to have gone through Pennsylvania, but the risk going up the Ohio river has caused me to go to Canada. Steamboat traveling is universally condemned; though many go in boats, consequently many get lost. Going in a skiff is new, and is approved of in my case. After I arrive at the mouth of the Tennessee river, I will go up the Ohio seventy-five miles, to the mouth of the Wabash, then up the Wabash, forty-four miles to New Harmony, where I shall go ashore by night, and go thirteen miles east, to Charles Grier, a farmer, (colored man), who will entertain us, and next night convey us sixteen miles to David Stormon, near Princeton, who will take the command, and I be released. ...

One half of my time has been used in trying to find persons to assist, when I may arrive on the Ohio river, in which I have failed, except Stormon.

Having no letter of introduction to Stormon from any source, on which I could fully rely, I traveled two hundred miles around, to find out his stability. I have found many abolitionists, nearly all who have made propositions, which themselves would not comply with, and nobody else would. Already I have traveled over three thousand miles. Two thousand and four hundred by steamboat, two hundred by railroad, one hundred by stage, four hundred on foot, forty-eight in a skiff.

I have yet five hundred miles to go to the plantation, to commence operations. I have been two weeks on the decks of steamboats, three nights out, two of which I got perfectly wet. If I had had paper money as McKim desired, it would have been destroyed. I have not been entertained gratis at any place except Stormon's. I had one hundred and twenty-six dollars when I left Philadelphia, one hundred from you, twenty-six mine.

Telegraphed to station at Evansville, thirty-three miles from Stormon's, and at Vinclure's, twenty-five miles from Stormon's. The Wabash route is considered the safest route. No one has ever been lost from Stormon's to Canada. Some have been lost between Stormon's and the Ohio. The wolves have never suspected Stormon. ...

SETH CONCKLIN, PRINCETON, GIBSON COUNTY, IND.

P. S. First of April, will be about the time Peter's family will arrive opposite Detroit. You should inform yourself how to find them there. I may have no opportunity.

I will look promptly for your letter at Princeton, till the 10th of March, and longer if there should have been any delay by the mails.

In March, as contemplated, Concklin arrived in Indiana, at the place designated, with Peter's wife and three children, and sent a thrilling letter to the writer, portraying in the most vivid light his adventurous flight from the hour they left Alabama until their arrival in Indiana. In this report he stated, that instead of starting early in the morning, owing to some unforeseen delay on the part of the family, they did not reach the designated place till towards day, which greatly exposed them in passing a certain town which he had hoped to avoid.

But as his brave heart was bent on prosecuting his journey without further delay, he concluded to start at all hazards, notwithstanding the dangers he apprehended from passing said town by daylight. For safety he endeavored to hide his freight by having them all lie flat down on the bottom of the skiff; covered them with blankets, concealing them from the effulgent beams of the early morning sun, or rather from the "Christian Wolves" who might perchance espy him from the shore in passing the town.

The wind blew fearfully. Concklin was rowing heroically when loud voices from the shore hailed him, but he was utterly deaf to the sound. Immediately one or two guns were fired in the direction of the skiff, but he heeded not this significant call; consequently here ended this difficulty. He supposed, as the wind was blowing so hard, those on shore who hailed him must have concluded that he did not hear them and that he meant no disrespect in treating them with seeming indifference. Whilst many straits and great dangers had to be passed, this was the greatest before reaching their destination.

But suffice it to say that the glad tidings which this letter contained filled the breast of Peter with unutterable delight and his friends and relations with wonder beyond degree.[2] No fond wife had ever waited with more longing desire for the return of her husband than Peter had for this blessed news. All doubts had disappeared, and a well grounded hope was cherished that within a few short days Peter and his fond wife and children would be reunited in Freedom on the Canada side, and that Concklin and the friends would be rejoicing with joy unspeakable over this great triumph. But alas, before the few days had expired the subjoined brief paragraph of news was discovered in the morning *Ledger*.

RUNAWAY NEGROES CAUGHT—At Vincennes, Indiana, on Saturday last, a white man and four negroes were arrested. The negroes belong to B. McKiernon of South Florence, Alabama, and the man who was running them off calls himself John H. Miller. The prisoners were taken charge of by the Marshall of Evansville—*April 9th.*

How suddenly these sad tidings turned into mourning and gloom the hope and joy of Peter and his relatives no pen could possibly describe; at least the writer will not attempt it here, but will at once introduce a witness who met the noble Concklin and the panting fugitives in Indiana and proffered them sympathy and advice. And it may safely be said from a truer and more devoted friend of the slave they could not have received counsel.

---

2 In some unaccountable manner this the last letter Concklin ever penned, perhaps, has been unfortunately lost. [Note by William Still.]

EVANSVILLE, INDIANA, MARCH 31ST, 1851.

WM. STILL: *Dear Sir,*—On last Tuesday I mailed a letter to you, written by Seth Concklin. I presume you have received that letter. It gave an account of his rescue of the family of your brother. If that is the last news you have had from them, I have very painful intelligence for you. They passed on from near Princeton, where I saw them and had a lengthy interview with them, up north, I think twenty-three miles above Vincennes, Ind., where they were seized by a party of men, and lodged in jail. Telegraphic dispatches were sent all through the South. I have since learned that the Marshall of Evansville received a dispatch from Tuscumbia, to look out for them. By some means, he and the master, so says report, went to Vincennes and claimed the fugitives, chained Mr. Concklin and hurried all off. Mr. Concklin wrote to Mr. David Stormon, Princeton, as soon as he was cast into prison, to find bail. So soon as we got the letter and could get off, two of us were about setting off to render all possible aid, when we were told they all had passed, a few hours before, through Princeton, Mr. Concklin in chains. What kind of process was had, if any, I know not. I immediately came down to this place, and learned that they had been put on a boat at 3 P.M. I did not arrive until 6. Now all hopes of their recovery are gone. No case ever so enlisted my sympathies. I had seen Mr. Concklin in Cincinnati. I had given him aid and counsel. I happened to see them after they landed in Indiana. I heard Peter and Levin tell their tale of suffering, shed tears of sorrow for them all; but now, since they have fallen a prey to the unmerciful bloodhounds of this state, and have again been dragged back to unrelenting bondage, I am entirely unmanned. And poor Concklin! I fear for him. When he is dragged back to Alabama, I fear they will go far beyond the utmost rigor of the law, and vent their savage cruelty upon him. It is with pain I have to communicate these things. But you may not hear them from him. I could not get to see him or them, as Vincennes is about thirty miles from Princeton, where I was when I heard of the capture.

I take pleasure in stating that, according to the letter he (Concklin) wrote to Mr. D. Stewart, Mr. Concklin did not abandon them, but risked his own liberty to save them. He was not with them when they were taken; but went afterwards to take them out of jail upon a writ of Habeas Corpus, when they seized him too and lodged him in prison.

I write in much haste. If I can learn any more facts of importance, I may write you. If you desire to hear from me again, or if you should learn any thing specific from Mr. Concklin, be pleased to write me at Cincinnati, where I expect to be in a short time. If curious to know your correspondent, I may say I was formerly Editor of the *New Concord Free Press*, Ohio. I only add that every case of this kind only tends to make me abhor my (no!) *this* country more and more. It is the Devil's Government, and God will destroy it.

YOURS FOR THE SLAVE, N. R. JOHNSTON.

P. S. I broke open this letter to write you some more. The foregoing pages were written at night. I expected to mail it next morning before leaving Evansville; but the boat for which I was waiting came down about three in the morning; so I had to hurry on board, bringing the letter along. As it now is I am not sorry, for coming down, on my way to St. Louis, as far as Paducah, there I learned from a colored man at the wharf that, that same day, in the morning, the master and the family of fugitives arrived off the boat, and had then gone on their journey to Tuscumbia, but that the "white man" (Mr. Concklin) had "got away from them," about twelve miles up the river. It seems he got off the boat some way, near or at Smithland, Ky., a town at the mouth of the Cumberland River. I presume the report is true, and hope he will finally escape, though I was also told that they were in pursuit of him. Would that the others had also escaped. Peter and Levin could have done so, I think, if they had had resolution. One of them rode a horse, he not tied either, behind the coach in which the others were. He followed apparently "contented and happy." From report, they told their master, and even their pursuers, before the master came, that Concklin had decoyed them away, they coming unwillingly. I write on a very unsteady boat.

YOURS, N. R. JOHNSTON.

A report found its way into the papers to the effect that "Miller," the white man arrested in connection with the capture of the family, was found drowned, with his hands and feet in chains and his skull fractured. It proved, as his friends feared, to be Seth Concklin. And in irons, upon the river bank, there is no doubt he was buried. …

Stunning and discouraging as this horrible ending was to all concerned, and serious as the matter looked in the eyes of Peter's friends with regard to Peter's family, he could not for a moment abandon the idea of rescuing them from the jaws of the destroyer. But most formidable difficulties stood in the way of opening correspondence with reliable persons in Alabama. Indeed it seemed impossible to find a merchant, lawyer, doctor, planter or minister, who was not too completely interlinked with slavery to be relied upon to manage a negotiation of this nature. Whilst waiting and hoping for something favorable to turn up, the subjoined letter from the owner of Peter's family was received and is here inserted precisely as it was written, spelled and punctuated—

MCKIERNON'S LETTER

SOUTH FLORENCE, ALA 6 AUGUST 1851

MR WILLIAM STILL *No 31 North Fifth street Philadelphia*

Sir a few days sinc mr Lewis Tharenton of Tuscumbia Ala showed me a letter dated 6 June 51 from cincinnati signd samuel Lewis in behalf of a Negro man by the name of peter Gist who informed the writer of the Letter that you ware his brother and wished an answer to be directed to you as he peter would be in philadelphi. the object of the letter was to purchis from me 4 Negros that is peters wife & 3 children 2 sons & 1 Girl the Name of said Negros are the woman Viney the (mother) Eldest son peter 21 or 2 years old second son Leven 19 or 20 years 1 Girl about 13 or 14 years old. the Husband & Father of these people once Belonged to a relation of mine by the name of Gist now Decest & some few years since he peter was sold to a. man by the Name of Freedman who removed to cincinnati ohio & Tuck peter with him of course peter became free by the volentary act of the master some time last march a white man by the name of Miller apperd in the nabourhood & abducted the bove negroes was caut at vincanes Indi with said negroes & was thare convicted of steling & remanded back to Ala to Abide the penalty of the law & on his return met his Just reward by Getting drownded at the month of cumberland River on the ohio in attempting to make his escape I recovered & Braught Back said 4 negroes or as You would say coulard people under the Belief that peter the Husband was accessery to the offence tharcby putting me to much Expense & Truble to the amt $1000 which if he gets them he or his Friends must refund these 4 negroes are worth in the market about 4000 for thea are Extraordinary fine & likely & but for the fact of Elopement I would not take 8000 Dollars for them but as the thing now stands you can say to peter & his new discovered Relations in philadelphia I will take 5000 for the 4 culerd people & if this will suite him & he can raise the money I will delever to him or his agent at paduca at month of Tennessee river said negroes but the money must be Deposeted in the Hands of some respectabl person at paduca before I remove the property it wold not be safe for peter to come to this countery write me a line on recpt of this & let me Know peters views on the above

I am Yours &c B. McKiernon

N B say to peter to write & let me Know his viewes amediately as I am determined to act in a way if he dont take this offer he will never have an other oppertunity

B. McKiernon

WM. STILL'S ANSWER

Philadelphia, Aug. 16th, 1851.

To B. McKiernon, Esq.: *Sir.*—I have received your letter from South Florence, Ala., under date of the 6th inst. To say that it took me by surprise, as well as afforded me pleasure, for which I feel to be very much indebted to you, is no more than true. In regard to your informants of myself—Mr. Thornton, of Ala., and Mr. Samuel Lewis, of Cincinnati—to them both I am a stranger. However, I am the brother of Peter, referred to, and with the fact of his having a wife and three children in your service I am also familiar. This brother, Peter, I have only had the pleasure of knowing for the brief space of one year and thirteen days, although he is now past forty and I twenty-nine years of age. Time will not allow me at present, or I should give you a detailed account of how Peter became a slave, the forty long years which intervened between the time he was kidnapped, when a boy, being only six years of age, and his arrival in this city, from Alabama, one year and fourteen days ago, when he was re-united to his mother, five brothers and three sisters.

None but a father's heart can fathom the anguish and sorrows felt by Peter during the many vicissitudes through which he has passed. He looked back to his boyhood and saw himself snatched from the tender embraces of his parents and home to be made a slave for life.

During all his prime days he was in the faithful and constant service of those who had no just claim upon him. In the meanwhile he married a wife, who bore him eleven children, the greater part of whom were emancipated from the troubles of life by death, and three only survived. To them and his wife he was devoted. Indeed I have never seen attachment between parents and children, or husband and wife, more entire than was manifested in the case of Peter.

Through these many years of servitude, Peter was sold and resold, from one State to another, from one owner to another, till he reached the forty-ninth year of his age, when, in a good Providence, through the kindness of a friend and the sweat of his brow, he regained the God-given blessings of liberty. He eagerly sought his parents and home with all possible speed and pains, when, to his heart's joy, he found his relatives.

Your present humble correspondent is the youngest of Peter's brothers, and the first one of the family he saw after arriving in this part of the country. I think you could not fail to be interested in hearing how we became known to each other, and the proof of our being brothers, etc., all of which I should be most glad to relate, but time will not permit me to do so. The news of this wonderful occurrence, of Peter finding his kindred, was published quite extensively, shortly afterwards, in various newspapers, in this quarter, which may account for the fact of "Miller's" knowledge of the whereabouts of the "fugitives." Let me say, it is my firm conviction that no one had any hand in persuading "Miller" to go down from Cincinnati, or any other place, after the family. As glad as I should be, and as much as I would do for the liberation of Peter's family (now no longer young), and his three "likely" children, in whom he prides himself how much, if you are a father, you can imagine; yet I would not, and could not, think of persuading any friend to peril his life, as would be the case, in an errand of that kind.

As regards the price fixed upon by you for the family, I must say I do not think it possible to raise half that amount, though Peter authorized me to say he would give you twenty-five hundred for them. Probably he is not as well aware as I am, how difficult it is to raise so large a sum of money from the public. The applications for such objects are so frequent among us in the North, and have always been so liberally met, that it is no wonder if many get tired of being called upon. To be sure some of us brothers own some property, but no great amount; certainly not enough to enable us to bear so great a burden. Mother owns a small farm in New Jersey, on which she has lived for nearly forty years, from which she derives her support in her old age. This small farm contains between forty and fifty acres, and is the fruit of my father's toil. Two of my brothers own small places also, but they have young families, and consequently consume nearly as much as they make, with the exception of adding some improvements to their places.

For my own part, I am employed as a clerk for a living, but my salary is quite too limited to enable me to contribute any great amount towards so large a sum as is demanded. Thus you see how we are situated financially. We have plenty of friends, but little money. Now, sir, allow me to make an appeal to your humanity, although we are aware of your power to hold as property those poor slaves, mother, daughter and two sons, that in no part of the United States could they escape and be secure from your claim nevertheless, would your understanding, your heart, or your conscience reprove you, should you restore to them, without price, that dear freedom, which is theirs by right of nature, or would you not feel a satisfaction in so doing which all the wealth of the world could not equal? At all events, could you not so reduce the price as to place it in the power of Peter's relatives and friends to raise the means for their purchase? At first, I doubt not, but that you will think my appeal very unreasonable; but, sir, serious reflection will decide, whether the money demanded by you, after all, will be of as great a benefit to you, as the satisfaction you would find in bestowing so great a favor upon those whose entire happiness in this life depends mainly upon your decision in the matter. If the entire family cannot be purchased or freed, what can Vina and her daughter be purchased for? Hoping, sir, to hear from you, at your earliest convenience, I subscribe myself,

Your obedient servant, WM. STILL.

No reply to this letter was ever received from McKiernon. The cause of his reticence can be as well conjectured by the reader as the writer.

Time will not admit of further details kindred to this narrative. The life, struggles, and success of Peter and his family were ably brought before the public in "The Kidnapped and the Ransomed," being the personal recollections of Peter Still and his wife "Vina," after forty years of slavery, by Mrs. Kate E. R. Pickard; with an introduction by Rev. Samuel J. May, and an appendix by William H. Furness, D. D., in 1856. But, of course, it was not prudent or safe, in the days of Slavery, to publish such facts as are now brought to light: all such had to be kept concealed in the breasts of the fugitives and their friends.

The following brief sketch, touching the separation of Peter and his mother, will fitly illustrate this point, and at the same time explain certain mysteries which have been hitherto kept hidden—

THE SEPARATION

WITH REGARD TO PETER'S SEPARATION from his mother, when a little boy, in few words, the facts were these: His parents, Levin and Sidney, were both slaves on the Eastern Shore of Maryland. "I will die before I submit to the yoke," was the declaration of his father to his young master before either was twenty-one years of age. Consequently he was allowed to buy himself at a very low figure, and he paid the required sum and obtained his "free papers" when quite a young man the young wife and mother remaining in slavery under Saunders Griffin, as also her children, the latter having increased to the number of four, two little boys and two little girls. But to escape from chains, stripes, and bondage, she took her four little children and fled to a place near Greenwich, New Jersey. Not a great while, however, did she remain there in a state of freedom before the slave-hunters pursued her, and one night they pounced upon the whole family, and, without judge or jury, hurried them all back to slavery. Whether this was kidnapping or not is for the reader to decide for himself.

Safe back in the hands of her owner, to prevent her from escaping a second time, every night for about three months she was cautiously "kept locked up in the garret," until, as they supposed, she was fully "cured of the desire to do so again." But she was incurable. She had been a witness to the fact that her own father's brains had been blown out by the discharge of a heavily loaded gun, deliberately aimed at his head by his drunken master. She only needed half a chance to make still greater struggles than ever for freedom.

She had great faith in God, and found much solace in singing some of the good old Methodist tunes, by day and night. Her owner, observing this apparently tranquil state of mind, indicating that she "seemed better contented than ever," concluded that it was safe to let the garret door remain unlocked at night. Not many weeks were allowed to pass before she resolved to again make a bold strike for freedom. This time she had to leave the two little boys, Levin and Peter, behind.

On the night she started she went to the bed where they were sleeping, kissed them, and, consigning them into the hands of God, bade her mother good-bye, and with her two little girls wended her way again to Burlington County, New Jersey, but to a different neighborhood from that where she had been seized. She changed her name to Charity, and succeeded in again joining her husband, but, alas, with the heart-breaking thought that she had been compelled to leave her two little boys in slavery and one of the little girls on the road for the father to go back after. Thus she began life in freedom anew.

Levin and Peter, eight and six years of age respectively, were now left at the mercy of the enraged owner, and were soon hurried off to a Southern market and sold, while their mother, for whom they were daily weeping, was they knew not where. They were too young to know that they were slaves, or to understand the nature of the afflicting separation. Sixteen years before Peter's return, his older brother (Levin) died a slave in the State of Alabama, and was buried by his surviving brother, Peter.

No idea other than that they had been "kidnapped" from their mother ever entered their minds; nor had they any knowledge of the State from whence they supposed they had been taken, the last names of their mother and father, or where they were born. On the other hand, the mother was aware that the safety of herself and her rescued children depended on keeping the whole transaction a strict family secret. During the forty years of separation, except two or three Quaker friends, including the devoted friend of the slave, Benjamin Lundy, it is doubtful whether any other individuals were let into the secret of her slave life. And when the account given of Peter's return, etc., was published in 1850, it led some of the family to apprehend serious danger from the partial revelation of the early condition of the mother, especially as it was about the time that the Fugitive Slave law was passed.

Hence, the author of "The Kidnapped and the Ransomed" was compelled to omit these dangerous facts, and had to confine herself strictly to the "personal recollections of Peter Still" with regard to his being "kidnapped." Likewise, in the sketch of Seth Concklin's eventful life, written by Dr. W. H. Furness, for similar reasons he felt obliged to make but bare reference to his wonderful agency in relation to Peter's family, although he was fully aware of all the facts in the case.

SOURCE: William Still, 1872 (see the Bibliography on p. 203 for complete information).

WILLIAM AND ELLEN CRAFT

Female Slave in Male Attire, Fleeing as a Planter, with Her Husband as Her Body Servant

[William Still]

William and Ellen Craft, married slaves from Georgia, escaped to the North by using clever disguises. Fair-skinned Ellen transformed herself into a white male planter, and William posed as the planter's slave and faithful servant. Although Georgia slave-hunters were unable to capture the couple, the Crafts moved to England (Still explains below) to avoid living "in daily fear of slave-catchers."

A QUARTER OF A CENTURY AGO, William and Ellen Craft were slaves in the State of Georgia. With them, as with thousands of others, the desire to be free was very strong. For this jewel they were willing to make any sacrifice, or to endure any amount of suffering. In this state of mind they commenced planning. After thinking of various ways that might be tried, it occurred to William and Ellen, that one might act the part of master and the other the part of servant.

Ellen being fair enough to pass for white, of necessity would have to be transformed into a young planter for the time being. All that was needed, however, to make this important change was that she should be dressed elegantly in a fashionable suit of male attire, and have her hair cut in the style usually worn by young planters. Her profusion of dark hair offered a fine opportunity for the change. So far this plan looked very tempting. But it occurred to them that Ellen was beardless. After some mature reflection, they came to the conclusion that this difficulty could be very readily obviated by having the face muffled up as though the young planter was suffering badly with the face or toothache; thus they got rid of this trouble. Straightway, upon further reflection, several other very serious difficulties stared them in the face. For instance, in traveling, they knew that they would be under the necessity of stopping repeatedly at hotels, and that the custom of registering would have to be conformed to, unless some very good excuse could be given for not doing so.

Here they again thought much over matters, and wisely concluded that the young man had better assume the attitude of a gentleman very much indisposed. He must have his right arm placed carefully in a sling; that would be a sufficient excuse for not registering, etc. Then he must be a little lame, with a nice cane in the left hand; he must have large green spectacles over his eyes, and withal he must be very hard of hearing and dependent on his faithful servant (as was no uncommon thing with slave-holders), to look after all his wants.

William was just the man to act this part. To begin with, he was very "likely-looking;" smart, active and exceedingly attentive to his young master—indeed he was almost eyes, ears, hands and feet for him. William knew that this would please the slave-holders. The young planter would have nothing to do but hold himself subject to his ailments and put on a bold air of superiority; he was not to deign to notice anybody. If, while traveling, gentlemen, either politely or rudely, should venture to scrape acquaintance with the young planter, in his deafness he was to remain mute; the servant was to explain. In every instance when this occurred, as it actually did, the servant was fully equal to the emergency—none dreaming of the disguises in which the Underground Rail Road passengers were traveling.

They stopped at a first-class hotel in Charleston, where the young planter and his body servant were treated, as the house was wont to treat the chivalry. They stopped also at a similar hotel in Richmond, and with like results.

They knew that they must pass through Baltimore, but they did not know the obstacles that they would have to surmount in the Monumental City. They proceeded to the depot in the usual manner, and the servant asked for tickets for his master and self. Of course the master could have a ticket, but "bonds will have to be entered before you can get a ticket," said the ticket master. "It is the rule of this office to require bonds for all negroes applying for tickets to go North, and none but gentlemen of well-known responsibility will be taken," further explained the ticket master.

The servant replied, that he knew "nothing about that"—that he was "simply traveling with his young master to take care of him—he being in a very delicate state of health, so much so, that fears were entertained that he might not be able to hold out to reach Philadelphia, where he was hastening for medical treatment," and ended his reply by saying, "my master can't be detained." Without further parley, the ticket master very obligingly waived the old "rule," and furnished the requisite tickets. The mountain being thus removed, the young planter and his faithful servant were safely in the cars for the city of Brotherly Love.

Scarcely had they arrived on free soil when the rheumatism departed—the right arm was unslung—the toothache was gone—the beardless face was unmuffled—the deaf heard and spoke—the blind saw—and the lame leaped as an hart, and in the presence of a few astonished friends of the slave, the facts of this unparalleled Underground Rail Road feat were fully established by the most unquestionable evidence.

The constant strain and pressure on Ellen's nerves, however, had tried her severely, so much so, that for days afterwards, she was physically very much prostrated, although joy and gladness beamed from her eyes, which bespoke inexpressible delight within.

Never can the writer forget the impression made by their arrival. Even now, after a lapse of nearly a quarter of a century, it is easy to picture them in a private room, surrounded by a few friends—Ellen in her fine suit of black, with her cloak and high-heeled boots, looking, in every respect, like a young gentleman; in an hour after having dropped her male attire, and assumed the habiliments of her sex the feminine only was visible in every line and feature of her structure.

Her husband, William, was thoroughly colored, but was a man of marked natural abilities, of good manners, and full of pluck, and possessed of perceptive faculties very large.

It was necessary, however, in those days, that they should seek a permanent residence, where their freedom would be more secure than in Philadelphia; therefore they were advised to go to headquarters, directly to Boston. There they would be safe, it was supposed, as it had then been about a generation since a fugitive had been taken back from the old Bay State, and through the incessant labors of William Lloyd Garrison, the great pioneer, and his faithful coadjutors, it was conceded that another fugitive slave case could never be tolerated on the free soil of Massachusetts. So to Boston they went.

On arriving, the warm hearts of abolitionists welcomed them heartily, and greeted and cheered them without let or hindrance. They did not pretend to keep their coming a secret, or hide it under a bushel; the story of their escape was heralded broadcast over the country— North and South, and indeed over the civilized world. For two years or more, not the slightest fear was entertained that they were not just as safe in Boston as if they had gone to Canada. But the day the Fugitive Bill passed, even the bravest abolitionist began to fear that a fugitive slave was no longer safe anywhere under the stars and stripes, North or South, and that William and Ellen Craft were liable to be captured at any moment by Georgia slave hunters. Many abolitionists counselled resistance to the death at all hazards. Instead of running to Canada, fugitives generally armed themselves and thus said, "Give me liberty or give me death."

William and Ellen Craft believed that it was their duty, as citizens of Massachusetts, to observe a more legal and civilized mode of conforming to the marriage rite than had been permitted them in slavery, and as Theodore Parker had shown himself a very warm friend of theirs, they agreed to have their wedding over again according to the laws of a free State. After performing the ceremony, the renowned and fearless advocate of equal rights (Theodore Parker), presented William with a revolver and a dirk-knife, counselling him to use them manfully in defence of his wife and himself, if ever an attempt should be made by his owners or anybody else to re-enslave them.

But, notwithstanding all the published declarations made by abolitionists and fugitives, to the effect, that slave-holders and slave-catchers in visiting Massachusetts in pursuit of their runaway property, would be met by just such weapons as Theodore Parker presented William with, to the surprise of all Boston, the owners of William and Ellen actually had the effrontery to attempt their recapture under the Fugitive Slave Law....

Ellen first received information that the slave-hunters from Georgia were after her through Mrs. Geo. S. Hilliard, of Boston, who had been a good friend to her from the day of her arrival from slavery. How Mrs. Hilliard obtained the information, the impression it made on Ellen, and where she was secreted, the following extract of a letter written by Mrs. Hilliard, touching the memorable event, will be found deeply interesting:

"In regard to William and Ellen Craft, it is true that we received her at our house when the first warrant under the act of eighteen hundred and fifty was issued.

"Dr. Bowditch called upon us to say, that the warrant must be for William and Ellen, as they were the only fugitives here known to have come from Georgia, and the Dr. asked what we could do. I went to the house of the Rev. F. T. Gray, on Mt. Vernon street, where Ellen was working with Miss Dean, an upholsteress, a friend of ours, who had told us she would teach Ellen her trade. I proposed to Ellen to come and do some work for me, intending not to alarm her. My manner, which I supposed to be indifferent and calm, *betrayed* me, and she threw herself into my arms, sobbing and weeping. She, however, recovered her composure as soon as we reached the street, and was *very firm* ever after.

"My husband wished her, by all means, to be brought to our house, and to remain under his protection, saying: 'I am perfectly willing to meet the penalty, should she be found here, but will never give her up.' The penalty, you remember, was six months' imprisonment and a thousand dollars fine. William Craft went, after a time, to Lewis Hayden. He was at first, as Dr. Bowditch told us, 'barricaded in his shop on Cambridge street.' I saw him there, and he said, 'Ellen must not be left at your house.' 'Why? William,' said I, 'do you think we would give her up?' 'Never,' said he, 'but Mr. Hilliard is not only our friend, but he is a U. S. Commissioner, and should Ellen be found in his house, he must resign his office, as well as incur the penalty of the law, and I will not subject a friend to such a punishment for the sake of our safety.' Was not this noble, when you think how small was the penalty that any one could receive for aiding slaves to escape, compared to the fate which threatened them in case they were captured? William C. made the same objection to having his wife taken to Mr. Ellis Gray Loring's, he also being a friend and a Commissioner."

This deed of humanity and Christian charity is worthy to be commemorated and classed with the act of the good Samaritan, as the same spirit is shown in both cases. Often was Mrs. Hilliard's house an asylum for fugitive slaves.

After the hunters had left the city in dismay, and the storm of excitement had partially subsided, the friends of William and Ellen concluded that they had better seek a country where they would not be in daily fear of slave-catchers, backed by the Government of the United States. They were, therefore, advised to go to Great Britain. Outfits were liberally provided for them, passages procured, and they took their departure for a habitation in a foreign land. ...

In England the Crafts were highly respected. While under her British Majesty's protection, Ellen became the mother of several children (having had none under the stars' and stripes). These they spared no pains in educating for usefulness in the world. Some two years since William and Ellen returned with two of their children to the United States, and after visiting Boston and other places, William concluded to visit Georgia, his old home, with a view of seeing what inducement war had opened up to enterprise, as he had felt a desire to remove his family thither, if encouraged. Indeed he was prepared to purchase a plantation, if he found matters satisfactory. This visit evidently furnished the needed encouragement, judging from the fact that he did purchase a plantation somewhere in the neighborhood of Savannah, and is at present living there with his family.

... Obviously the Fugitive Slave Law in its crusade against William and Ellen Craft, reaped no advantages, but on the contrary, liberty was greatly the gainer.

SOURCE: William Still, 1872 (see the Bibliography on p. 203 for complete information).

FREDERICK DOUGLASS

Narrative of the Life of Frederick Douglass (1845)

(excerpt, Chapter 11)

After escaping from slavery in Maryland, Douglass (1818–1895) became a fierce advocate for abolition; he wrote sharply argued articles and gave stern speeches on the politics of slavery. In the first edition of his brilliant autobiography, which he supplemented and edited over the course of his life, he concludes with the story of the circumstances preceding his Underground Railroad escape—the details of which he purposefully withheld to prevent slaveholders learning of further preventative measures—and of his new life in the North.

I NOW COME to that part of my life during which I planned, and finally succeeded in making, my escape from slavery. But before narrating any of the peculiar circumstances, I deem it proper to make known my intention not to state all the facts connected with the transaction. My reasons for pursuing this course may be understood from the following: First, were I to give a minute statement of all the facts, it is not only possible, but quite probable, that others would thereby be involved in the most embarrassing difficulties. Secondly, such a statement would most undoubtedly induce greater vigilance on the part of slaveholders than has existed heretofore among them;

which would, of course, be the means of guarding a door whereby some dear brother bondman might escape his galling chains. I deeply regret the necessity that impels me to suppress any thing of importance connected with my experience in slavery. It would afford me great pleasure indeed, as well as materially add to the interest of my narrative, were I at liberty to gratify a curiosity, which I know exists in the minds of many, by an accurate statement of all the facts pertaining to my most fortunate escape. But I must deprive myself of this pleasure, and the curious of the gratification which such a statement would afford. I would allow myself to suffer under the greatest imputations which evil-minded men might suggest, rather than exculpate myself, and thereby run the hazard of closing the slightest avenue by which a brother slave might clear himself of the chains and fetters of slavery.

I have never approved of the very public manner in which some of our western friends have conducted what they call the *underground railroad,* but which, I think, by their open declarations, has been made most emphatically the *upperground railroad.* I honor those good men and women for their noble daring, and applaud them for willingly subjecting themselves to bloody persecution, by openly avowing their participation in the escape of slaves. I, however, can see very little good resulting from such a course, either to themselves or the slaves escaping; while, upon the other hand, I see and feel assured that those open declarations are a positive evil to the slaves remaining, who are seeking to escape. They do nothing towards enlightening the slave, whilst they do much towards enlightening the master. They stimulate him to greater watchfulness, and enhance his power to capture his slave. We owe something to the slaves south of the line as well as to those north of it; and in aiding the latter on their way to freedom, we should be careful to do nothing which would be likely to hinder the former from escaping from slavery. I would keep the merciless slave-holder profoundly ignorant of the means of flight adopted by the slave. I would leave him to imagine himself surrounded by myriads of invisible tormentors, ever ready to snatch from his infernal grasp his trembling prey. Let him be left to feel his way in the dark; let darkness commensurate with his crime hover over him; and let him feel that at every step he takes, in pursuit of the flying bondman, he is running the frightful risk of having his hot brains dashed out by an invisible agency. Let us render the tyrant no aid; let us not hold the light by which he can trace the footprints of our flying brother. But enough of this, I will now proceed to the statement of those facts, connected with my escape, for which I am alone responsible, and for which no one can be made to suffer but myself.

In the early part of the year 1838, I became quite restless. I could see no reason why I should, at the end of each week, pour the reward of my toil into the purse of my master. When I carried to him my weekly wages, he would, after counting the money, look me in the face with a robber-like fierceness, and ask, "Is this all?" He was satisfied with nothing less than the last cent. He would, however, when I made him six dollars, sometimes give me six cents, to encourage me. It had the opposite effect. I regarded it as a sort of admission of my right to the whole. The fact that he gave me any part of my wages was proof, to my mind, that he believed me entitled to the whole of them. I always felt worse for having received any thing; for I feared that the giving me a few cents would ease his conscience, and make him feel himself to be a pretty honorable sort of robber. My discontent grew upon me. I was ever on the look-out for means of escape; and, finding no direct means, I determined to try to hire my time, with a view of getting money with which to make my escape. In the spring of 1838, when Master Thomas came to Baltimore to purchase his spring goods, I got an opportunity, and applied to him to allow me to hire my time. He unhesitatingly refused my request, and told me this was another stratagem by which to escape. He told me I could go nowhere but that he could get me; and that, in the event of my running away, he should spare no pains in his efforts to catch me. He exhorted me to content myself, and be obedient. He told me, if I would be happy, I must lay out no plans for the future. He said, if I behaved myself properly, he would take care of me. Indeed, he advised me to complete thoughtlessness of the future, and taught me to depend solely upon him for happiness. He seemed to see fully the pressing necessity of setting aside my intellectual nature, in order to contentment in slavery. But in spite of him, and even in spite of myself, I continued to think, and to think about the injustice of my enslavement, and the means of escape.

About two months after this, I applied to Master Hugh for the privilege of hiring my time. He was not acquainted with the fact that I had applied to Master Thomas, and had been refused. He too, at first, seemed disposed to refuse; but, after some reflection, he granted me the privilege, and proposed the following terms: I was to be allowed all my time, make all contracts with those for whom I worked, and find my own employment; and, in return for this liberty, I was to pay him three dollars at the end of each week; find myself in calking tools, and in board and clothing. My board was two dollars and a half per week.

This, with the wear and tear of clothing and calking tools, made my regular expenses about six dollars per week. This amount I was compelled to make up, or relinquish the privilege of hiring my time. Rain or shine, work or no work, at the end of each week the money must be forthcoming, or I must give up my privilege. This arrangement, it will be perceived, was decidedly in my master's favor. It relieved him of all need of looking after me. His money was sure. He received all the benefits of slaveholding without its evils; while I endured all the evils of a slave, and suffered all the care and anxiety of a freeman. I found it a hard bargain. But, hard as it was, I thought it better than the old mode of getting along. It was a step towards freedom to be allowed to bear the responsibilities of a freeman, and I was determined to hold on upon it. I bent myself to the work of making money. I was ready to work at night as well as day, and by the most untiring perseverance and industry, I made enough to meet my expenses, and lay up a little money every week. I went on thus from May till August. Master Hugh then refused to allow me to hire my time longer. The ground for his refusal was a failure on my part, one Saturday night, to pay him for my week's time. This failure was occasioned by my attending a camp meeting about ten miles from Baltimore. During the week, I had entered into an engagement with a number of young friends to start from Baltimore to the camp ground early Saturday evening; and being detained by my employer, I was unable to get down to Master Hugh's without disappointing the company. I knew that Master Hugh was in no special need of the money that night. I therefore decided to go to camp meeting, and upon my return pay him the three dollars. I staid at the camp meeting one day longer than I intended when I left. But as soon as I returned, I called upon him to pay him what he considered his due. I found him very angry; he could scarce restrain his wrath. He said he had a great mind to give me a severe whipping. He wished to know how I dared go out of the city without asking his permission. I told him I hired my time, and while I paid him the price which he asked for it, I did not know that I was bound to ask him when and where I should go. This reply troubled him; and, after reflecting a few moments, he turned to me, and said I should hire my time no longer; that the next thing he should know of, I would be running away. Upon the same plea, he told me to bring my tools and clothing home forthwith. I did so; but instead of seeking work, as I had been accustomed to do previously to hiring my time, I spent the whole week without the performance of a single stroke of work. I did this in retaliation. Saturday night, he called upon me as usual for my week's wages. I told

him I had no wages; I had done no work that week. Here we were
upon the point of coming to blows. He raved, and swore his determination to get hold of me. I did not allow myself a single word; but was
resolved, if he laid the weight of his hand upon me, it should be blow
for blow. He did not strike me, but told me that he would find me in
constant employment in future. I thought the matter over during the
next day, Sunday, and finally resolved upon the third day of September,
as the day upon which I would make a second attempt to secure my
freedom. I now had three weeks during which to prepare for my journey. Early on Monday morning, before Master Hugh had time to make
any engagement for me, I went out and got employment of Mr. Butler,
at his ship-yard near the drawbridge, upon what is called the City
Block, thus making it unnecessary for him to seek employment for me.
At the end of the week, I brought him between eight and nine dollars.
He seemed very well pleased, and asked me why I did not do the same
the week before. He little knew what my plans were. My object in
working steadily was to remove any suspicion he might entertain of my
intent to run away; and in this I succeeded admirably. I suppose he
thought I was never better satisfied with my condition than at the very
time during which I was planning my escape. The second week passed,
and again I carried him my full wages; and so well pleased was he, that
he gave me twenty-five cents, (quite a large sum for a slaveholder to
give a slave,) and bade me to make a good use of it. I told him I would.

Things went on without very smoothly indeed, but within there
was trouble. It is impossible for me to describe my feelings as the time
of my contemplated start drew near. I had a number of warm-hearted
friends in Baltimore,—friends that I loved almost as I did my life,—
and the thought of being separated from them forever was painful
beyond expression. It is my opinion that thousands would escape
from slavery, who now remain, but for the strong cords of affection
that bind them to their friends. The thought of leaving my friends was
decidedly the most painful thought with which I had to contend. The
love of them was my tender point, and shook my decision more than
all things else. Besides the pain of separation, the dread and apprehension of a failure exceeded what I had experienced at my first attempt.
The appalling defeat I then sustained returned to torment me. I felt
assured that, if I failed in this attempt, my case would be a hopeless
one—it would seal my fate as a slave forever. I could not hope to get
off with any thing less than the severest punishment, and being placed
beyond the means of escape. It required no very vivid imagination to
depict the most frightful scenes through which I should have to pass,

in case I failed. The wretchedness of slavery, and the blessedness of freedom, were perpetually before me. It was life and death with me. But I remained firm, and, according to my resolution, on the third day of September, 1838, I left my chains, and succeeded in reaching New York without the slightest interruption of any kind. How I did so,—what means I adopted,—what direction I travelled, and by what mode of conveyance,—I must leave unexplained, for the reasons before mentioned.

I have been frequently asked how I felt when I found myself in a free State. I have never been able to answer the question with any satisfaction to myself. It was a moment of the highest excitement I ever experienced. I suppose I felt as one may imagine the unarmed mariner to feel when he is rescued by a friendly man-of-war from the pursuit of a pirate. In writing to a dear friend, immediately after my arrival at New York, I said I felt like one who had escaped a den of hungry lions. This state of mind, however, very soon subsided; and I was again seized with a feeling of great insecurity and loneliness. I was yet liable to be taken back, and subjected to all the tortures of slavery. This in itself was enough to damp the ardor of my enthusiasm. But the loneliness overcame me. There I was in the midst of thousands, and yet a perfect stranger; without home and without friends, in the midst of thousands of my own brethren—children of a common Father, and yet I dared not to unfold to any one of them my sad condition. I was afraid to speak to any one for fear of speaking to the wrong one, and thereby falling into the hands of money-loving kidnappers, whose business it was to lie in wait for the panting fugitive, as the ferocious beasts of the forest lie in wait for their prey. The motto which I adopted when I started from slavery was this—"Trust no man!" I saw in every white man an enemy, and in almost every colored man cause for distrust. It was a most painful situation; and, to understand it, one must needs experience it, or imagine himself in similar circumstances. Let him be a fugitive slave in a strange land— a land given up to be the hunting-ground for slaveholders—whose inhabitants are legalized kidnappers—where he is every moment subjected to the terrible liability of being seized upon by his fellowmen, as the hideous crocodile seizes upon his prey!—say, let him place himself in my situation—without home or friends—without money or credit—wanting shelter, and no one to give it—wanting bread, and no money to buy it,—and at the same time let him feel that he is pursued by merciless men-hunters, and in total darkness as to what to do, where to go, or where to stay,—perfectly helpless both as to the means of defence and means of escape,—in the midst of plenty, yet suffering the terrible gnawings of hunger,—in the midst of houses, yet having no home,—among fellow-men, yet feeling as if in the midst of wild beasts, whose greediness to swallow up the trembling and half-famished fugitive is only equalled by that with which the monsters of the deep swallow up the helpless fish upon which they subsist,—I say, let him be placed in this most trying situation,—the situation in which I was placed,—then, and not till then, will he fully appreciate the hardships of, and know how to sympathize with, the toil-worn and whip-scarred fugitive slave.

Thank Heaven, I remained but a short time in this distressed situation. I was relieved from it by the humane hand of Mr. DAVID RUGGLES, whose vigilance, kindness, and perseverance, I shall never forget. I am glad of an opportunity to express, as far as words can, the love and gratitude I bear him. Mr. Ruggles is now afflicted with blindness, and is himself in need of the same kind offices which he was once so forward in the performance of toward others. I had been in New York but a few days, when Mr. Ruggles sought me out, and very kindly took me to his boarding-house at the corner of Church and Lespenard Streets. Mr. Ruggles was then very deeply engaged in the memorable *Darg* case, as well as attending to a number of other fugitive slaves, devising ways and means for their successful escape; and, though watched and hemmed in on almost every side, he seemed to be more than a match for his enemies.

Very soon after I went to Mr. Ruggles, he wished to know of me where I wanted to go; as he deemed it unsafe for me to remain in New York. I told him I was a calker, and should like to go where I could get work. I thought of going to Canada; but he decided against it, and in favor of my going to New Bedford, thinking I should be able to get work there at my trade. At this time, Anna,[1] my intended wife, came on; for I wrote to her immediately after my arrival at New York, (notwithstanding my homeless, houseless, and helpless condition,) informing her of my successful flight, and wishing her to come on forthwith. In a few days after her arrival, Mr. Ruggles called in the Rev. J. W. C. Pennington, who, in the presence of Mr. Ruggles, Mrs. Michaels, and two or three others, performed the marriage ceremony, and gave us a certificate, of which the following is an exact copy:—

---

1 She was free. [Note by Frederick Douglass.]

"This may certify, that I joined together in holy matrimony Frederick Johnson[2] and Anna Murray, as man and wife, in the presence of Mr. David Ruggles and Mrs. Michaels.

"JAMES W. C. PENNINGTON. NEW YORK, SEPT. 15, 1838."

Upon receiving this certificate, and a five-dollar bill from Mr. Ruggles, I shouldered one part of our baggage, and Anna took up the other, and we set out forthwith to take passage on board of the steamboat *John W. Richmond* for Newport, on our way to New Bedford. Mr. Ruggles gave me a letter to a Mr. Shaw in Newport, and told me, in case my money did not serve me to New Bedford, to stop in Newport and obtain further assistance; but upon our arrival at Newport, we were so anxious to get to a place of safety, that, notwithstanding we lacked the necessary money to pay our fare, we decided to take seats in the stage, and promise to pay when we got to New Bedford. We were encouraged to do this by two excellent gentlemen, residents of New Bedford, whose names I afterward ascertained to be Joseph Ricketson and William C. Taber. They seemed at once to understand our circumstances, and gave us such assurance of their friendliness as put us fully at ease in their presence. It was good indeed to meet with such friends, at such a time. Upon reaching New Bedford, we were directed to the house of Mr. Nathan Johnson, by whom we were kindly received, and hospitably provided for. Both Mr. and Mrs. Johnson took a deep and lively interest in our welfare. They proved themselves quite worthy of the name of abolitionists. When the stage-driver found us unable to pay our fare, he held on upon our baggage as security for the debt. I had but to mention the fact to Mr. Johnson, and he forthwith advanced the money.

We now began to feel a degree of safety, and to prepare ourselves for the duties and responsibilities of a life of freedom. On the morning after our arrival at New Bedford, while at the breakfast-table, the question arose as to what name I should be called by. The name given me by my mother was, "Frederick Augustus Washington Bailey." I, however, had dispensed with the two middle names long before I left Maryland, so that I was generally known by the name of "Frederick Bailey." I started from Baltimore bearing the name of "Stanley." When I got to New York, I again changed my name to "Frederick

---

2 I had changed my name from Frederick *Bailey* to that of *Johnson*. [Note by Frederick Douglass.]

Johnson," and thought that would be the last change. But when I got to New Bedford, I found it necessary again to change my name. The reason of this necessity was, that there were so many Johnsons in New Bedford, it was already quite difficult to distinguish between them. I gave Mr. Johnson the privilege of choosing me a name, but told him he must not take from me the name of "Frederick." I must hold on to that, to preserve a sense of my identity. Mr. Johnson had just been reading the "Lady of the Lake," and at once suggested that my name be "Douglass." From that time until now I have been called "Frederick Douglass;" and as I am more widely known by that name than by either of the others, I shall continue to use it as my own.

I was quite disappointed at the general appearance of things in New Bedford. The impression which I had received respecting the character and condition of the people of the north, I found to be singularly erroneous. I had very strangely supposed, while in slavery, that few of the comforts, and scarcely any of the luxuries, of life were enjoyed at the north, compared with what were enjoyed by the slaveholders of the south. I probably came to this conclusion from the fact that northern people owned no slaves. I supposed that they were about upon a level with the non-slaveholding population of the south. I knew *they* were exceedingly poor, and I had been accustomed to regard their poverty as the necessary consequence of their being non-slaveholders. I had somehow imbibed the opinion that, in the absence of slaves, there could be no wealth, and very little refinement. And upon coming to the north, I expected to meet with a rough, hard-handed, and uncultivated population, living in the most Spartan-like simplicity, knowing nothing of the ease, luxury, pomp, and grandeur of southern slaveholders. Such being my conjectures, any one acquainted with the appearance of New Bedford may very readily infer how palpably I must have seen my mistake.

In the afternoon of the day when I reached New Bedford, I visited the wharves, to take a view of the shipping. Here I found myself surrounded with the strongest proofs of wealth. Lying at the wharves, and riding in the stream, I saw many ships of the finest model, in the best order, and of the largest size. Upon the right and left, I was walled in by granite warehouses of the widest dimensions, stowed to their utmost capacity with the necessaries and comforts of life. Added to this, almost every body seemed to be at work, but noiselessly so, compared with what I had been accustomed to in Baltimore. There were no loud songs heard from those engaged in loading and unloading ships. I heard no deep oaths or horrid curses on the laborer. I saw no whipping of men; but all seemed to go smoothly on. Every man appeared to understand his work, and went at it with a sober, yet cheerful earnestness, which betokened the deep interest which he felt in what he was doing, as well as a sense of his own dignity as a man. To me this looked exceedingly strange. From the wharves I strolled around and over the town, gazing with wonder and admiration at the splendid churches, beautiful dwellings, and finely-cultivated gardens; evincing an amount of wealth, comfort, taste, and refinement, such as I had never seen in any part of slaveholding Maryland.

Every thing looked clean, new, and beautiful. I saw few or no dilapidated houses, with poverty-stricken inmates; no half-naked children and barefooted women, such as I had been accustomed to see in Hillsborough, Easton, St. Michael's, and Baltimore. The people looked more able, stronger, healthier, and happier, than those of Maryland. I was for once made glad by a view of extreme wealth, without being saddened by seeing extreme poverty. But the most astonishing as well as the most interesting thing to me was the condition of the colored people, a great many of whom, like myself, had escaped thither as a refuge from the hunters of men. I found many, who had not been seven years out of their chains, living in finer houses, and evidently enjoying more of the comforts of life, than the average of slaveholders in Maryland. I will venture to assert that my friend Mr. Nathan Johnson (of whom I can say with a grateful heart, "I was hungry, and he gave me meat; I was thirsty, and he gave me drink; I was a stranger, and he took me in") lived in a neater house; dined at a better table; took, paid for, and read, more newspapers; better understood the moral, religious, and political character of the nation,—than nine tenths of the slaveholders in Talbot county, Maryland. Yet Mr. Johnson was a working man. His hands were hardened by toil, and not his alone, but those also of Mrs. Johnson. I found the colored people much more spirited than I had supposed they would be. I found among them a determination to protect each other from the blood-thirsty kidnapper, at all hazards. Soon after my arrival, I was told of a circumstance which illustrated their spirit. A colored man and a fugitive slave were on unfriendly terms. The former was heard to threaten the latter with informing his master of his whereabouts. Straightway a meeting was called among the colored people, under the stereotyped notice, "Business of importance!" The betrayer was invited to attend. The people came at the appointed hour, and organized the meeting by appointing a very religious old gentleman as president, who, I believe, made a prayer, after which he addressed the meeting as follows:

"Friends, we have got him here, and I would recommend that you young men just take him outside the door, and kill him!" With this, a number of them bolted at him; but they were intercepted by some more timid than themselves, and the betrayer escaped their vengeance, and has not been seen in New Bedford since. I believe there have been no more such threats, and should there be hereafter, I doubt not that death would be the consequence.

I found employment, the third day after my arrival, in stowing a sloop with a load of oil. It was new, dirty, and hard work for me; but I went at it with a glad heart and a willing hand. I was now my own master. It was a happy moment, the rapture of which can be understood only by those who have been slaves. It was the first work, the reward of which was to be entirely my own. There was no Master Hugh standing ready, the moment I earned the money, to rob me of it. I worked that day with a pleasure I had never before experienced. I was at work for myself and newly-married wife. It was to me the starting-point of a new existence. When I got through with that job, I went in pursuit of a job of calking; but such was the strength of prejudice against color, among the white calkers, that they refused to work with me, and of course I could get no employment.[3] Finding my trade of no immediate benefit, I threw off my calking habiliments, and prepared myself to do any kind of work I could get to do. Mr. Johnson kindly let me have his wood-horse and saw, and I very soon found myself a plenty of work. There was no work too hard—none too dirty. I was ready to saw wood, shovel coal, carry the hod, sweep the chimney, or roll oil casks,—all of which I did for nearly three years in New Bedford, before I became known to the anti-slavery world.

In about four months after I went to New Bedford, there came a young man to me, and inquired if I did not wish to take the *Liberator*. I told him I did; but, just having made my escape from slavery, I remarked that I was unable to pay for it then. I, however, finally became a subscriber to it. The paper came, and I read it from week to week with such feelings as it would be quite idle for me to attempt to describe. The paper became my meat and my drink. My soul was set all on fire. Its sympathy for my brethren in bonds—its scathing denunciations of slaveholders—its faithful exposures of slavery—and

---

3 I am told that colored persons can now get employment at calking in New Bedford—a result of anti-slavery effort. [Note by Frederick Douglass.]

its powerful attacks upon the upholders of the institution—sent a thrill of joy through my soul, such as I had never felt before!

I had not long been a reader of the *Liberator,* before I got a pretty correct idea of the principles, measures and spirit of the anti-slavery reform. I took right hold of the cause. I could do but little; but what I could, I did with a joyful heart, and never felt happier than when in an anti-slavery meeting. I seldom had much to say at the meetings, because what I wanted to say was said so much better by others. But, while attending an anti-slavery convention at Nantucket, on the 11th of August, 1841, I felt strongly moved to speak, and was at the same time much urged to do so by Mr. William C. Coffin, a gentleman who had heard me speak in the colored people's meeting at New Bedford. It was a severe cross, and I took it up reluctantly. The truth was, I felt myself a slave, and the idea of speaking to white people weighed me down. I spoke but a few moments, when I felt a degree of freedom, and said what I desired with considerable ease. From that time until now, I have been engaged in pleading the cause of my brethren—with what success, and with what devotion, I leave those acquainted with my labors to decide.

SOURCE: Frederick Douglass. *Narrative of the Life of Frederick Douglass.* Mineola, New York: Dover Publications, 1995. (Original edition, 1845.)

ABRAM GALLOWAY AND RICHARD EDEN

Blood Flowed Freely: Two Passengers Secreted in a Vessel Loaded with Spirits of Turpentine—Shrouds Prepared to Prevent Being Smoked to Death

[William Still]

Abram Galloway and Richard Eden were two extraordinary friends, "heroes who were worthy to be classed among the bravest of the brave," who contrived a perilous but successful escape from North Carolina. Still relates not only the details of their escape but its happy aftermath.

THE PHILADELPHIA BRANCH of the Underground Rail Road was not fortunate in having very frequent arrivals from North Carolina. Of course such of her slave population as managed to become initiated in the mysteries of traveling North by the Underground Rail Road were sensible enough to find out nearer and safer routes than through Pennsylvania. Nevertheless the Vigilance Committee of Philadelphia occasionally had the pleasure of receiving some heroes who were worthy to be classed among the bravest of the brave, no matter who they may be who have claims to this distinction.

In proof of this bold assertion the two individuals whose names stand at the beginning of this chapter are presented. Abram was only twenty-one years of age, mulatto, five feet six inches high, intelligent and the picture of good health. "What was your master's name?" inquired a member of the Committee. "Milton Hawkins," answered Abram. "What business did Milton Hawkins follow?" again queried said member. "He was chief engineer on the Wilmington and Manchester Rail Road" (not a branch of the Underground Rail Road), responded Richard. "Describe him," said the member. "He was a slim built, tall man with whiskers. He was a man of very good disposition. I always belonged to him; he owned three. He always said he would sell before he would use a whip. His wife was a very mean woman; she would whip contrary to his orders." "Who was your father?" was further inquired. "John Wesley Galloway," was the prompt response. "Describe your father?" "He was captain of a government vessel; he recognized me as his son, and protected me as far as he was allowed so to do; he lived at Smithfield, North Carolina. Abram's master, Milton Hawkins, lived at Wilmington, N. C." "What prompted you to escape?" was next asked. "Because times were hard and I could not come up with my wages as I was required to do, so thought I would try and do better." At this juncture Abram explained substantially in what sense times were hard, &c. In the first place he was not allowed to own himself; he, however, preferred hiring his time to serving in the usual way. This favor was granted Abram; but he was compelled to pay $15 per month for his time, besides finding himself in clothing, food, paying doctor bills, and a head tax of $15 a year.

Even under this master, who was a man of very good disposition, Abram was not contented. In the second place, he "always thought Slavery was wrong," although he had "never suffered any personal abuse." Toiling month after month the year round to support his master and not himself, was the one intolerable thought. Abram and

Richard were intimate friends, and lived near each other. Being similarly situated, they could venture to communicate the secret feelings of their hearts to each other. Richard was four years older than Abram, with not quite so much Anglo-Saxon blood in his veins, but was equally as intelligent, and was by trade, a "fashionable barber," well-known to the ladies and gentlemen of Wilmington. Richard owed service to Mrs. Mary Loren, a widow. "She was very kind and tender to all her slaves." "If I was sick," said Richard, "she would treat me the same as a mother would." She was the owner of twenty, men, women and children, who were all hired out, except the children too young for hire. Besides having his food, clothing and doctor's expenses to meet, he had to pay the "very kind and tender-hearted widow" $12.50 per month, and head tax to the State, amounting to twenty-five cents per month. It so happened, that Richard at this time, was involved in a matrimonial difficulty. Contrary to the laws of North Carolina, he had lately married a free girl, which was an indictable offence, and for which the penalty was, then in soak for him—said penalty to consist of thirty-nine lashes, and imprisonment at the discretion of the judge.

So Abram and Richard put their heads together, and resolved to try the Underground Rail Road. They concluded that liberty was worth dying for, and that it was their duty to strike for Freedom even if it should cost them their lives. The next thing needed, was information about the Underground Rail Road. Before a great while the captain of a schooner turned up, from Wilmington, Delaware. Learning that his voyage extended to Philadelphia, they sought to find out whether this captain was true to Freedom. To ascertain this fact required no little address. It had to be done in such a way, that even the captain would not really understand what they were up to, should he be found untrue. In this instance, however, he was the right man in the right place, and very well understood his business.

Abram and Richard made arrangements with him to bring them away; they learned when the vessel would start, and that she was loaded with tar, rosin, and spirits of turpentine, amongst which the captain was to secrete them. But here came the difficulty. In order that slaves might not be secreted in vessels, the slave-holders of North Carolina had procured the enactment of a law requiring all vessels coming North to be smoked.

To escape this dilemma, the inventive genius of Abram and Richard soon devised a safe-guard against the smoke. This safe-guard consisted in silk oil-cloth shrouds, made large, with drawing strings, which, when pulled over their heads, might be drawn very tightly around their waists, whilst the process of smoking might be in operation. A bladder of water and towels were provided, the latter to be wet and held to their nostrils, should there be need. In this manner they had determined to struggle against death for liberty. The hour approached for being at the wharf. At the appointed time they were on hand ready to go on the boat; the captain secreted them, according to agreement. They were ready to run the risk of being smoked to death; but as good luck would have it, the law was not carried into effect in this instance, so that the "smell of smoke was not upon them." The effect of the turpentine, however, of the nature of which they were totally ignorant, was worse, if possible, than the smoke would have been. The blood was literally drawn from them at every pore in frightful quantities. But as heroes of the bravest type they resolved to continue steadfast as long as a pulse continued to beat, and thus they finally conquered.

The invigorating northern air and the kind treatment of the Vigilance Committee acted like a charm upon them, and they improved very rapidly from their exhaustive and heavy loss of blood. Desiring to retain some memorial of them, a member of the Committee begged one of their silk shrouds, and likewise procured an artist to take the photograph of one of them; which keepsakes have been valued very highly. In the regular order of arrangements the wants of Abram and Richard were duly met by the Committee, financially and otherwise, and they were forwarded to Canada. After their safe arrival in Canada, Richard addressed a member of the Committee thus:

KINGSTON, July 20, 1857.

MR. WILLIAM STILL—*Dear Friend*:—I take the opertunity Of wrighting a few lines to let you no that we air all in good health hoping thos few lines may find you and your family engoying the same blessing. We arived in King all saft Canada West Abram Galway gos to work this morning at $1 75 per day and John pediford is at work for mr george mink and i will opne a shop for my self in a few days My wif will send a daugretipe to your cair whitch you will pleas to send on to me Richard Edons to the cair of George Mink Kingston C W

Yours with Respect, RICHARD EDONS.

Abram, his comrade, allied himself faithfully to John Bull until Uncle Sam became involved in the contest with the rebels. In this hour of need Abram hastened back to North Carolina to help fight the battles of Freedom. How well he acted his part, we are not informed. We only know that, after the war was over, in the reconstruction of North Carolina, Abram was promoted to a seat in its Senate. He died in office only a few months since. ...

SOURCE: William Still, 1872 (see the Bibliography on p. 203 for complete information).

MARGARET GARNER

The Slave Mother Who Killed Her Child Rather Than See It Taken Back to Slavery

[Levi Coffin]

Margaret Garner, fugitive slave and mother of four, declared that she would kill herself and her children before she returned to slavery or allowed her sons and daughters to be enslaved. When hunted by her owner and his posse, Garner resisted capture by slitting her daughter's throat and attempting to kill her other children as well as herself. Garner's story was the inspiration for Toni Morrison's Beloved *(1987) and for the opera* Margaret Garner *(2005), composed by Richard Danielpour with the libretto by Toni Morrison. In the following narrative, Levi Coffin, known as the "President of the Underground Railroad," discusses Garner's experiences and her sad return to "the seething hell of American slavery."*

PERHAPS NO CASE that came under my notice, while engaged in aiding fugitive slaves, attracted more attention and aroused deeper interest and sympathy than the case of Margaret Garner, the slave mother, who killed her child rather than see it taken back to slavery. This happened in the latter part of January, 1856. The Ohio River was frozen over at the time, and the opportunity thus offered for escaping to a free State was embraced by a number of slaves living in Kentucky, several miles back from the river. A party of seventeen, belonging to different masters in the same neighborhood, made arrangements to escape together. There was snow on the ground and the roads were smooth, so the plan of going to the river on a sled naturally suggested itself. The time fixed for their flight was Sabbath night, and having managed to get a large sled and two good horses, belonging to one of their masters, the party of seventeen crowded into the sled and started on their hazardous journey in the latter part of the night. They drove the horses at full speed, and at daylight reached the river below Covington, opposite Western Row. They left the sled and horses here, and as quickly as possible crossed the river on foot. It was now broad daylight, and people were beginning to pass about the streets, and the fugitives divided their company that they might not attract so much notice.

An old slave man named Simon, and his wife Mary, together with their son Robert and his wife Margaret Garner and four children, made their way to the house of a colored man named Kite, who had formerly lived in their neighborhood and had been purchased from slavery by his father, Joe Kite. They had to make several inquiries in order to find Kite's house, which was below Mill Creek, in the lower part of the city. This afterward led to their discovery; they had been seen by a number of persons on their way to Kite's, and were easily traced by pursuers. The other nine fugitives were more fortunate. They made their way up town and found friends who conducted them to safe hiding-places, where they remained until night. They were then put on the Underground Railroad, and went safely through to Canada.

Kite felt alarmed for the safety of the party that had arrived at his house, and as soon as breakfast was over, he came to my store, at the corner of Sixth and Elm Streets, to ask counsel regarding them. I told him that they were in a very unsafe place and must be removed at once. I directed him how to conduct them from his house to the outskirts of the city, up Mill Creek, to a settlement of colored people in the western part of the city, where fugitives were often harbored. I would make arrangements to forward them northward, that night, on the Underground Railroad. Kite returned to his house at once, according to my directions, but he was too late; in a few minutes after his return, the house was surrounded by pursuers—the masters of the fugitives, with officers and a posse of men. The door and windows were barred, and those inside refused to give admittance. The fugitives were determined to fight, and to die, rather than to be taken back to slavery. Margaret, the mother of the four children, declared that she would kill herself and her children before she would return to bondage. The slave men were armed and fought bravely. The window was first battered down with a stick of wood, and one of the deputy marshals attempted to enter, but a pistol shot from within made a flesh wound on his arm and caused him to abandon the attempt. The pursuers then battered down the door with some timber and rushed in. The husband of Margaret fired several shots, and wounded one of the officers, but was soon overpowered and dragged out of the house. At this moment, Margaret Garner, seeing that their hopes of freedom were vain seized a butcher knife that lay on the table, and with one stroke cut the throat of her little daughter, whom she probably loved the best. She then attempted to take the life of the other children and to kill herself, but she was overpowered and hampered before she could complete her desperate work. The whole party was then arrested and lodged in jail.

The trial lasted two weeks, drawing crowds to the court-room every day. Colonel Chambers, of this city, and two lawyers from Covington—Wall and Tinnell—appeared for the claimants, and Messrs. Jolliffe and Getchell for the slaves. The counsel for the defense brought witnesses to prove that the fugitives had been permitted to visit the city at various times previously. It was claimed that Margaret Garner had been brought here by her owners a number of years before, to act as nurse girl, and according to the law which liberated slaves who were brought into free States by the consent of their masters, she had been free from that time, and her children, all of whom had been born since then—following the condition of the mother—were likewise free.

The Commissioner decided that a voluntary return to slavery, after a visit to a free State, re-attached the conditions of slavery, and that the fugitives were legally slaves at the time of their escape.

Early in the course of the trial, Lawyer Jolliffe announced that warrants had been issued by the State authorities to arrest the fugitives on a criminal charge—Margaret Garner for murder, and the others for complicity in murder—and moved that the papers should be served on them immediately. Commissioner Pendery wished that to be deferred until he had given his decision, and the fugitives were out of the jurisdiction of his court, but Jolliffe pressed the motion to have the warrants served—"For," said he, "the fugitives have all assured me that they will *go singing to the gallows* rather than be returned to slavery." He further said that it might appear strange for him to be urging that his clients should be indicted for murder, but he was anxious that this charge should be brought against them before they passed from the jurisdiction of the Commissioner's Court, for the infamous law of 1850 provided that no warrant in any event should be served upon the fugitives in case they were remanded to the custody of their owners. Not even a warrant for murder could prevent their being returned to bondage.

Jolliffe said that in the final argument of the case he intended not only to allege, but to demonstrate, conclusively, to the Court, that the Fugitive Slave law was unconstitutional, and as part and parcel of that argument he wished to show the effects of carrying it out. It had driven a frantic mother to murder her own child rather than see it carried back to the seething hell of American slavery. This law was of such an order that its execution required human hearts to be wrung and human blood to be spilt.

"The Constitution," said he, "expressly declared that Congress should pass no law prescribing any form of religion or preventing the free exercise thereof. If Congress could not pass any law requiring you to worship God, still less could they pass one requiring you to carry fuel to hell." These ringing words called forth applause from all parts of the court-room. Jolliffe said: "It is for the Court to decide whether the Fugitive Slave law overrides the law of Ohio to such an extent that it can not arrest a fugitive slave even for a crime of murder."

The fugitives were finally indicted for murder, but we will see that this amounted to nothing.

Margaret Garner, the chief actor in the tragedy which had occurred, naturally excited much attention. She was a mulatto, about five feet high, showing one-fourth or one-third white blood. She had a high forehead, her eyebrows were finely arched and her eyes bright and intelligent, but the African appeared in the lower part of her face, in her broad nose and thick lips. On the left side of her forehead was an old scar, and on the cheekbone, on the same side, another one. When asked what caused them, she said: "White man struck me." That was all, but it betrays a story of cruelty and degradation, and, perhaps, gives the key-note to Margaret's hate of slavery, her revolt against its thralldom, and her resolve to die rather than go back to it.

She appeared to be twenty-two or twenty-three years old. While in the court-room she was dressed in dark calico, with a white handkerchief pinned around her neck, and a yellow cotton handkerchief, arranged as a turban, around her head. The babe she held in her arms was a little girl, about nine months old, and was much lighter in color than herself, light enough to show a red tinge in its cheeks. During the trial she would look up occasionally, for an instant, with a timid, apprehensive glance at the strange faces around her, but her eyes were generally cast down. The babe was continually fondling her face with its little hands, but she rarely noticed it, and her general expression was one of extreme sadness. The little boys, four and six years old, respectively, were bright-eyed, woolly-headed little fellows, with fat dimpled cheeks. During the trial they sat on the floor near their mother, playing together in happy innocence, all unconscious of the gloom that shrouded their mother, and of the fact that their own future liberty was at stake. The murdered child was almost white, a little girl of rare beauty.

The case seemed to stir every heart that was alive to the emotions of humanity. The interest manifested by all classes was not so much for the legal principles involved, as for the mute instincts that mold every human heart—the undying love of freedom that is planted in every breast—the resolve to die rather than submit to a life of degradation and bondage.

A number of people, who were deeply interested in the fugitives, visited them in prison and conversed with them. Old Simon, his wife Mary, and their son Robert, while expressing their longing for freedom, said that they should not attempt to kill themselves if they were returned to slavery. Their trust in God seemed to have survived all the wrong and cruelty inflicted upon them by man, and though they felt often like crying bitterly, "How long, O Lord, how long?" they still trusted and endured. But Margaret seemed to have a different nature; she could see nothing but woe for herself and her children. Who can fathom the depths of her heart as she brooded over the wrongs and insults that had been heaped upon her all her life? Who can wonder if her faith staggered when she saw her efforts to gain freedom frustrated, when she saw the gloom of her old life close around her again, without any hope of deliverance? Those who came to speak words of comfort and cheer felt them die upon their lips, when they looked into her face, and marked its expression of settled despair. Her sorrow was beyond the reach of any words of encouragement and consolation, and can be realized in all its fullness only by those who have tasted of a cup equally bitter.

Among those who visited Margaret in prison was Lucy Stone, the well-known eloquent public speaker. It was reported that she gave Margaret a knife, and told her to kill herself and her children rather than be taken back to slavery. Colonel Chambers, the counsel for the claimants, referred to this rumor in court, and Lucy Stone, coming in shortly afterward, was informed of it. She requested to say a few words in reply, and when the court had adjourned, the greater part of the crowd remained to hear her. She said: "I am only sorry that I was not in when Colonel Chambers said what he did about me, and my giving a knife to Margaret. When I saw that poor fugitive, took her toil-hardened hand in mine, and read in her face deep suffering and an ardent longing for freedom, I could not help bid her be of good cheer. I told her that a thousand hearts were aching for her, and that they were glad one child of hers was safe with the angels. Her only reply was a look of deep despair, of anguish such as no words can speak. I thought the spirit she manifested was the same with that of our ancestors to whom we had erected the monument at Bunker Hill—the spirit that would rather let us all go back to God than back to slavery. The faded faces of the negro children tell too plainly to what degradation female slaves must submit. Rather than give her little daughter to that life, she killed it. If in her deep maternal love she felt the impulse to send her child back to God, to save it from coming woe, who shall say she had no right to do so? That desire had its root in the deepest and holiest feelings of our nature—implanted alike in black and white by our common Father. With my own teeth I would tear open my veins and let the earth drink my blood, rather than to wear the chains of slavery. How then could I blame her for wishing her child to find freedom with God and the angels, where no chains are? I know not whether this Commissioner has children, else I would appeal to him to know how he would feel to have them torn from him, but I feel that he will not disregard the Book which says: 'Thou shalt not deliver unto his master the servant which is escaped from his master unto thee: he shall dwell with thee, even among you, in that place which he shall choose in one of thy gates, where it liketh him best.'"

But in spite of touching appeals, of eloquent pleadings, the Commissioner remanded the fugitives back to slavery. He said that it was not a question of feeling to be decided by the chance current of his sympathies; the law of Kentucky and of the United States made it a question of property.

In regard to the claim, plainly established by the evidence, that the fugitives had previously been brought to this State by the consent of their masters, he said: "Had the slaves asserted their freedom, they would have been practically free, but they voluntarily returned to slavery. In allowing them to come to Ohio, the master voluntarily abandoned his claim upon them, and they, in returning, abandoned their claim to freedom."

By a provision of the law, previously referred to, they could not be tried on the warrant for murder, and their indictment on that charge was practically ignored. Jolliffe said, indignantly, that even a savage tribe reserved to itself the right to investigate a charge for murder committed within its border, but the sovereign State of Ohio allowed itself and its laws to be overruled by the infamous Fugitive Slave law, made in the interests of slaveholders. The question of bringing the case before a superior court, and trying the slaves for murder was agitated, and Gaines, the master of Margaret, promised to have her in safe-keeping on the opposite side of the river, to be delivered up to the authorities of the State of Ohio, if a requisition for her was made.

The fugitives were then delivered to their owners, who conveyed them in an omnibus to the wharf of the Covington ferry-boat. A crowd followed them to the river, but there was no demonstration. The masters were surrounded by large numbers of their Kentucky friends, who had stood by them and guarded their interests during the trial, and there was great rejoicing among them, on account of their victory.

The masters kept their slaves in jail in Covington, a few days, then took them away. When the requisition was made for Margaret, Gaines said that he had kept her in Covington for some time according to the agreement, then, as the writ was not served, he had sent her down the river. This was a violation of the spirit of the agreement, and much indignation was manifested by Margaret's friends in Ohio, but nothing further was done. Margaret was lost, in what Jolliffe called, "the seething hell of American slavery." It was reported that on her way down the river she sprang from the boat into the water with her babe in her arms; that when she rose she was seized by some of the boat hands and rescued, but that her child was drowned.

After the trial of the fugitives, a committee of citizens presented a purse to Jolliffe, accompanied by an address, in token of their appreciation of his services. He returned thanks in an eloquent letter, setting forth his views on the unconstitutionality of the Fugitive Slave law.

SOURCE: Levi Coffin. *Reminiscences of Levi Coffin, the Reputed President of the Underground Railroad; Being a Brief History of the Labors of a Lifetime in Behalf of the Slave, with the Stories of Numerous Fugitives, Who Gained Their Freedom Through His Instrumentality, and Many Other Incidents*. Second edition. Cincinnati: Robert Clarke and Company, 1880.

CHARLES GILBERT

Fleeing from Davis, a Negro Trader, Secreted Under a Hotel, Up a Tree, Under a Floor, in a Thicket, on a Steamer

[William Still]

Still delights in Charles Gilbert's "marvellous" escape, appreciating the intelligence that rescued him from numerous desperate situations on his way to freedom.

IN 1854 CHARLES WAS OWNED in the city of Richmond by Benjamin Davis, a notorious negro trader. Charles was quite a "likely-looking article," not too black or too white, but rather of a nice "ginger-bread color." Davis was of opinion that this "article" must bring him a tip-top price. For two or three months the trader advertised Charles for sale in the papers, but for some reason or other Charles did not command the high price demanded.

While Davis was thus daily trying to sell Charles, Charles was contemplating how he might escape. Being uncommonly shrewd he learned something about a captain of a schooner from Boston, and determined to approach him with regard to securing a passage. The captain manifested a disposition to accommodate him for the sum of ten dollars, provided Charles could manage to get to Old Point Comfort, there to embark. The Point was about one hundred and sixty miles distant from Richmond.

A man of ordinary nerve would have declined this condition unhesitatingly. On the other hand it was not Charles' intention to let any offer slide; indeed he felt that he must make an effort. If he failed, he could not see how his lot could be made more miserable by attempting to flee. In full view of all the consequences he ventured to take the hazardous step, and to his great satisfaction he reached Old Point Comfort safely. In that locality he was well known, unfortunately too well known, for he had been raised partly there, and, at the same time, many of his relatives and acquaintances were still living there. These facts were evidently well known to the trader, who unquestionably had snares set in order to entrap Charles should he seek shelter among his relatives, a reasonable supposition. Charles had scarcely reached his old home before he was apprised of the fact that the hunters and watch dogs of Slavery were eagerly watching for him. Even his nearest relatives, through fear of consequences had to hide their faces as it were from him. None dare offer him a night's lodging, scarcely a cup of water, lest such an act might be discovered by the hunters, whose fiendish hearts would have found pleasure in meting out the most dire punishments to those guilty of thus violating the laws of Slavery. The prospect, if not utterly hopeless, was decidedly discouraging. The way to Boston was entirely closed. A "reward of $200" was advertised for his capture. For the first week after arriving at Old Point he entrusted himself to a young friend by the name of E. S. The fear of the pursuers drove him from his hiding-place at the expiration of the week. Thence he sought shelter neither with kinfolks, Christians, nor infidels, but in this hour of his calamity he made up his mind that he would try living under a large hotel for a while. Having watched his opportunity, he managed to reach Higee hotel, a very large house without a cellar, erected on pillars three or four feet above the ground. One place alone, near the cistern, presented some chance for a hiding-place, sufficient to satisfy him quite well under the circumstances. This dark and gloomy spot he at once willingly occupied rather than return to Slavery. In this refuge he remained four weeks. Of course he could not live without food; but to communicate with man or woman would inevitably subject him to danger. Charles' experience in the neighborhood of his old home left no ground for him to hope that he would be likely to find friendly aid anywhere under the shadow of Slavery. In consequence of these fears he received his food from the "slop tub," securing this diet in the darkness of night after all was still and quiet around the hotel. To use his own language, the meals thus obtained were often "sweet" to his taste.

One evening, however, he was not a little alarmed by the approach of an Irish boy who came under the hotel to hunt chickens. While prowling around in the darkness he appeared to be making his way unconsciously to the very spot where Charles was reposing. How to meet the danger was to Charles' mind at first very puzzling, there was no time now to plan. As quick as thought he feigned the bark of a savage dog accompanied with a furious growl and snarl which he was confident would frighten the boy half out of his senses, and cause him to depart quickly from his private apartment. The trick succeeded admirably, and the emergency was satisfactorily met, so far as the boy was concerned, but the boy's father, hearing the attack of the dog, swore that he would kill him. Charles was a silent listener to the threat, and he saw that he could no longer remain in safety in his present quarter. So that night he took his departure for Bay Shore; here he decided to pass a day in the woods, but the privacy of this place was not altogether satisfactory to Charles' mind; but where to find a more secure retreat he could not,—dared not venture to ascertain that day. It occurred to him, however, that he would be much safer up a tree than hid in the bushes and undergrowth. He therefore climbed up a large acorn tree and there passed an entire day in deep meditation. No gleam of hope appeared, yet he would not suffer himself to think of returning to bondage. In this dilemma he remembered a poor washer-woman named Isabella, a slave who had charge of a wash-house. With her he resolved to seek succor. Leaving the woods he proceeded to the wash-house and was kindly received by Isabella, but what to do with him or how to afford him any protection she could see no way whatever. The schooling which Charles had been receiving a number of weeks in connection with the most fearful looking-for of the threatened wrath of the trader made it much easier for him than for her to see how he could be provided for. A room and comforts he was not accustomed to. Of course he could not expect such comforts now. Like many another escaping from the relentless tyrant, Charles could contrive methods which to his venturesome mind would afford hope, however desperate they might appear to others. He thought that he might be safe under the floor. To Isabella the idea was new, but her sympathies were strongly with Charles, and she readily consented to accommodate him under the floor of the wash-house. Isabella and a friend of Charles, by the name of John Thomas, were the only persons who were cognizant of this arrangement. The kindness of these friends, manifested by their willingness to do anything in their power to add to the comfort of Charles, was proof to him that his efforts and sufferings had not been altogether in vain. He remained under the floor two weeks, accessible to kind voices and friendly ministrations. At the end of this time his repose was again sorely disturbed by reports from without that suspicion had been awakened towards the washhouse. How this happened neither Charles nor his friends could conjecture. But the arrival of six officers whom he could hear talking very plainly in the house, whose errand was actually to search for him, convinced him that he had never for a single moment been in greater danger. The officers not only searched the house, but they offered his friend John Thomas $25 if he would only put them on Charles' track. John professed to know nothing; Isabella was equally ignorant. Discouraged with their efforts on this occasion, the officers gave up the hunt and left the house. Charles, however, had had enough of the floor accommodations. He left that night and returned to his old quarters under the hotel. Here he stayed one week, at the expiration of which time the need of fresh air was so imperative, that he resolved to go out at night to Allen's cottage and spend a day in the woods. He had knowledge of a place where the undergrowth and bushes were almost impenetrable. To rest and refresh himself in this thicket he felt would be a great comfort to him. Without serious difficulty he reached the thicket, and while pondering over the all-absorbing matter as to how he should ever manage to make his escape, an old man approached. Now while Charles had no reason to think that he was sought by the old intruder, his very near approach admonished him that it would neither be safe nor agreeable to allow him to come nearer. Charles remembering that his trick of playing the dog, when previously in danger under the hotel, had served a good end, thought that it would work well in the thicket. So he again tried his power at growling and barking hideously for a moment or two, which at once caused the man to turn his course. Charles could hear him distinctly retreating, and at the same time cursing the dog. The owner of the place had the reputation of keeping "bad dogs," so the old man poured out a dreadful threat against "Stephens' dogs," and was soon out of the reach of the one in the thicket.

Notwithstanding his success in frightening off the old man, Charles felt that the thicket was by no means a safe place for him. He concluded to make another change. This time he sought a marsh; two hours' stay there was sufficient to satisfy him, that that too was no place to tarry in, even for a single night. He, therefore, left immediately. A third time, he returned to the hotel, where he remained only two days. His appeals had at last reached the heart of his mother—she could no longer bear to see him struggling, and suffering, and not render him aid, whatever the consequences might be. If she at first feared to lend him a helping hand, she now resolutely worked with a view of saving money to succor him. Here the prospect began to brighten.

A passage was secured for him on a steamer bound for Philadelphia. One more day, and night must elapse, ere he could be received on board. The joyful anticipations which now filled his breast left no room for fear; indeed, he could scarcely contain himself; he was drunk with joy. In this state of mind he concluded that nothing would afford him more pleasure before leaving, than to spend his last hours at the wash-house, "under the floor." To this place he went with no fear of hunters before his eyes. Charles had scarcely been three hours in this place, however, before three officers came in search of him. Two of them talked with Isabella, asked her about her "boarders," etc.; in the meanwhile, one of them uninvited, made his way up stairs. It so happened, that Charles was in this very portion of the house. His case now seemed more hopeless than ever. The officer up stairs was separated from him simply by a thin curtain. Women's garments hung all around. Instead of fainting or surrendering, in the twinkling of an eye, Charles' inventive intellect, led him to enrobe himself in female attire. Here, to use his own language, a "thousand thoughts" rushed into his mind in a minute. The next instant he was going down stairs in the presence of the officers, his old calico dress, bonnet and rig, attracting no further attention than simply to elicit the following simple questions: "Whose gal are you?" "Mr. Cockling's, sir." "What is your name?" "Delie, sir." "Go on then!" said one of the officers, and on Charles went to avail himself of the passage on the steamer which his mother had procured for him for the sum of thirty dollars.

In due time, he succeeded in getting on the steamer, but he soon learned, that her course was not direct to Philadelphia, but that some stay would be made in Norfolk, Va. Although disappointed, yet this being a step in the right direction, he made up his mind to be patient. He was delayed in Norfolk four weeks. From the time Charles first escaped, his owner (Davis the negro trader), had kept a standing reward of $550 advertised for his recovery. This showed that Davis was willing to risk heavy expenses for Charles as well as gave evidence that he believed him still secreted either about Richmond, Petersburg, or

Old Point Comfort. In this belief he was not far from being correct, for Charles spent most of his time in either of these three places, from the day of his escape until the day that he finally embarked. At last, the long looked-for hour arrived to start for Philadelphia.

He was to leave his mother, with no hope of ever seeing her again, but she had purchased herself and was called free. Her name was Margaret Johnson. Three brothers likewise were ever in his thoughts, (in chains), "Henry," "Bill," and "Sam," (half brothers). But after all the hope of freedom outweighed every other consideration, and he was prepared to give up all for liberty. To die rather than remain a slave was his resolve.

Charles arrived per steamer, from Norfolk, on the 11th day of November, 1854. The Richmond papers bear witness to the fact, that Benjamin Davis advertised Charles Gilbert, for months prior to this date, as has been stated in this narrative. As to the correctness of the story, all that the writer has to say is, that he took it down from the lips of Charles, hurriedly, directly after his arrival, with no thought of magnifying a single incident. On the contrary, much that was of interest in the story had to be omitted. Instead of being overdrawn, not half of the particulars were recorded. Had the idea then been entertained, that the narrative of this young slave-warrior was to be brought to light in the manner and time that it now is, a far more thrilling account of his adventures might have been written. Other colored men who knew both Davis and Charles, as well as one man ordinarily knows another, rejoiced at seeing Charles in Philadelphia, and they listened with perfect faith to his story. So marvellous were the incidents of his escape, that his sufferings in Slavery, previous to his heroic struggles to throw off the yoke, were among the facts omitted from the records. While this may be regretted it is, nevertheless, gratifying on the whole to have so good an account of him as was preserved. It is needless to say, that the Committee took especial pleasure in aiding him, and listening to so remarkable a story narrated so intelligently by one who had been a slave.

SOURCE: William Still, 1872 (see the Bibliography on p. 203 for complete information).

ARNOLD GRAGSTON

"How Their Grandpa Brought Emancipation to Loads of Slaves"

[Federal Writers' Project American Guide, Pearl Randolph]

In 1936-37, the federal government commissioned reporters to interview former slaves. Arnold Gragston had not only conducted hundreds of slaves from Kentucky across the Ohio River to freedom in Ohio, he finally at the end of the Civil War conducted himself and his wife.

★

Verbatim Interview with Arnold Gragston, 97-year-old ex-slave whose early life was spent helping slaves to freedom across the Ohio River, while he, himself, remained in bondage. As he puts it, he guesses he could be called a "conductor" on the underground railway, "only we didn't call it that then. I don't know as we called it anything—we just knew there was a lot of slaves always a-wantin' to get free, and I had to help 'em." Interview with subject, Arnold Gragston, present address, Robert Hungerford College Campus, Eatonville (P.O. Maitland), Florida. (Subject is relative of President of Hungerford College and stays several months in Eatonville at frequent intervals. His home is Detroit, Michigan.)

★

MOST OF THE SLAVES DIDN'T KNOW when they was born, but I did. You see, I was born on a Christmas mornin'—it was in 1840; I was a full grown man when I finally got my freedom.

Before I got it, though, I helped a lot of others get theirs. Lawd only knows how many; might have been as much as two-three hundred. It was 'way more than a hundred, I know.

But that all came after I was a young man—grown enough to know a pretty girl when I saw one, and to go chasing after her, too. I was born on a plantation that b'longed to Mr. Jack Tabb in Mason County, just across the river in Kentucky.

Mr. Tabb was a pretty good man. He used to beat us, sure; but not nearly so much as others did, some of his own kin people, even. But he was kinda funny sometimes; he used to have a special slave who didn't have nothin' to do but teach the rest of us—we had about ten on the plantation, and a lot on the other plantations near us—how to read and write and figger. Mr. Tabb liked us to know how to figger. But sometimes when he would send for us and we would be a long time comin', he would ask us where we had been. If we told him we had been learnin' to read, he would near beat the daylights out of us—after gettin' somebody to teach us; I think he did some of that so that the other owners wouldn't say he was spoilin' his slaves.

He was funny about us marryin', too. He would let us go a-courtin' on the other plantations near anytime we liked, if we were good, and if we found somebody we wanted to marry, and she was on a plantation that b'longed to one of his kin folks or a friend, he would swap a slave so that the husband and wife could be together. Sometimes, when he couldn't do this, he would let a slave work all day on his plantation, and live with his wife at night on her plantation. Some of the other owners was always talking about his spoilin' us.

He wasn't a Dimmacrat like the rest of 'em in the county; he belonged to the "Know-nothin' Party" and he was a real leader in it. He used to always be makin' speeches, and sometimes his best friends wouldn't be speaking to him for days at a time.

Mr. Tabb was always specially good to me. He used to let me go all about—I guess he had to; couldn't get too much work out of me even when he kept me right under his eyes. I learned fast, too, and I think he kinda liked that. He used to call Sandy Davis, the slave who taught me, "the smartest Nigger in Kentucky."

It was 'cause he used to let me go around in the day and night so much that I came to be the one who carried the runnin' away slaves over the river. It was funny the way I started it too.

I didn't have no idea of ever gettin' mixed up in any sort of business like that until one special night. I hadn't even thought of rowing across the river myself.

But one night I had gone on another plantation courtin', and the old woman whose house I went to told me she had a real pretty girl there who wanted to go across the river and would I take her? I was scared and backed out in a hurry. But then I saw the girl, and she was such a pretty little thing, brown-skinned and kinda rosy, and looking as scared as I was feelin', so it wasn't long before I was listenin' to the old woman tell me when to take her and where to leave her on the other side.

I didn't have nerve enough to do it that night, though, and I told them to wait for me until tomorrow night. All the next day I kept seeing Mister Tabb laying a rawhide across my back, or shootin' me, and kept seeing that scared little brown girl back at the house, looking at me with her big eyes and asking me if I wouldn't just row her across to Ripley. Me and Mr. Tabb lost, and soon as dust settled that night, I was at the old lady's house.

I don't know how I ever rowed the boat across the river—the current was strong and I was trembling. I couldn't see a thing there in the dark, but I felt that girl's eyes. We didn't dare to whisper, so I couldn't tell her how sure I was that Mr. Tabb or some of the other owners would tear me up when they found out what I had done. I just knew they would find out.

I was worried, too, about where to put her out of the boat. I couldn't ride her across the river all night, and I didn't know a thing about the other side. I had heard a lot about it from other slaves but I thought it was just about like Mason County, with slaves and masters, overseers and rawhides; and so, I just knew that if I pulled the boat up and went to asking people where to take her I would get a beating or get killed.

I don't know whether it seemed like a long time or a short time, now—it's so long ago; I know it was a long time rowing there in the cold and worryin'. But it was short, too, 'cause as soon as I did get on the other side the big-eyed, brown-skin girl would be gone. Well, pretty soon I saw a tall light and I remembered what the old lady had told me about looking for that light and rowing to it. I did; and when I got up to it, two men reached down and grabbed her; I started tremblin' all over again, and prayin'. Then, one of the men took my arm and I just felt down inside of me that the Lord had got ready for me. "You hungry, Boy?" is what he asked me, and if he hadn't been holdin' me I think I would have fell backward into the river.

That was my first trip; it took me a long time to get over my scared feelin', but I finally did, and I soon found myself goin' back across the river, with two and three people, and sometimes a whole boatload. I got so I used to make three and four trips a month.

What did my passengers look like? I can't tell you any more about it than you can, and wasn't there. After that first girl—no, I never did see her again—I never saw my passengers. It would have to be the "black nights" of the moon when I would carry them, and I would meet 'em out in the open or in a house without a single light. The only way I knew who they were was to ask them; "What you say?" And they would answer, "Menare." I don't know what that word meant—it came from the Bible. I only know that that was the password I used, and all of them that I took over told it to me before I took them.

I guess you wonder what I did with them after I got them over the river. Well, there in Ripley was a man named Mr. Rankins; I think the rest of his name was John. He had a regular station there on his place for escaping slaves. You see, Ohio was a free state and once they got over the river from Kentucky or Virginia, Mr. Rankins could strut them all around town, and nobody would bother 'em. The only reason we used to land quietly at night was so that whoever brought 'em could go back for more, and because we had to be careful that none of the owners had followed us. Every once in a while they would follow a boat and catch their slaves back. Sometimes they would shoot at whoever was trying to save the poor devils.

Mr. Rankins had a regular station for the slaves. He had a big lighthouse in his yard, about thirty feet high and he kept it burnin' all night. It always meant freedom for a slave if he could get to this light.

Sometimes Mr. Rankins would have twenty or thirty slaves that had run away on his place at the time. It must have cost him a whole lots to keep them and feed 'em, but I think some of his friends helped him.

Those who wanted to stay around that part of Ohio could stay, but didn't many of 'em do it, because there was too much danger that you would be walking along free one night, feel a hand over your mouth, and be back across the river and in slavery again in the morning. And nobody in the world ever got a chance to know as much misery as a slave that had escaped and been caught.

So a whole lot of 'em went on North to other parts of Ohio, or to New York, Chicago or Canada; Canada was popular then because all of the slaves thought it was the last gate before you got all the way *inside* of heaven. I don't think there was much chance for a slave to make a living in Canada, but didn't many of 'em come back. They seem like they rather starve up there in the cold than to be back in slavery.

The Army soon started taking a lot of 'em, too. They could enlist in the Union Army and get good wages, more food than they ever had, and have all the little gals wavin' at 'em when they passed. Them blue uniforms was a nice change, too.

No, I never got anything from a single one of the people I carried over the river to freedom. I didn't want anything; after I had made a few trips I got to like it, and even though I could have been free any night myself, I figgered I wasn't getting along so bad so I would stay on Mr. Tabb's place and help the others get free. I did it for four years.

I don't know to this day how he never knew what I was doing; I used to take some awful chances, and he knew I must have been up to something; I wouldn't do much work in the day, would never be in my house at night, and when he would happen to visit the plantation where I had said I was goin' I wouldn't be there. Sometimes I think he did know and wanted me to get the slaves away that way so he wouldn't have to cause hard feelins' by freein' 'em.

I think Mr. Tabb used to talk a lot to Mr. John Fee; Mr. Fee was a man who lived in Kentucky, but Lord! how that man hated slavery! He used to always tell us (we never let our owners see us listenin' to him, though) that God didn't intend for some men to be free and some men be in slavery. He used to talk to the owners, too, when they would listen to him, but mostly they hated the sight of John Fee.

In the night, though, he was a different man, for every slave who came through his place going across the river he had a good word, something to eat and some kind of rags, too, if it was cold. He always knew just what to tell you to do if anything went wrong, and sometimes I think he kept slaves there on his place 'till they could be rowed across the river. Helped us a lot.

I almost ran the business in the ground after I had been carrying the slaves across for nearly four years. It was in 1863, and one night I carried across about twelve on the same night. Somebody must have seen us, because they set out after me as soon as I stepped out of the boat back on the Kentucky side; from that time on they were after me. Sometimes they would almost catch me; I had to run away from Mr. Tabb's plantation and live in the fields and in the woods. I didn't know what a bed was from one week to another. I would sleep in a cornfield tonight, up in the branches of a tree tomorrow night, and buried in a haypile the next night; the River, where I had carried so many across myself, was no good to me; it was watched too close.

Finally, I saw that I could never do any more good in Mason County, so I decided to take my freedom, too. I had a wife by this time, and one night we quietly slipped across and headed for Mr. Rankin's bell and light. It looked like we had to go almost to China to get across that river: I could hear the bell and see the light on Mr. Rankin's place, but the harder I rowed, the farther away it got, and I knew if I didn't make it I'd get killed. But finally, I pulled up by the lighthouse, and went on to my freedom—just a few months before all of the slaves got theirs. I didn't stay in Ripley, though; I wasn't taking no chances. I went on to Detroit and still live there with most of my 10 children and 31 grandchildren.

The bigger ones don't care so much about hearin' it now, but the little ones never get tired of hearin' how their grandpa brought Emancipation to loads of slaves he could touch and feel, but never could see.

SOURCE: *Federal Writers' Project American Guide (Negro Writers' Unit)*. Pearl Randolph, Field Worker. Jacksonville, Florida, December 18, 1936. [Library of Congress website: *"Born in Slavery: Slave Narratives from the Federal Writers' Project, 1936–1938* contains more than 2,300 first-person accounts of slavery and 500 black-and-white photographs of former slaves. These narratives were collected in the 1930s as part of the Federal Writers' Project of the Works Progress Administration (WPA) and assembled and microfilmed in 1941 as the seventeen-volume *Slave Narratives: A Folk History of Slavery in the United States from Interviews with Former Slaves."*]

SAMUEL GREEN, *alias* WESLEY KINNARD

Ten Years in the Penitentiary for Having a Copy *of* Uncle Tom's Cabin

[William Still]

Harriet Beecher Stowe's novel Uncle Tom's Cabin, *published in 1852, seems to have influenced more Americans (and worldwide readers) to comprehend the blatant wrongs of slavery than all previous abolitionist writings put together. In many states in the South, legislators deemed such moral awakening dangerous; the novel was banned, and its possession was criminalized. An escaped slave's father, Sam Green, who had bought himself out of slavery, was, after a visit to his son in Canada, "indicted for having in his possession, papers, pamphlets and pictorial representations, having a tendency to create discontent, etc., among the people of color in the State." Still dated this story August 28, 1854.*

THE PASSENGER ANSWERING to the above name, left Indian Creek, Chester Co., Md., where he had been held to service or labor, by Dr. James Muse. One week had elapsed from the time he set out until his arrival in Philadelphia. Although he had never enjoyed school privileges of any kind, yet he was not devoid of intelligence. He had profited by his daily experience as a slave, and withal, had managed to learn to read and write a little, despite law and usage to the contrary. Sam was about twenty-five years of age and by trade, a blacksmith. Before running away, his general character for sobriety, industry, and religion, had evidently been considered good, but in coveting his freedom and running away to obtain it, he had sunk far below the utmost limit of forgiveness or mercy in the estimation of the slave-holders of Indian Creek.

During his intercourse with the Vigilance Committee, while rejoicing over his triumphant flight, he gave, with no appearance of excitement, but calmly, and in a common-sense like manner, a brief description of his master, which was entered on the record book substantially as follows: "Dr. James Muse is thought by the servants to be the worst man in Maryland, inflicting whipping and all manner of cruelties upon the servants."

While Sam gave reasons for this sweeping charge, which left no room for doubt, on the part of the Committee, of his sincerity and good judgment, it was not deemed necessary to make a note of more of the doctor's character than seemed actually needed, in order to show why "Sam" had taken passage on the Underground Rail Road. For several years, "Sam" was hired out by the doctor at blacksmithing; in this situation, daily wearing the yoke of unrequited labor, through the kindness of Harriet Tubman (sometimes called "Moses"), the light of the Underground Rail Road and Canada suddenly illuminated his mind. It was new to him, but he was quite too intelligent and liberty-loving, not to heed the valuable information which this sister of humanity imparted. Thenceforth he was in love with Canada, and likewise a decided admirer of the U. R. Road. Harriet was herself a shrewd and fearless agent, and well understood the entire route from that part of the country to Canada. The spring previous, she had paid a visit to the very neighborhood in which "Sam" lived, expressly to lead her own brothers out of "Egypt." She succeeded. To "Sam" this was cheering and glorious news, and he made up his mind, that before a great while, Indian Creek should have one less slave and that Canada should have one more citizen. Faithfully did he watch an opportunity to carry out his resolution. In due time a good Providence opened the way, and to "Sam's" satisfaction he reached Philadelphia, having encountered no peculiar difficulties. The Committee, perceiving that he was smart, active, and promising, encouraged his undertaking, and having given him friendly advice, aided him in the usual manner. Letters of introduction were given him, and he was duly forwarded on his way. He had left his father, mother, and one sister behind. Samuel and Catharine were the names of his parents. Thus far, his escape would seem not to affect his parents, nor was it apparent that there was any other cause why the owner should revenge himself upon them.

The father was an old local preacher in the Methodist Church—much esteemed as an inoffensive, industrious man; earning his bread by the sweat of his brow, and contriving to move along in the narrow road allotted colored people bond or free, without exciting a spirit of ill will in the proslavery power of his community. But the rancor awakened in the breast of slave-holders in consequence of the high-handed step the son had taken, brought the father under suspicion and hate. Under the circumstances, the eye of Slavery could do nothing more than watch for an occasion to pounce upon him. It was not long before the desired opportunity presented itself. Moved by parental affection, the old man concluded to pay a visit to his boy, to see how he was faring in a distant land, and among strangers. This resolution he quietly carried into effect. He found his son in Canada, doing well; industrious; a man of sobriety, and following his father's footsteps religiously. That the old man's heart was delighted with what his eyes saw and his ears heard in Canada, none can doubt. But in the simplicity of his imagination, he never dreamed that this visit was to be made the means of his destruction. During the best portion of his days he had faithfully worn the badge of slavery, had afterwards purchased his freedom, and thus become a free man. He innocently conceived the idea that he was doing no harm in availing himself not only of his God-given rights, but of the rights that he had also purchased by the hard toil of his own hands. But the enemy was lurking in ambush for him—thirsting for his blood. To his utter consternation, not long after his return from his visit to his son "a party of gentlemen from the New Market district, went at night to Green's house and made search, whereupon was found a copy of *Uncle Tom's Cabin*. This was enough—the hour had come, wherein to wreak vengeance upon poor Green. The course pursued and the result, may be seen in the following statement taken from the *Cambridge* (Md.)

Democrat, of April 29th, 1857, and communicated by the writer to the *Provincial Freeman*:

SAM GREEN

THE CASE OF THE STATE AGAINST SAM GREEN (free negro) indicted for having in his possession, papers, pamphlets and pictorial representations, having a tendency to create discontent, etc., among the people of color in the State, was tried before the court on Friday last.

This case was of the utmost importance, and has created in the public mind a great deal of interest—it being the first case of the kind ever having occurred in our country.

It appeared, in evidence, that this Green has a son in Canada, to whom Green made a visit last summer. Since his return to this county, suspicion has fastened upon him, as giving aid and assisting slaves who have since absconded and reached Canada, and several weeks ago, a party of gentlemen from New Market district, went at night, to Green's house and made search, whereupon was found a volume of *Uncle Tom's Cabin*, a map of Canada, several schedules of routes to the North, and a letter from his son in Canada, detailing the pleasant trip he had, the number of friends he met with on the way, with plenty to eat, drink, etc., and concludes with a request to his father, that he shall tell certain other slaves, naming them, to come on, which slaves, it is well known, did leave shortly afterwards, and have reached Canada. The case was argued with great ability, the counsel on both sides displaying a great deal of ingenuity, learning and eloquence. The first indictment was for the having in possession the letter, map and route schedules.

Notwithstanding the mass of evidence given, to show the prisoner's guilt, in unlawfully having in his possession these documents, and the nine-tenths of the community in which he lived, believed that he had a hand in the running away of slaves, it was the opinion of the court, that the law under which he was indicted, was not applicable to the case, and that he must, accordingly, render a verdict of not guilty.

He was immediately arraigned upon another indictment, for having in possession *Uncle Tom's Cabin*, and tried; in this case the court has not yet rendered a verdict, but holds it under curia till after the Somerset county court. It is to be hoped, the court will find the evidence in this case sufficient to bring it within the scope of the law under which the prisoner is indicted (that of 1842, chap. 272), and that the prisoner may meet his due reward—be that what it may.

That there is something required to be done by our Legislators, for the protection of slave property, is evident from the variety of constructions put upon the statute in this case, and we trust, that at the next meeting of the Legislature there will be such amendments, as to make the law on this subject, perfectly clear and comprehensible to the understanding of every one.

In the language of the assistant counsel for the State, "Slavery must be protected or it must be abolished."

From the same sheet, of May 20th, the terrible doom of Samuel Green, is announced in the following words:

In the case of the State against Sam Green, (free negro) who was tried at the April term of the Circuit Court of this county, for having in his possession abolition pamphlets, among which was *Uncle Tom's Cabin*, has been found guilty by the court, and sentenced to the penitentiary for the term of ten years—until the 14th of May, 1867.

The son, a refugee in Canada, hearing the distressing news of his father's sad fate in the hands of the relentless "gentlemen," often wrote to know if there was any prospect of his deliverance. The subjoined letter is a fair sample of his correspondence:

SALFORD, 22, 1857.

DEAR SIR I take my pen in hand to Request a faver of you if you can by any means without duin InJestus to your self or your Bisness to grant it as I Bleve you to be a man that would Sympathize in such a ones Condition as my self I Reseved a letter that Stats to me that mv Fater has ben Betraed in the act of helping sum frend to Canada and the law has Convicted and Sentanced him to the Stats prison for 10 years his White Frands ofered 2 thousen Dollers to Redem him but they would not short three thousen. I am in Canada and it is a Difficult thing to get a letter to any of my Frands in Maryland so as to get prop per information abot it—if you can by any means get any in telligence from Baltimore City a bot this Event Plese do so and Rit word and all so all the inform mation that you think prop per as Regards the Evant and the best mathod to Redeme him and so Plese Rite soon as you can You will oblige your sir Frand and Drect your letter to Salford P. office C. W. —SAMUEL GREEN.

In this dark hour the friends of the Slave could do but little more than sympathize with this heart-stricken son and grey-headed father.

The aged follower of the Rejected and Crucified had like Him to bear the "reproach of many," and make his bed with the wicked in the Penitentiary. Doubtless there were a few friends in his neighborhood who sympathized with him, but they were powerless to aid the old man. But thanks to a kind Providence, the great deliverance brought about during the Rebellion by which so many captives were freed, also unlocked Samuel Green's prison doors and he was allowed to go free.

After his liberation from the Penitentiary, we had from his own lips narrations of his years of suffering—of the bitter cup, that he was compelled to drink, and of his being sustained by the Almighty Arm ...

SOURCE: William Still, 1872 (see the Bibliography on p. 203 for complete information).

JAMIE GRIFFIN, *alias* THOMAS BROWN

Slave-Holder in Maryland with Three Colored Wives

[William Still]

We enjoy again and again in Still's narrations the matter-of-factness of slaves' dramatic decisions to escape. Jamie Griffin simply "examined his feet and legs, found that they were in good order, and his faith and hope strong enough to remove a mountain."

JAMES WAS A TILLER OF THE SOIL under the yoke of Joshua Hitch, who lived on a farm about seventeen miles from Baltimore. James spoke rather favorably of him; indeed, it was through a direct act of kindness on the part of his master that he procured the opportunity to make good his escape. It appeared from his story, that his master's affairs had become particularly embarrassed, and the Sheriff was making frequent visits to his house. This sign was interpreted to mean that James, if not others, would have to be sold before long. The master was much puzzled to decide which way to turn. He owned but three other adult slaves besides James, and they were females. One of them was his chief housekeeper, and with them all his social relations were of such a nature as to lead James and others to think and say that they "were all his wives." Or to use James's own language, "he had three slave women; two were sisters, and he lived with them all as his wives; two of them he was very fond of," and desired to keep them from being sold if possible. The third, he concluded he could not save, she would have to be sold. In this dilemma, he was good enough to allow James a few days' holiday, for the purpose of finding him a good master. Expressing his satisfaction and gratification, James, armed with full authority from his master to select a choice specimen, started for Baltimore.

On reaching Baltimore, however, James carefully steered clear of all slave-holders, and shrewdly turned his attention to the matter of getting an Underground Rail Road ticket for Canada. After making as much inquiry as he felt was safe, he came to the conclusion to walk of nights for a long distance. He examined his feet and legs, found that they were in good order, and his faith and hope strong enough to remove a mountain. Besides several days still remained in which he was permitted to look for a new master; and these he decided could be profitably spent in making his way towards Canada. So off he started, at no doubt a very diligent pace, for at the end of the first night's journey, he had made much headway, but at the expense of his feet.

His faith was stronger than ever. So he rested next day in the woods, concealed, of course, and the next evening started with fresh courage and renewed perseverance. Finally, he reached Columbia, Pennsylvania, and there he had the happiness to learn, that the mountain which at first had tried his faith so severely, was removed, and friendly hands were reached out and a more speedy and comfortable mode of travel advised. He was directed to the Vigilance Committee in Philadelphia, from whom he received friendly aid, and all necessary information respecting Canada and how to get there.

James was thirty-one years of age, rather a fine-looking man, of a chestnut color, and quite intelligent. He had been a married man, but for two years before his escape, he had been a widower—that is, his wife had been sold away from him to North Carolina, and in that space of time he had received only three letters from her; he had given up all hope of ever seeing her again. He had two little boys living in Baltimore, whom he was obliged to leave. Their names were Edward and William. What became of them afterwards was never known at the Philadelphia station.

James's master was a man of about fifty years of age—who had never been lawfully married, yet had a number of children on his place who were of great concern to him in the midst of other pressing embarrassments. Of course, the Committee never learned how matters were settled after James left, but, in all probability, his wives, Nancy and Mary (sisters), and Lizzie, with all the children, had to be sold.

SOURCE: William Still, 1872 (see the Bibliography on p. 203 for complete information).

HARRY GRIMES

Arrival from North Carolina, 1857—Feet Slit for Running Away, Flogged, Stabbed, Stayed in the Hollow of a Big Poplar Tree, Visited by a Snake, Abode in a Cave

[William Still]

Grimes suffered terribly as a slave, and at the request of William Still recounted some of the more shocking details of his life story.

THE COMING OF THE PASSENGERS here noticed was announced in the subjoined letter from Thomas Garrett:

WILMINGTON, 11th Mo. 25th, 1857.

RESPECTED FRIEND, WILLIAM STILL:—I write to inform thee, that Captain Fountain has arrived this evening from the South with three men, one of which is nearly naked, and very lousy. He has been in the swamps of Carolina for eighteen months past. One of the others has been some time out. I would send them on to-night, but will have to provide two of them with some clothes before they can be sent by rail road. I have forgotten the number of thy house. As most likely all are more or less lousy, having been compelled to sleep together, I thought best to write thee so that thee may get a suitable place to take them to, and meet them at Broad and Prime streets on the arrival of the cars, about 11 o'clock to-morrow evening. I have engaged one of our men to take them to his house, and go to Philadelphia with them to-morrow evening. Johnson who will accompany them is a man in whom we can confide. Please send me the number of thy house when thee writes.

THOMAS GARRETT.

This epistle from the old friend of the fugitive, Thomas Garrett, excited unusual interest. Preparation was immediately made to give the fugitives a kind reception, and at the same time to destroy their plagues, root and branch, without mercy.

They arrived according to appointment. The cleansing process was carried into effect most thoroughly, and no vermin were left to tell the tale of suffering they had caused. Straightway the passengers were made comfortable in every way, and the spirit of freedom seemed to be burning like "fire shut up in the bones." The appearance alone of these men indicated their manhood, and wonderful natural ability. The examining Committee were very desirous of hearing their story without a moment's delay.

As Harry, from having suffered most, was the hero of this party, and withal was an intelligent man, he was first called upon to make his statement as to how times had been with him in the prison house, from his youth up. He was about forty-six years of age, according to his reckoning, full six feet high, and in muscular appearance was very rugged, and in his countenance were evident marks of firmness. He said that he was born a slave in North Carolina, and had been sold three times. He was first sold when a child three years of age, the second time when he was thirteen years old, and the third and last time he was sold to Jesse Moore, from whom he fled. Prior to his coming into the hands of Moore he had not experienced any very hard usage, at least nothing more severe than fell to the common lot of slave-boys, therefore the period of his early youth was deemed of too little interest to record in detail. In fact time only could be afforded for noticing very briefly some of the more remarkable events of his bondage. The examining Committee confined their interrogations to his last taskmaster.

"How did Moore come by you?" was one of the inquiries. "He bought me," said Harry, "of a man by the name of Taylor, nine or ten years ago; he was as bad as he could be, couldn't be any worse to be alive. He was about fifty years of age, when I left him, a right red-looking man, big bellied old fellow, weighs about two hundred and forty pounds. He drinks hard, he is just like a rattlesnake, just as cross and crabbed when he speaks, seems like he could go through you. He flogged Richmond for not ploughing the corn good, that was what he pretended to whip him for. Richmond ran away, was away four months, as nigh as I can guess, then they cotched him, then struck him a hundred lashes, and then they split both feet to the bone, and split both his insteps, and then master took his knife and stuck it into him in many places; after he done him that way, he put him into the barn to shucking corn. For a long time he was not able to work; when he did partly recover, he was set to work again."

We ceased to record anything further concerning Richmond, although not a fourth part of what Harry narrated was put upon paper. The account was too sickening and the desire to hear Harry's account of himself too great to admit of further delay; so Harry confined himself to the sufferings and adventures which had marked his own life. Briefly he gave the following facts: "I have been treated bad! One day we were grabbing and master said we didn't do work enough. 'How came there was no more work done that day?' said master to me. I told him I did work. In a more stormy manner he 'peated the question. I then spoke up and said: 'Massa, I don't know what to say.' At once massa plunged his knife into my neck causing me to stagger. Massa was drunk. He then drove me down to the black folk's houses (cabins of the slaves). He then got his gun, called the overseer, and told him to get some ropes. While he was gone I said, 'Massa, now you are going to tie me up and cut me all to pieces for nothing. I would just as leave you would take your gun and shoot me down as to tie me up and cut me all to pieces for nothing.' In a great rage he said 'go.' I jumped, and he put up his gun and snapped both barrels at me. He then set his dogs on me, but as I had been in the habit of making much of them, feeding them, &c., they would not follow me, and I kept on straight to the woods. My master and the overseer cotched the horses and tried to run me down, but as the dogs would not follow me they couldn't make nothing of it. It was the last of August a year ago. The devil was into him, and he flogged and beat four of the slaves, one man and three of the women, and said if he could only get hold of me he wouldn't strike me, 'nary-a-lick,' but would tie me to a tree and empty both barrels into me.

"In the woods I lived on nothing, you may say, and something too. I had bread, and roasting ears, and 'taters. I stayed in the hollow of a big poplar tree for seven months; the other part of the time I stayed in a cave. I suffered mighty bad with the cold and for something to eat. Once I got me some charcoal and made me a fire in my tree to warm me, and it liked to killed me, so I had to take the fire out. One time a snake come to the tree, poked its head in the hollow and was coming in, and I took my axe and chopped him in two. It was a poplar leaf moccasin, the poisonest kind of a snake we have. While in the woods all my thoughts was how to get away to a free country."

Subsequently, in going back over his past history, he referred to the fact, that on an occasion long before the cave and tree existence, already noticed, when suffering under this brutal master, he sought protection in the woods and abode twenty-seven months in a cave, before he surrendered himself, or was captured. His offence, in this instance, was simply because he desired to see his wife, and "stole" away from his master's plantation and went a distance of five miles, to where she lived, to see her. For this grave crime his master threatened to give him a hundred lashes, and to shoot him; in order to avoid this punishment, he escaped to the woods, etc. The lapse of a dozen years and recent struggles for an existence, made him think lightly of his former troubles and he would, doubtless, have failed to recall his earlier conflicts but for the desire manifested by the Committee to get all the information out of him they could. He was next asked, "Had you a wife and family?" "Yes, sir," he answered, "I had a wife and eight children, belonged to the widow Slade." Harry gave the names of his wife and children as follows: Wife, Susan, and children, Oliver, Sabey, Washington, Daniel, Jonas, Harriet, Moses and Rosetta, the last named he had never seen. "Between my mistress and my master there was not much difference."

SOURCE: William Still, 1872 (see the Bibliography on p. 203 for complete information).

JAMES HAMLET AND OTHERS

The Slave-Hunting Tragedy in Lancaster County, in
September 1851: Treason at Christiana

[William Still]

Although the Fugitive Slave Act gave slave-owners authority to reclaim
their "property," fugitives rejected the law,[1] attempting to elude slave-
hunters and defend their freedom. In September 1851, plans to capture
seven fugitive slaves in Lancaster County were thwarted by the fugitives
and their supporters, but this did not happen without bloodshed, man-
hunts, arrests, and charges of treason.

HAVING INSERTED the Fugitive Slave Bill in these records of the
Underground Rail Road, one or two slave cases will doubtless suffice
to illustrate the effect of its passage on the public mind, and the colored people in particular. The deepest feelings of loathing, contempt
and opposition were manifested by the opponents of Slavery on every
hand. Antislavery papers, lecturers, preachers, etc., arrayed themselves
boldly against it on the ground of its inhumanity and violation of the
laws of God.

On the other hand, the slave-holders South, and their pro-slavery
adherents in the North demanded the most abject obedience from all
parties, regardless of conscience or obligation to God. In order to
compel such obedience, as well as to prove the practicability of the
law, unbounded zeal daily marked the attempt on the part of slave-
holders and slave-catchers to refasten the fetters on the limbs of fugitives in different parts of the North, whither they had escaped.

In this dark hour, when colored men's rights were so insecure, as
a matter of self-defence, they felt called upon to arm themselves and
resist all kidnapping intruders, although clothed with the authority of
wicked law. ...

And, as if gloating over their repeated successes, and utterly regardless of all caution, about one year after the passage of this nefarious
bill, a party of slave-hunters arranged for a grand capture at Christiana.

---

1 See the Appendix below.

One year from the passage of the law, at a time when alarm and excitement were running high, the most decided stand was taken at Christiana, in the State of Pennsylvania, to defeat the law, and defend freedom. Fortunately for the fugitives the plans of the slave-hunters and officials leaked out while arrangements were making in Philadelphia for the capture, and, information being sent to the Anti-slavery office, a messenger was at once dispatched to Christiana to put all persons supposed to be in danger on their guard.

Among those thus notified, were brave hearts, who did not believe in running away from slave-catchers. They resolved to stand up for the right of self-defence. They loved liberty and hated Slavery, and when the slave-catchers arrived, they were prepared for them. Of the contest, on that bloody morning, we have copied a report, carefully written at the time, by C. M. Burleigh, editor of the *Pennsylvania Freeman*, who visited the scene of battle, immediately after it was over, and doubtless obtained as faithful an account of all the facts in the case, as could then be had.

Last Thursday morning, (the 11th inst), a peaceful neighborhood in the borders of Lancaster county, was made the scene of a bloody battle, resulting from an attempt to capture seven colored men as fugitive slaves. As the reports of the affray which came to us were contradictory, and having good reason to believe that those of the daily press were grossly one-sided and unfair, we repaired to the scene of the tragedy, and, by patient inquiry and careful examination, endeavored to learn the real facts. To do this, from the varying and conflicting statements which we encountered, scarcely two of which agreed in every point, was not easy; but we believe the account we give below, as the result of these inquiries, is substantially correct.

Very early on the 11th inst. a party of slave-hunters went into a neighborhood about two miles west of Christiana, near the eastern border of Lancaster county, in pursuit of fugitive slaves. The party consisted of Edward Gorsuch, his son, Dickerson Gorsuch, his nephew, Dr. Pearce, Nicholas Hutchins, and others, all from Baltimore county, Md., and one Henry H. Kline, a notorious slave-catching constable from Philadelphia, who had been deputized by Commissioner Ingraham for this business. At about day-dawn they were discovered lying in an ambush near the house of one William Parker, colored man, by an inmate of the house, who had started for his work. He fled back to the house, pursued by the slave-hunters, who entered the lower part of the house, but were unable to force their way into the upper part, to which the family had retired. A horn was blown from an upper window; two shots were fired, both, as we believe, though we are not certain, by the assailants, one at the colored man who fled into the house, and the other at the inmates, through the window. No one was wounded by either. A parley ensued. The slave-holder demanded his slaves, who he said were concealed in the house. The colored men presented themselves successively at the window, and asked if they were the slaves claimed; Gorsuch said, that neither of them was his slave. They told him that they were the only colored men in the house, and were determined never to be taken alive as slaves. Soon the colored people of the neighborhood, alarmed by the horn, began to gather, armed with guns, axes, corn-cutters, or clubs. Mutual threatenings were uttered by the two parties. The slave-holders told the blacks that resistance would be useless, as they had a party of thirty men in the woods near by. The blacks warned them again to leave, as they would die before they would go into Slavery.

From an hour to an hour and a half passed in these parleyings, angry conversations, and threats; the blacks increasing by new arrivals, until they probably numbered from thirty to fifty, most of them armed in some way. About this time, Castner Hanaway, a white man, and a Friend, who resided in the neighborhood, rode up, and was soon followed by Elijah Lewis, another Friend, a merchant, in Cooperville, both gentlemen highly esteemed as worthy and peaceable citizens. As they came up, Kline, the deputy marshal, ordered them to aid him, as a United States officer, to capture the fugitive slaves. They refused of course, as would any man not utterly destitute of honor, humanity, and moral principle, and warned the assailants that it was madness for them to attempt to capture fugitive slaves there, or even to remain, and begged them if they wished to save their own lives, to leave the ground. Kline replied, "Do you really think so?" "Yes," was the answer, "the sooner you leave, the better, if you would prevent bloodshed." Kline then left the ground, retiring into a very safe distance into a corn-field, and toward the woods. The blacks were so exasperated by his threats, that, but for the interposition of the two white Friends, it is very doubtful whether he would have escaped without injury. Messrs. Hanaway and Lewis both exerted their influence to dissuade the colored people from violence, and would probably have succeeded in restraining them, had not the assailing party fired upon them. Young Gorsuch asked his father to leave, but the old man refused, declaring, as it is said and believed, that he would "go to hell, or have his slaves."

Finding they could do nothing further, Hanaway and Lewis both started to leave, again counselling the slave-hunters to go away, and the colored people to peace, but had gone but a few rods, when one of the inmates of the house attempted to come out at the door. Gorsuch presented his revolver, ordering him back. The colored man replied, "You had better go away, if you don't want to get hurt," and at the same time pushed him aside and passed out. Maddened at this, and stimulated by the question of his nephew, whether he would "take such an insult from a d——d nigger," Gorsuch fired at the colored man, and was followed by his son and nephew, who both fired their revolvers. The fire was returned by the blacks, who made a rush upon them at the same time. Gorsuch and his son fell, the one dead, the other wounded. The rest of the party after firing their revolvers, fled precipitately through the corn and to the woods, pursued by some of the blacks. One was wounded, the rest escaped unhurt. Kline, the deputy marshal, who now boasts of his miraculous escape from a volley of musketballs, had kept at a safe distance, though urged by young Gorsuch to stand by his father and protect him, when he refused to leave the ground. He of course came off unscathed. Several colored men were wounded, but none severely. Some had their hats or their clothes perforated with bullets; others had flesh wounds. They said that the Lord protected them, and they shook the bullets from their clothes. One man found several shot in his boot, which seemed to have spent their force before reaching him, and did not even break the skin. The slave-holders having fled, several neighbors, mostly Friends and anti-slavery men, gathered to succor the wounded and take charge of the dead. We are told that Parker himself protected the wounded man from his excited comrades, and brought water and a bed from his own house for the invalid, thus showing that he was as magnanimous to his fallen enemy as he was brave in the defence of his own liberty. The young man was then removed to a neighboring house, where the family received him with the tenderest kindness and paid him every attention, though they told him in Quaker phrase, that "they had no unity with his cruel business," and were very sorry to see him engaged in it. He was much affected by their kindness, and we are told, expressed his regret that he had been thus engaged, and his determination, if his life was spared, never again to make a similar attempt. His wounds are very severe, and it is feared mortal. All attempts to procure assistance to capture the fugitive slaves failed, the people in the neighborhood either not relishing the business of slave-catching, or at least, not choosing to risk their lives in it. There was a very great reluctance felt to going even to remove the body and the wounded man, until several abolitionists and Friends had collected for that object, when others found courage to follow on. The excitement caused by this most melancholy affair is very great among all classes. The abolitionists, of course, mourn the occurrence, while they see in it a legitimate fruit of the Fugitive Slave Law, just such a harvest of blood as they had long feared that the law would produce, and which they had earnestly labored to prevent. We believe that they alone, of all classes of the nation, are free from responsibility for its occurrence, having wisely foreseen the danger, and faithfully labored to avert it by removing its causes, and preventing the inhuman policy which has hurried on the bloody convulsion.

The enemies of the colored people are making this the occasion of fresh injuries, and a more bitter ferocity toward that defenceless people, and of new misrepresentation and calumnies against the abolitionists.

The colored people, though the great body of them had no connection with this affair, are hunted like partridges upon the mountains, by the relentless horde which has been poured forth upon them, under the pretense of arresting the parties concerned in the fight. When we reached Christiana, on Friday afternoon, we found that the Deputy-Attorney Thompson, of Lancaster, was there, and had issued warrants, upon the depositions of Kline and others, for the arrest of all suspected persons. A company of police were scouring the neighborhood in search of colored people, several of whom were seized while at their work near by, and brought in.

CASTNER HANAWAY AND ELIJAH LEWIS, hearing that warrants were issued against them, came to Christiana, and voluntarily gave themselves up, calm and strong in the confidence of their innocence. They, together with the arrested colored men, were sent to Lancaster jail that night.

The next morning we visited the ground of the battle, and the family where young Gorsuch now lives, and while there, we saw a deposition which he had just made, that he believed no white persons were engaged in the affray, beside his own party. As he was on the ground during the whole controversy, and deputy Marshall Kline had discreetly run off into the corn-field, before the fighting began, the hireling slave-catcher's eager and confident testimony against our white friends, will, we think, weigh lightly with impartial men.

On returning to Christiana, we found that the United States Marshal from the city, had arrived at that place, accompanied by Commissioner Ingraham, Mr. Jones, a special commissioner of the United States, from Washington, the U.S. District Attorney Ashmead, with forty-five U.S. Marines from the Navy Yard, and a posse of about forty of the City Marshal's police, together with a large body of special constables, eager for such a manhunt, from Columbia and Lancaster and other places. This crowd divided into parties, of from ten to twenty-five, and scoured the country, in every direction, for miles around, ransacking the houses of the colored people, and captured every colored man they could find, with several colored women, and two other white men. Never did our heart bleed with deeper pity for the peeled and persecuted colored people, than when we saw this troop let loose upon them, and witnessed the terror and distress which its approach excited in families, wholly innocent of the charges laid against them. ...

Although the government had summoned its ablest legal talent and the popular sentiment was as a hundred to one against William Parker and his brave comrades who had made the slave-hunter "bite the dust," most nobly did Thaddeus Stevens prove that he was not to be cowed, that he believed in the stirring sentiment so much applauded by the American people, "Give me liberty, or give me death," not only for the white man but for all men. Thus standing upon such great and invulnerable principles, it was soon discovered that one could chase a thousand, and two put ten thousand to flight in latter as well as in former times.

At first even the friends of freedom thought that the killing of Gorsuch was not only wrong, but unfortunate for the cause. Scarcely a week passed, however, before the matter was looked upon in a far different light, and it was pretty generally thought that, if the Lord had not a direct hand in it, the cause of Freedom at least would be greatly benefited thereby.

And just in proportion as the masses cried, Treason! Treason! the hosts of freedom from one end of the land to the other were awakened to sympathize with the slave. Thousands were soon amused to show sympathy who had hitherto been dormant. Hundreds visited the prisoners in their cells to greet, cheer, and offer them aid and counsel in their hour of sore trial.

The friends of freedom remained calm even while the pro-slavery party were fiercely raging and gloating over the prospect, as they evidently thought of the satisfaction to be derived from teaching the abolitionists a lesson from the scaffold, which would in future prevent Underground Rail Road passengers from killing their masters when in pursuit of them.

Through the efforts of the authorities three white men, and twenty-seven colored had been safely lodged in Moyamensing prison, under the charge of treason. The authorities, however, had utterly failed to catch the hero, William Parker, as he had been sent to Canada, via the Underground Rail Road, and was thus "sitting under his own vine and fig tree, where none dared to molest, or make him afraid."

As an act of simple justice it may here be stated that the abolitionists and prisoners found a true friend and ally at least in one United States official, who, by the way, figured prominently in making arrests, etc., namely: the United States Marshal, A. E. Roberts. In all his intercourse with the prisoners and their friends, he plainly showed that all his sympathies were on the side of Freedom, and not with the popular pro-slavery sentiment which clamored so loudly against traitors and abolitionists.

Two of his prisoners had been identified in the jail as fugitive slaves by their owners. When the trial came on these two individuals were among the missing. How they escaped was unknown—the Marshal, however, was strongly suspected of being a friend of the Underground Rail Road, and to add now, that those suspicions were founded on fact, will, doubtless, do him no damage.

In order to draw the contrast between Freedom and Slavery, simply with a view of showing how the powers that were acted and judged in the days of the reign of the Fugitive Slave Law, unquestionably nothing better could be found to meet the requirements of this issue than the charge of Judge Kane, coupled with the indictment of the Grand Jury. In the light of the Emancipation and the Fifteenth Amendment, they are too transparent to need a single word of comment. Judge and jury having found the accused chargeable with Treason, nothing remained, so far as the men were concerned, but to bide their time as best they could in prison. Most of them were married, and had wives and children clinging to them in this hour of fearful looking for of judgment.

SOURCE: William Still, 1872 (see the Bibliography on p. 203 for complete information).

ELIZA HARRIS

*The Slave Woman Who Crossed the Ohio River on the
Drifting Ice with Her Child in Her Arms*

[Levi Coffin]

*Eliza Harris ran away from her owner when she learned that he planned to sepa-
rate her from her only living child. With slave-hunters in pursuit, she crossed the
Ohio River by jumping from one piece of drifting ice to another. After surviving
that perilous part of her journey, she was directed to a station on the Underground
Railroad and then to the home of Levi Coffin, who had assisted thousands of
fugitives in their quests for freedom. Harris and her child eventually settled in
Canada, where they were "comfortable and contented." Years later, Harris enjoyed an unexpected reunion with the Coffins in Canada, a meeting that allowed
her to reiterate her feelings for the people who had helped her escape from the harsh
realities of enslavement. Harris's story, as Coffin notes, was the inspiration for a
famous episode in Harriet Beecher Stowe's* Uncle Tom's Cabin *(1852).*

ELIZA HARRIS, of *Uncle Tom's Cabin* notoriety, the slave woman who
crossed the Ohio River, near Ripley, on the drifting ice with her
child in her arms, was sheltered under our roof and fed at our table
for several days. This was while we lived at Newport, Indiana, which
is six miles west of the State line of Ohio. To elude the pursuers who
were following closely on her track, she was sent across to our line of
the Underground Railroad.

The story of this slave woman, so graphically told by Harriet
Beecher Stowe in *Uncle Tom's Cabin,* will, no doubt, be remembered
by every reader of that deeply interesting book. The cruelties of slavery depicted in that remarkable work are not overdrawn. The stories
are founded on facts that really occurred, real names being wisely
withheld, and fictitious names and imaginary conversations often inserted. From the fact that Eliza Harris was sheltered at our house several days, it was generally believed among those acquainted with the
circumstances that I and my wife were the veritable Simeon and
Rachel Halliday, the Quaker couple alluded to in *Uncle Tom's Cabin.*
I will give a short sketch of the fugitive's story, as she related it.

She said she was a slave from Kentucky, the property of a man
who lived a few miles back from the Ohio River, below Ripley,

Ohio. Her master and mistress were kind to her, and she had a comfortable home, but her master got into some pecuniary difficulty, and she found that she and her only child were to be separated. She had buried two children, and was doubly attached to the one she had left, a bright, promising child, over two years old. When she found that it was to be taken from her, she was filled with grief and dismay, and resolved to make her escape that night if possible. She watched her opportunity, and when darkness had settled down and all the family had retired to sleep, she started with her child in her arms and walked straight toward the Ohio River. She knew that it was frozen over, at that season of the year, and hoped to cross without difficulty on the ice, but when she reached its banks at daylight, she found that the ice had broken up and was slowly drifting in large cakes. She ventured to go to a house near by, where she was kindly received and permitted to remain through the day. She hoped to find some way to cross the river the next night, but there seemed little prospect of any one being able to cross in safety, for during the day the ice became more broken and dangerous to cross. In the evening she discovered pursuers nearing the house, and with desperate courage she determined to cross the river, or perish in the attempt. Clasping her child in her arms she darted out of the back door and ran toward the river, followed by her pursuers, who had just dismounted from their horses when they caught sight of her. No fear or thought of personal danger entered Eliza's mind, for she felt that she had rather be drowned than to be captured and separated from her child. Clasping her babe to her bosom with her left arm, she sprang on to the first cake of ice, then from that to another and another. Some times the cake she was on would sink beneath her weight, then she would slide her child on to the next cake, pull herself on with her hands, and so continue her hazardous journey. She became wet to the waist with ice water and her hands were benumbed with cold, but as she made her way from one cake of ice to another, she felt that surely the Lord was preserving and upholding her, and that nothing could harm her.

When she reached the Ohio side, near Ripley, she was completely exhausted and almost breathless. A man, who had been standing on the bank watching her progress with amazement and expecting every moment to see her go down, assisted her up the bank. After she had recovered her strength a little he directed her to a house on the hill, on the outskirts of town. She made her way to the place, and was kindly received and cared for. It was not considered safe for her to remain there during the night, so, after resting a while and being provided with food and dry clothing, she was conducted to a station on the Underground Railroad, a few miles farther from the river. The next night she was forwarded on from station to station to our house in Newport, where she arrived safely and remained several days.

Other fugitives arrived in the meantime, and Eliza and her child were sent with them, by the Greenville branch of the Underground Railroad, to Sandusky, Ohio. They reached that place in safety, and crossed the lake to Canada, locating finally at Chatham, Canada West.

In the summer of 1854 I was on a visit to Canada, accompanied by my wife and daughter, and Laura S. Haviland, of Michigan. At the close of a meeting which we attended, at one of the colored churches, a woman came up to my wife, seized her hand, and exclaimed: "How are you, Aunt Katie? God bless you!" etc. My wife did not recognize her, but she soon called herself to our remembrance by referring to the time she was at our house in the days of her distress, when my wife gave her the name of Eliza Harris, and by relating other particulars. We visited her at her house while at Chatham, and found her comfortable and contented.

Many other fugitives came and spoke to us, whom we did not recognize or remember until they related some incident that recalled them to mind. Such circumstances occurred in nearly every neighborhood we visited in Canada. Hundreds who had been sheltered under our roof and fed at our table, when fleeing from the land of whips and chains, introduced themselves to us and referred to the time, often fifteen or twenty years before, when we had aided them. ...

At ... many other places, we met with many, both men and women, whom we had assisted on their way to liberty, and their expressions of thankfulness and regard were very gratifying to us.

SOURCE: Levi Coffin. *Reminiscences of Levi Coffin, the Reputed President of the Underground Railroad; Being a Brief History of the Labors of a Lifetime in Behalf of the Slave, with the Stories of Numerous Fugitives, Who Gained Their Freedom Through His Instrumentality, and Many Other Incidents. Second edition.* Cincinnati: Robert Clarke and Company, 1880.

JOSIAH HENSON

The Life of Josiah Henson, Formerly a Slave, Now an Inhabitant of Canada, as Narrated by Himself (1849)

(excerpts)

One of the more famous of pre-Civil War escaped-slave narratives was Henson's; he tells here of his decision to escape from the slaveholders who, in spite of his having paid a large sum for his freedom and having given life-saving service to them, were trying to sell him away. He rallied his wife to join him and their children in their quest to reach Canada. On their way, they were aided by, among others, American Indians. Safely in Canada, Henson reminds us, "I was a stranger, in a strange land, and had to look about me at once, for refuge and resource." After years of farming, he resumed his calling of Sunday preaching.

WE ARRIVED HOME about the tenth of July, but it was not till the middle of August that Amos was well enough to move out of his chamber, though he had been convalescent all the while. As soon as he could speak, he told all I had done for him, and said, "If I had sold him, I should have died;" but it never seemed to occur to him or the rest of the family that they were under any, the slightest, obligation to me on that account. I had done well as a slave, and to have it acknowledged, and to be praised for it, was compensation enough for me. My merits, whatever they were, instead of exciting sympathy, or any feeling of attachment to me, seemed only to enhance my money value to them. This was not the view which I took of the case myself; and as soon as Amos began to recover, I began to meditate upon a plan of escape from the danger, in which I constantly stood, of a repetition of the attempt to sell me in the highest market. Providence seemed to have interfered once to defeat the scheme, but I could not expect such extraordinary circumstances to be repeated, and I was bound to do every thing in my power to secure myself and my family from the wicked conspiracy of Isaac and Amos R. against my life, as well as against my natural rights in my own person, and those which I had acquired, under even the barbarous laws of slavery, by the money I had paid for myself. If Isaac would only have been honest enough to adhere to his own bargain, I would have adhered to mine, and paid him all I had promised. But his attempt to kidnap me again, after having pocketed three-fourths of my market value, absolved me from all obligation, in my opinion, to pay him any more, or to continue in a position which exposed me to his machinations. I determined to make my escape to Canada, about which I had heard something, as beyond the limits of the United States; for, notwithstanding there were free States in the Union, I felt that I should be safer under an entirely foreign jurisdiction. The slave States had their emissaries in the others, and I feared that I might fall into their hands, and need a stronger protection than might be afforded me by public opinion in the northern States at that time.

It was not without long thought on the subject that I devised a plan of escape; but when I had fully made up my mind, I communicated my intention to my wife, who was too much terrified by the dangers of the attempt to do any thing, at first, but endeavor to dissuade me from it, and try to make me contented with my condition as it was. In vain I explained to her the liability we were in of being separated from our children as well as from each other; and presented every argument which had weighed with my own mind, and had at last decided me. She had not gone through my trials, and female timidity overcame her sense of the evils she had experienced. I argued the matter with her, at various times, till I was satisfied that argument alone would not prevail; and then I said to her, very deliberately, that though it was a cruel thing for me to part with her, yet I would do it, and take all the children with me but the youngest, rather than run the risk of forcible separation from them all, and of a much worse captivity besides, which we were constantly exposed to here. She wept and entreated, but found I was resolute, and after a whole night spent in talking over the matter, I left her to go to my work for the day. I had not gone far when I heard her voice calling me;—I waited till she came up to me, and then, finding me as determined as ever, she said, at last, she would go with me. It was an immense relief to my nerves, and my tears flowed as fast as hers had done before. I rode off with a heart a good deal lighter.

She was living, at the time, near the landing I have mentioned; for the plantation extended the whole five miles from the house to the river, and there were several different farms, all of which I was overseeing, and, therefore, riding about from one to another every day. The oldest boy was at the house with Master Amos, the rest were all with her. Her consent was given on Thursday morning, and on the night of the following Saturday, I had decided to set out, as it would then be several days before I should be missed, and I should get a good start. Some time previously I had got my wife to make me a large knapsack, big enough to hold the two smallest children; and I had arranged it that she should lead the second boy, while the oldest was stout enough to go by himself, and to help me carry the necessary food. I used to pack the little ones on my back, of an evening, after I had got through my day's work, and trot round the cabin with them, and go some little distance from it, in order to accustom both them and myself to the task before us.

At length the eventful night came. I went up to the house to ask leave to take Tom home with me, that he might have his clothes mended. No objection was made, and I bade Master Amos "good night" for the last time. It was about the middle of September, and by nine o'clock in the evening all was ready. It was a dark, moonless night, and we got into the little skiff in which I had induced a fellow-slave to take us across the river. It was an agitating and solemn moment. The good fellow who was rowing us over, said this affair might end in his death; "but," said he, "you will not be brought back alive, will you?" "Not if I can help it," I answered. "And if you are overpowered and return," he asked, "will you conceal my part of the business?" "That I will, so help me God," I replied. "Then I am easy," he answered, "and wish you success." We landed on the Indiana shore, and I began to feel that I was my own master. But in what circumstances of fear and misery still! We were to travel by night, and rest by day, in the woods and bushes. We were thrown absolutely upon our own poor and small resources, and were to rely on our own strength alone. The population was not so numerous as now, nor so well disposed to the slave. We dared look to no one for help. But my courage was equal to the occasion, and we trudged on cautiously and steadily, and as fast as the darkness, and the feebleness of my wife and boys would allow.

It was nearly a fortnight before we reached Cincinnati; and a day or two previous to getting there, our provisions were used up, and I had the misery to hear the cry of hunger and exhaustion from those I loved so dearly. It was necessary to run the risk of exposure by daylight upon the road; so I sprung upon it boldly from our hiding place one morning, and turned towards the south, to prevent the suspicion of my going the other way. I approached the first house I saw, and asked if they would sell me a little bread and meat. No, they had nothing for black fellows. At the next I succeeded better, but had to make as good a bargain as I could, and that was not very successful, with a man who wanted to see how little he could give me for my quarter of a dollar. As soon as I had succeeded in making a purchase, I followed the road, still towards the south, till I got out of sight of the house, and then darted into the woods again, and returned northward, just out of sight of the road. The food which I bought, such as it was, put new life and strength into my wife and children when I got back to them again, and we at length arrived safe at Cincinnati. There we were kindly received and entertained for several days, my wife and little ones were refreshed, and then we were carried on our way thirty miles in a wagon.

We followed the same course as before, of travelling by night, and resting by day, till we arrived at the Scioto, where we had been told we should strike the military road of General Hull, in the last war with Great Britain, and might then safely travel by day. We found the road, accordingly, by the large sycamore and elm which marked its beginning, and entered upon it with fresh spirits early in the day. Nobody had told us that it was cut through the wilderness, and I had neglected to provide any food, thinking we should soon come to some habitation, where we could be supplied. But we travelled on all day without seeing one, and laid down at night, hungry and weary enough. I thought I heard the howling of wolves, and the terror inspired by this, and the exertions I used to keep them off, by making as much noise as I could, took away all power of sleeping, till daylight, and rendered a little delay inevitable. In the morning we were as hungry as ever, but had nothing to relieve our appetites but a little piece of dried beef. I divided some of this all round, and then started for a second day's trip in the wilderness. It was a hard trial, and this day is a memorable one in my life. The road was rough, of course, being neglected, and the logs lying across it constantly; the underbrush was somewhat cleared away, and that was about all to mark the track. As we went wearily on, I was a little ahead of my wife and the boys, when I heard them call to me, and, turning round, saw that my wife had fallen over a log, and was prostrate on the ground. "Mother's dying," cried Tom; and when I reached her, it seemed really so. She had fainted. I did not know but it might be fatal, and was half distracted with the fear and the uncertainty. In a few minutes, however, she recovered sufficiently to take a few mouthfuls of the beef, and this, with a little rest, revived her so much that she bravely set out once more.

We had not gone far, and I suppose it was about three o'clock in the afternoon, when we discerned some persons approaching us at no great distance. We were instantly on the alert, as we could hardly expect them to be friends. The advance of a few paces showed me they were Indians, with packs on their shoulders; and they were so near that if they were hostile, it would be useless to try to escape. So I walked along boldly, till we came close upon them. They were bent down with their burdens, and had not raised their eyes till now; and when they did so, and saw me coming towards them, they looked at me in a frightened sort of way for a moment, and then, setting up a peculiar howl, turned round, and ran as fast as they could. There were three or four of them, and what they were afraid of I could not imagine, unless they supposed I was the devil, whom they had perhaps heard of as black. But even then one would have thought my wife and children might have reassured them. However, there was no doubt they were well frightened, and we heard their wild and prolonged howl, as they ran, for a mile or more. My wife was alarmed too, and thought they were merely running back to collect more of a party, and then to come and murder us, and she wanted to turn back. I told her they were numerous enough to do that, if they wanted to, without help; and that as for turning back, I had had quite too much of the road behind us, and that it would be a ridiculous thing that both parties should run away. If they were disposed to run, I would follow. We did follow on, and soon the noise was stopped; and, as we advanced, we could discover Indians peeping at us from behind the trees, and dodging out of our sight, if they thought we were looking at them. Presently we came upon their wigwams, and saw a fine looking, stately Indian, with his arms folded, waiting for us to approach. He was apparently the chief, and, saluting us civilly, he soon discovered that we were human beings, and spoke to his young men, who were scattered about, and made them come in, and give up their foolish fears. And now curiosity seemed to prevail. Each one wanted to touch the children, who were shy as partridges, with their long life in the woods; and as they shrunk away, and uttered a little cry of alarm, the Indian would jump back too, as if he thought they would bite him. However, a little while sufficed to make them understand what we were, and whither we were going, and what we needed; and as little, to set them about supplying our wants, feeding us bountifully, and giving us a comfortable wigwam for our night's rest. The next day we resumed our march, and found, from the Indians, that we were only about twenty-five miles from the lake. They sent some of their young men to point out the place where we were to turn off, and parted from us with as much kindness as possible.

In passing over the part of Ohio near the lake, where such an extensive plain is found, we came to a spot overflowed by a stream, across which the road passed. I forded it first, with the help of a sounding-pole, and then taking the children on my back, first, the two little ones, and then the others, one at a time, and, lastly, my wife, I succeeded in getting them all safely across, where the ford was one hundred to one hundred and fifty yards wide, and the deepest part perhaps four feet deep. At this time the skin was worn from my back to an extent almost equal to the size of my knapsack.

One night more was passed in the woods, and in the course of the next forenoon we came out upon the wide plain, without trees, which lies south and west of Sandusky city. We saw the houses of the village, and kept away from them for the present, till I should have an opportunity to reconnoitre a little. When about a mile from the lake, I hid my companions in the bushes, and pushed forward. Before I had gone far, I observed on the left, on the opposite side from the town, something which looked like a house, between which and a vessel, a number of men were passing and repassing with activity. I promptly decided to approach them; and, as I drew near, I was hailed by one of the number, who asked me if I wanted to work. I told him yes; and it was scarcely a minute before I had hold of a bag of corn, which, like the rest, I emptied into the hold of the vessel lying at anchor a few rods off. I got into the line of laborers hurrying along the plank next to the only colored man I saw engaged, and soon entered into conversation with him; in the course of which I inquired of him where they were going, the best route to Canada, who was the captain, and other particulars interesting to me, and communicated to him where I came from, and whither I wished to go. He told the captain, who called me to one side, and by his frank look and manner soon induced me to acknowledge my condition and purpose. I found I had not mistaken him. He sympathized with me, at once, most heartily; and offered to take me and my family to Buffalo, whither they were bound, and where they might arrive the next evening, if the favorable wind continued, of which they were hurrying to take advantage. Never did men work with a better will, and soon two or three hundred bushels were thrown on board, the hatches were fastened down, the anchor raised, and the sails hoisted. The captain had agreed to send a boat for me, after sundown, rather than take me on board at the landing; as there were Kentucky spies, he said, on the watch for slaves, at Sandusky, who might get a glimpse of me, if I brought my party out of the bush by daylight. I watched the vessel, as she left her moorings, with intense interest, and began to fear that she would go without me, after all; she stretched off to so great a distance, as it seemed to me, before she rounded to. At length, however, I saw her come up to the wind, and lower a boat for the shore; and, in a few minutes, my black friend and two sailors jumped out upon the beach. They went with me, immediately, to bring my wife and children. But what was my alarm when I came back to the place where I had left them, to find they had gone! For a moment, my fears were overpowering; but I soon discerned them, in the fading twilight, at no great distance. My wife had been alarmed by my long absence, and thought I must have been discovered by some of our watchful enemies, and had given up all for lost. Her fears were not removed by seeing me returning with three other men; and she tried to hide herself. It was not without difficulty that I satisfied her all was right, for her agitation was so great that she could not, at once, understand what I said. However, this was soon over, and the kindness of my companions facilitated the matter very much. Before long, we were all on the way to the boat, and it did not require much time or labor to embark our luggage. A short row brought us to the vessel, and, to my astonishment, we were welcomed on board, with three hearty cheers; for the crew were as much pleased as the captain, with the help they were giving us to escape. A fine run brought us to Buffalo the next evening, but it was too late to cross the river that night. The next morning we dropped down to Black Rock, and the friendly captain, whose name I have gratefully remembered as Captain Burnham, put us on board the ferry-boat to Waterloo, paid the passage money, and gave me a dollar at parting. He was a Scotchman, and had done enough to win my enduring gratitude, to prove himself a kind and generous man, and to give me a pleasant association with his dialect and his country.

When I got on the Canada side, on the morning of the 28th of October, 1830, my first impulse was to throw myself on the ground, and giving way to the riotous exultation of my feelings, to execute sundry antics which excited the astonishment of those who were looking on. A gentleman of the neighborhood, Colonel Warren, who happened to be present, thought I was in a fit, and as he inquired what was the matter with the poor fellow, I jumped up and told him I was free. "O," said he, with a hearty laugh, "is that it? I never knew freedom make a man roll in the sand before." It is not much to be wondered at, that my certainty of being free was not quite a sober one at the first moment; and I hugged and kissed my wife and children all round, with a vivacity which made them laugh as well as myself. There was not much time to be lost, though, in frolic, even at this extraordinary moment. I was a stranger, in a strange land, and had to look about me at once, for refuge and resource. I found a lodging for the night; and the next morning set about exploring the interior for the means of support. I knew nothing about the country, or the people; but kept my eyes and ears open, and made such inquiries as opportunity afforded. I heard, in the course of the day, of a Mr. Hibbard, who lived some six or seven miles off, and who was a rich man, as riches were counted there, with a large farm, and several small tenements on it, which he was in the habit of letting to his laborers. To him I went, immediately, though the character given him by his neighbors was not, by any means, unexceptionably good. But I thought he was not probably any worse than those I had been accustomed to serve, and that I could get along with him, if honest and faithful work would satisfy him. In the afternoon I found him, and soon struck a bargain with him for employment. I asked him if there was any house where he would let me live. He said yes, and led the way to an old two story sort of shanty, into the lower story of which the pigs had broken, and had apparently made it their resting-place for some time. Still, it was a house, and I forthwith expelled the pigs, and set about cleaning it for the occupancy of a better sort of tenants. With the aid of hoe and shovel, hot-water and a mop, I got the floor into a tolerable condition by midnight, and only then did I rest from my labor. The next day I brought the rest of the Hensons to my house, and though there was nothing there but bare walls and floors, we were all in a state of great delight, and my old woman laughed and acknowledged that it was worth while, and that it was better than a log-cabin with an earth-floor. I begged some straw of Mr. Hibbard, and confining it by logs in the corners of the room, I made beds of it three feet thick, upon which we reposed luxuriously after our long fatigues.

Another trial awaited me which I had not anticipated. In consequence of the great exposures we had gone through, my wife and all the children fell sick; and it was not without extreme peril that they escaped with their lives.

My employer soon found that my labor was of more value to him than that of those he was accustomed to hire; and as I consequently gained his favor, and his wife took quite a fancy to mine, we soon procured some of the comforts of life, while the necessaries of food and fuel were abundant. I remained with Mr. Hibbard three years, sometimes working on shares, and sometimes for wages; and I managed in that time to procure some pigs, a cow, and a horse. Thus my condition gradually improved, and I felt that my toils and sacrifices for freedom had not been in vain. Nor were my labors for the improvement of myself and others, in more important things than food and clothing, without effect. It so happened that one of my Maryland friends arrived in this neighborhood, and hearing of my being here, inquired if I ever preached now, and spread the reputation I had acquired elsewhere, for my gifts in the pulpit. I had said nothing myself, and had not intended to say any thing, of my having ever officiated in that way. I went to meeting with others, when I had an opportunity, and enjoyed the quiet of the Sabbath when there was no assembly. I would not refuse to labor in this field, however, when desired to do so; and I hope it is no violation of modesty to state the fact that I was frequently called upon, not by blacks alone, but by all classes in my vicinity, the comparatively educated, as well as the lamentably ignorant, to speak to them on their duty, responsibility, and immortality, on their obligations to their Maker, their Saviour, and themselves.

Source: Josiah Henson. *The Life of Josiah Henson, Formerly a Slave, Now an Inhabitant of Canada, as Narrated by Himself.* Boston: Arthur D. Phelps, 1849.

JOHN HENRY HILL

Five Years and One Month Secreted

[William Still]

In introducing this narrative of a slave who hid out for years before succeeding in his escape, we quote a reflection by Still: "It was … one of the most gratifying facts connected with the fugitives, the strong love and attachment that they constantly expressed for their relatives left in the South … But few probably are aware how deeply these feelings were cherished in the breasts of this people. Forty, fifty, or sixty years, in some instances elapsed, but this ardent sympathy and love continued warm and unwavering as ever. ... Therefore it is a source of great satisfaction to be able, in relating these heroic escapes, to present the evidences of the strong affections of this greatly oppressed race."

MANY LETTERS FROM JOHN HENRY show how incessantly his mind ran out towards the oppressed, and the remarkable intelligence and ability he displayed with the pen, considering that he had no chance to acquire book knowledge. After having fled for refuge to Canada and having become a partaker of impartial freedom under the government of Great Britain, to many it seemed that the fugitive should be perfectly satisfied. Many appeared to think that the fugitive, having secured freedom, had but little occasion for anxiety or care, even for his nearest kin. "Change your name." "Never tell any one how you escaped." "Never let any one know where you came from." "Never think of writing back, not even to your wife; you can do your kin no good, but may do them harm by writing." "Take care of yourself." "You are free, well, be satisfied then." "It will do you no good to fret about your wife and children; that will not get them out of Slavery." Such was the advice often given to the fugitive Men who had been slaves themselves, and some who had aided in the escape of individuals, sometimes urged these sentiments on men and women whose hearts were almost breaking over the thought that their dearest and best friends were in chains in the prison-house. Perhaps it was thoughtlessness on the part of some, and a wish to inspire due cautiousness on the part of others, that prompted this advice. Doubtless some did soon forget their friends. They saw no way by which they could readily communicate with them. Perhaps Slavery had dealt with them so cruelly, that little hope or aspiration was left in them.

It was, however, one of the most gratifying facts connected with the fugitives, the strong love and attachment that they constantly expressed for their relatives left in the South; the undying faith they had in God as evinced by their touching appeals on behalf of their fellow-slaves. But few probably are aware how deeply these feelings were cherished in the breasts of this people. Forty, fifty, or sixty years, in some instances elapsed, but this ardent sympathy and love continued warm and unwavering as ever. Children left to the cruel mercy of slaveholders, could never be forgotten. Brothers and sisters could not refrain from weeping over the remembrance of their separation on the auction block: of having seen innocent children, feeble and defenceless women in the grasp of a merciless tyrant, pleading, groaning, and crying in vain for pity. Not to remember those thus bruised and mangled, it would seem alike unnatural, and impossible. Therefore it is a source of great satisfaction to be able, in relating these heroic escapes, to present the evidences of the strong affections of this greatly oppressed race.

JOHN HENRY never forgot those with whom he had been a fellow-sufferer in Slavery; he was always fully awake to their wrongs, and longed to be doing something to aid and encourage such as were striving to get their Freedom. He wrote many letters in behalf of others, as well as for himself, the tone of which, was always marked by the most zealous devotion to the slave, a high sense of the value of Freedom, and unshaken confidence that God was on the side of the oppressed, and a strong hope, that the day was not far distant, when the slave power would be "suddenly broken and that without remedy."

Notwithstanding the literary imperfections of these letters, they are deemed well suited to these pages. Of course, slaves were not allowed book learning. Virginia even imprisoned white women for teaching free colored children the alphabet. Who has forgotten the imprisonment of Mrs. Douglass for this offense? In view of these facts, no apology is needed on account of Hill's grammar and spelling.

In these letters, may be seen, how much liberty was valued, how the taste of Freedom moved the pen of the slave; how the thought of fellow-bondmen, under the heel of the slave-holder, aroused the spirit of indignation and wrath; how importunately appeals were made for help from man and from God; how much joy was felt at the arrival of a fugitive, and the intense sadness experienced over the news of a failure or capture of a slave. Not only are the feelings of John Henry Hill represented in these epistles, but the feelings of very many others amongst the intelligent fugitives all over the country are also represented to the letter. It is more with a view of doing justice to a brave, intelligent class, whom the public are ignorant of, than merely to give special prominence to John and his relatives as individuals, that these letters are given.

ESCAPE OF JOHN HENRY HILL FROM THE SLAVE AUCTION IN RICHMOND, ON THE FIRST DAY OF JANUARY, 1853.

JOHN HENRY AT THAT TIME, was a little turned of twenty-five years of age, full six feet high, and remarkably well proportioned in every respect. He was rather of a brown color, with marked intellectual features. John was by trade, a carpenter, and was considered a competent workman. The year previous to his escape, he hired his time, for which he paid his owner $150. This amount John had fully settled up the last day of the year. As he was a young man of steady habits, a husband and father, and withal an ardent lover of Liberty; his owner, John Mitchell, evidently observed these traits in his character, and concluded that he was a dangerous piece of property to keep; that his worth in money could be more easily managed than the man. Consequently, his master unceremoniously, without intimating in any way to John, that he was to be sold, took him to Richmond, on the first day of January (the great annual sale day), and directly to the slave-auction. Just as John was being taken into the building, he was invited to submit to hand-cuffs. As the thought flashed upon his mind that he was about to be sold on the auction-block, he grew terribly desperate. "Liberty or death" was the watchword of that awful moment. In the twinkling of an eye, he turned on his enemies, with his fist, knife, and feet, so tiger-like, that he actually put four or five men to flight, his master among the number. His enemies thus suddenly baffled, John wheeled, and, as if assisted by an angel, strange as it may appear, was soon out of sight of his pursuers, and securely hid away. This was the last hour of John Henry's slave life, but not, however, of his struggles and sufferings for freedom, for before a final chance to escape presented itself, nine months elapsed. The mystery as to where, and how he fared, the following account, in his own words, must explain—

Nine months I was trying to get away. I was secreted for a long time in a kitchen of a merchant near the corner of Franklyn and 7th streets, at Richmond, where I was well taken care of, by a lady friend of my mother. When I got Tired of staying in that place, I wrote myself a pass to pass myself to Petersburg, here I stopped with a very prominent Colored person, who was a friend to Freedom stayed here until two white friends told other friends if I was in the city to tell me to go at once, and stand not upon the order of going, because they had hard a plot. I wrot a pass, started for Richmond, Reached Manchester, cot off the Cars walked into Richmond, once more got back into the same old Den, Stayed here from the 16th of Aug. to 12th Sept. On the 11th of Sept. 8 o'clock P. M. a message came to me that there had been a State Room taken on the steamer City of Richmond for my benefit, and I assured the party that it would be occupied if God be willing. Before

10 o'clock the next morning, on the 12th, two beautiful Sept. day, I arose early, wrote my pass for Norfolk left my old Den with a many a good bye, turned out the back way to 7th St., thence to Main, down Main behind 4 night watch to old Rockett's and after about 20 minutes of delay I succeed in Reaching the State Room. My Conductor was very much Excited, but I felt as Composed as I do at this moment, for I had started from my Den that morning for Liberty or for Death providing myself with a Brace of Pistels. Yours truly J. H. HILL.

A private berth was procured for him on the steamship City of Richmond, for the amount of $125, and thus he was brought on safely to Philadelphia. While in the city, he enjoyed the hospitalities of the Vigilance Committee, and the greetings of a number of friends, during the several days of his sojourn. The thought of his wife, and two children, left in Petersburg, however, naturally caused him much anxiety. Fortunately, they were free, therefore, he was not without hope of getting them; moreover, his wife's father (Jack McCraey), was a free man, well known, and very well to do in the world, and would not be likely to see his daughter and grandchildren suffer. In this particular, Hill's lot was of a favorable character, compared with that of most slaves leaving their wives and children.

FIRST LETTER

On Arriving in Canada

TORONTO, October 4th, 1853.

DEAR SIR:—I take this method of informing you that I am well, and that I got to this city all safe and sound, though I did not get here as soon as I expect. I left your city on Saterday and I was on the way until the Friday following. I got to New York the same day that I left Philadelphia, but I had to stay there until Monday evening. I left that place at six o'clock, I got to Albany next morning in time to take the half past six o'clock train for Rochester, here I stay until Wensday night. The reason I stay there so long Mr. Gibbs given me a letter to Mr Morris at Rochester. I left that place Wensday, but I only got five miles from that city that night. I got to Lewiston on Thursday afternoon, but too late for the boat to this city. I left Lewiston on Friday at one o'clock, got to this city at five. Sir I found this to be a very handsome city. I like it better than any city I ever saw. It are not as large as the city that you live in, but it is very large place much more so than I expect to find it. I seen the gentleman that you given me letter to. I think him much of a gentleman, I got into work on Monday. The man whom I am working for is name Myers; but I expect to go to work for another man by name of Tinsly, who is a master workman in this city. He says that he will give me work next week and everybody advises me to work for Mr. Tinsly as there is more purity in him.

Mr. Still, I have been looking and looking for my friends for several days, but have not seen nor heard of them. I hope and trust in the Lord Almighty that all things are well with them. My dear sir, I could feel so much better satisfied if I could hear from my wife. Since I reached this city I have talagraphed to friend Brown to send my thing to me, but I cannot hear a word from no one at all. I have written to Mr. Brown two or three times since I left the city. I trust that he has gotten my wife's letters, that is if she has written Please direct your letters to me, near the corner Sarah and Edward street, until I give you further notice. You will tell friend B. how to direct his letters, as I forgotten it when I writt to him, and ask him if he has heard anything from Virginia. Please to let me hear from him without delay for my very soul is trubled about my friends whom I expected to of seen here before this hour. Whatever you do please to write, I shall look for you paper shortly. Believe me sir to be your well wisher.—JOHN H. HILL.

SECOND LETTER.

Expressions of gratitude—The Custom House refuses to charge him duty—He is greatly concerned for his wife

TORONTO, October 30th, 1853.

MY DEAR FRIEND:—I now write to inform you that I have received my things all safe and sound, and also have shuck hand with the friend that you send on to this place one of them is stopping with me. His name is Chas. Stuart, he seemes to be a tolerable smart fellow. I Rec'd my letters. I have taken this friend to see Mr. Smith. However will give him a place to board untell he can get to work. I shall do every thing I can for them all that I see the gentleman wish you to see his wife and let her know that he arrived safe, and present his love to her and to all the friend. Mr. Still, I am under ten thousand obligation to you for your kindness when shall I ever repay? S. speek very highly of you. I will state to you what Custom house master said to me. He ask me when he presented my efects are these your efects. I answered yes. He then ask me was I going to settle in Canada. I told him I was. He then ask me of my case. I told all about it. He said I am happy to see you and all that will come. He ask me how much I had to pay for my Paper. I told him half dollar. He then told me that I should have my money again. He a Rose from his seat and got my money. So my friend you can see the people and tell them all this is a land of liberty and believe they will find friends here. My best love to all.

My friend I must call upon you once more to do more kindness for me that is to write to my wife as soon as you get this, and tell her when she gets ready to come she will pack and consign her things to you. You will give her some instruction, but not to your expenses but to her own.

When you write direct your letter to Phillip Ubank, Petersburg, Va. My Box arrived here the 27th.

My dear sir I am in a hurry to take this friend to church, so I must close by saying I am your humble servant in the cause of liberty and humanity.—JOHN H. HILL.

THIRD LETTER.

Canada is highly praised—The Vigilance Committee is implored to send all the Fugitives there— "Farmers and Mechanics wanted" — "No living in Canada for Negroes," as argued by "Masters," flatly denied, &c., &c., &c.

SO I ASK YOU to send the fugitives to Canada. I don't know much of this Province but I beleaves that there is Rome enough for the colored and whites of the United States. We wants farmers mechanic men of all qualification &c., if they are not made we will make them, if we cannot make the old, we will make our children.

Now concerning the city toronto this city is Beautiful and Prosperous Levele city. Great many wooden codages more than what should be but I am in hopes there will be more of the Brick and Stone. But I am not done about your Republicanism. Our masters have told us that there was no living in Canada for a Negro but if it may Please your gentlemanship to publish these facts that we are here able to earn our bread and money enough to make us comfortable. But I say give me freedom, and the United States may have all her money and her Luxtures, yeas give Liberty or Death. I'm in America, but not under Such a Government that I cannot express myself, speak, think or write So as I am able, and if my master had allowed me to have an education

I would make them American Slave-holders feel me, Yeas I would make them tremble when I spoke, and when I take my Pen in hand their knees smote together. My Dear Sir suppose I was an educated man. I could write you something worth reading, but you know we poor fugitives whom has just come over from the South are not able to write much on no subject whatever, but I hope by the aid of my God I will try to use my midnight lamp, until I can have some influence upon the American Slavery. If some one would say to me, that they would give my wife bread until I could be Educated I would stoop my trade this day and take up my books.

But a crisis is approaching when essential requisite to the American Slaveholders when blood Death or Liberty will be required at their hands, I think our people have depened too long and too much on false legislator let us now look for ourselves. It is true that England however the Englishman is our best friend but we as men ought not to depened upon her Remonstrace with the Americans because she loves her commercial trade as any Nations do. But I must say, while we look up and acknowledge the Power greatness and honor of old England, and believe that while we sit beneath the Silken folds of her flag of Perfect Liberty, we are secure, beyond the reach of the aggressions of the Blood hounds and free from the despotism that would wrap around our limbs by the damable Slaveholder. Yet we would not like spoiled children depend upon her, but upon ourselves and as one means of strengthening ourselves, we should agitate the emigration to Canada. I here send you a paragraph which I clpted from the weekly Glob. I hope you will publish so that Mr. Williamson may know that men are not chattel here but reather they are men and if he wants his chattle let him come here after it or his thing, I wants you to let the whole United States know we are satisfied here because I have seen more Pleasure since I came here then I saw in the U. S. the 24 years that I served my master. Come Poor distress men women and come to Canada where colored men are free. Oh how sweet the word do sound to me years when I contemplate of these things, my very flesh creaps my heart thrub when I think of my beloved friends whom I left in that cursed hole. Oh my God what can I do for them or shall I do for them. Lord help them. Suffer them to be no longer depressed beneath the Bruat Creation but may they be looked upon as men made of the Bone and Blood as the Anglo-Americans. May God in his mercy Give Liberty to all this world. I must close as it am late hour at night. I Remain your friend in the cause of Liberty and humanity,—JOHN H. HILL, a fugitive.

If you know any one who would give me an education write and let me know for I am in want of it very much. Your with Respect, —J. H. H.

If the sentiments in the above letter do not indicate an uncommon degree of natural intelligence, a clear perception of the wrongs of Slavery, and a just appreciation of freedom, where shall we look for the signs of intellect and manhood?

FOURTH LETTER

Longs for his wife—In hearing of the return of a Fugitive from Philadelphia is made sorrowful—His love of Freedom increases, &c., &c.

TORONTO, November 12th, 1853.

MY DEAR STILL:—Your letter of the 31h came to hand thursday and also three copies all of which I was glad to Received they have taken my attention all together Every Time I got them. I also Rec'd. a letter from my friend Brown. Mr. Brown stated to me that he had heard from my wife but he did not say what way he heard. I am looking for my wife every day. Yes I want her to come then I will be better sattisfied. My friend I am a free man and feeles alright about that matter. I am doing tolrable well in my line of business, and think I will do better after little. I hope you all will never stop any of our Brotheran that makes their Escep from the South but send them on to this place where they can be free man and woman. We want them here and not in your State where they can be taken away at any hour. Nay but let him ccme here where he can Enjoy the Rights of a human being and not to be trodden under the feet of men like themselves All the People that come here does well. Thanks be to God that I came to this place. I would like very well to see you all but never do I expect to see you in the United States. I want you all to come to this land of Liberty where the bondman can be free. Come one come all come to this place, and I hope my dear friend you will send on here, I shall do for them as you all done for me when I came on here however I will do the best I can for them if they can they shall do if they will do, but some comes here that can't do well because they make no efford. I hope my friend you will teach them such lessons as Mrs. Moore Give me before I left your city. I hope she may live a hundred years longer and enjoy good health. May God bless her for the good cause which she are working in. Mr.

Still you ask me to remember you to Nelson. I will do so when I see him, he are on the lake so is Stewart. I received a letter to-day for Stewart from your city which letter I will take to him when he comes to the city. He are not stoping with us at this time. I was very sorry a few days ago when I heard that a man was taken from your city.

Send them over here, then let him come here and take them away and I will try to have a finger in the Pie myself. You said that you had written to my wife ten thousand thanks for what you have done and what you are willing to do. My friend whenever you hear from my wife please write to me. Whenever she come to your city please give instruction how to travel. I wants her to come the faster way. I wish she was here now. I wish she could get a ticket through to this place, I have mail a paper for you to day.

We have had snow but not to last long. Let me hear from you. My Respect friend Brown. I will write more when I have the opportunity.

Yours with Respect, —John H. Hill.

P. S. My dear Sir. Last night after I had written the above, and had gone to bed; I heard a strange voice in the house, Saying to Mr. Myers to come quickly to one of our colod Brotheran out of the street. We went and found a man a Carpenter laying on the side walk woltun in his Blood. Done by some unknown Person as yet but if they stay on the earth the law will deteck them. It is said that party of colord people done it, which party was seen to come out an infame house.

Mr. Myers have been down to see him and Brought the Sad news that the Poor fellow was dead. Mr. Scott for Henry Scott was the name, he was a fugitive from Virginia he came here from Pittsburg Pa. Oh, when I went where he laid what a shock, it taken my Sleep altogether night. When I got to Sopt his Body was surrounded by the Policeman. The law has taken the woman in cusidy. I write and also send you a paper of the case when it comes out. —J. H. Hill.

Source: William Still, 1872 (see the Bibliography on p. 203 for complete information).

ANN MARIA JACKSON AND HER SEVEN CHILDREN

Arrival from Maryland, 1859

[William Still]

Still relates the heartbreaking story of a woman who, after the descent into madness of her freed-slave husband on account of the sale of his own children, escaped with her children to Canada.

THE COMING OF THE ABOVE named was duly announced by Thomas Garrett:

WILMINGTON, 11th mo., 21st, 1858.

DEAR FRIENDS—McKIM AND STILL:—I write to inform you that on the 16th of this month, we passed on four able bodied men to Pennsylvania, and they were followed last night by a woman and her six children, from three or four years of age, up to sixteen years; I believe the whole belonged to the same estate, and they were to have been sold at public sale, I was informed yesterday, but preferred seeking their own master; we had some trouble in getting those last safe along, as they could not travel far on foot, and could not safely cross any of the bridges on the canal, either on foot or in carriage. A man left here two days since, with carriage, to meet them this side of the canal, but owing to spies they did not reach him till 10 o'clock last night; this morning he returned, having seen them about one or two o'clock this morning in a second carriage, on the border of Chester county, where I think they are all safe, if they can be kept from Philadelphia. If you see them they can tell their own tales, as I have seen one of them. May He, who feeds the ravens, care for them. Yours,—THOS. GARRETT.

The fire of freedom obviously burned with no ordinary fervor in the breast of this slave mother, or she never would have ventured with the burden of seven children, to escape from the hell of Slavery.

Ann Maria was about forty years of age, good-looking, pleasant countenance, and of a chestnut color, height medium, and intellect above the average. Her bearing was humble, as might have been expected, from the fact that she emerged from the lowest depths of Delaware Slavery. During the Fall prior to her escape, she lost her husband under most trying circumstances: he died in the poor-house, a raving maniac. Two of his children had been taken from their mother by her owner, as was usual with slave-holders, which preyed so severely on the poor father's mind that it drove him into a state of hopeless insanity. He was a "free man" in the eye of Delaware laws, yet he was not allowed to exercise the least authority over his children.

Prior to the time that the two children were taken from their mother, she had been allowed to live with her husband and children, independently of her master, by supporting herself and them with the white-wash brush, wash-tub, etc. For this privilege the mother doubtless worked with double energy, and the master, in all probability, was largely the gainer, as the children were no expense to him in their infancy; but when they began to be old enough to hire out, or bring high prices in the market, he snatched away two of the finest articles, and the powerless father was immediately rendered a fit subject for the mad-house; but the brave hearted mother looked up to God, resolved to wait patiently until in a good Providence the way might open to escape with her remaining children to Canada.

Year in and year out she had suffered to provide food and raiment for her little ones. Many times in going out to do days' work she would be compelled to leave her children, not knowing whether during her absence they would fall victims to fire, or be carried off by the master. But she possessed a well tried faith, which in her flight kept her from despondency. Under her former lot she scarcely murmured, but declared that she had never been at ease in Slavery a day after the birth of her first-born. The desire to go to some part of the world where she could have the control and comfort of her children, had always been a prevailing idea with her. "It almost broke my heart," she said, "when he came and took my children away as soon as they were big enough to hand me a drink of water. My husband was always very kind to me, and I had often wanted him to run away with me and the children, but I could not get him in the notion he did not feel that he could, and so he stayed, and died broken-hearted, crazy. I was owned by a man named Joseph Brown; he owned property in

Milford, and he had a place in Vicksburg, and some of his time he spends there, and some of the time he lives in Milford. This Fall he said he was going to take four of my oldest children and two other servants to Vicksburg. I just happened to hear of this news in time. My master was wanting to keep me in the dark about taking them, for fear that something might happen. My master is very sly; he is a tall, slim man, with a smooth face, bald head, light hair, long and sharp nose, swears very hard, and drinks. He is a widower, and is rich."

On the road the poor mother, with her travel-worn children became desperately alarmed, fearing that they were betrayed. But God had provided better things for her; her strength and hope were soon fully restored, and she was lucky enough to fall into the right hands. It was a special pleasure to aid such a mother. Her arrival in Canada was announced by Rev. H. Wilson as follows:

NIAGARA CITY, Nov. 30th, 1858.

DEAR BRO. STILL:—I am happy to inform you that Mrs. Jackson and her interesting family of seven children arrived safe and in good health and spirits at my house in St. Catharines, on Saturday evening last. With sincere pleasure I provided for them comfortable quarters till this morning, when they left for Toronto. I got them conveyed there at half fare, and gave them letters of introduction to Thomas Henning, Esq., and Mrs. Dr. Willis, trusting that they will be better cared for in Toronto than they could be at St. Catharines. We have so many coming to us we think it best for some of them to pass on to other places. My wife gave them all a good supply of clothing before they left us. James Henry, an older son is, I think, not far from St. Catharine, but has not as yet reunited with the family. Faithfully and truly yours, — HIRAM WILSON.

SOURCE: William Still, 1872 (see the Bibliography on p. 203 for complete information).

HARRIET JACOBS

Incidents in the Life of a Slave Girl (1861)

(excerpts)

Harriet Jacobs ("Linda Brent") became a fugitive when she was 21 years old and could no longer endure enslavement or the sexual abuse that was the slave woman's particular torment. In her 1861 autobiography, Incidents in the Life of a Slave Girl, *she recounts her experiences, hoping to further alert the men and women of the North to the awful truth about slavery. "I can testify," she writes, "from my own experiences and observations, that slavery is a curse to the whites as well as to the blacks. It makes the white fathers cruel and sensual; the sons violent and licentious; it contaminates the daughters, and makes the wives wretched. And as for the colored race, it needs an abler pen than mine to describe the extremity of their sufferings, the depth of their degradation."[1] In the following excerpts from her autobiography, Jacobs discusses her escape, the help she received from family and friends, her interactions with a ship captain and members of the Anti-Slavery Society, her concern for her children, and her dread of the Fugitive Slave Act.[2]*

★

"The Flight"

$300 REWARD! Ran away from the subscriber, an intelligent, bright, mulatto girl, named Linda, 21 years of age. Five feet four inches high. Dark eyes, and black hair inclined to curl; but it can be made straight. Has a decayed spot on a front tooth. She can read and write, and in all probability will try to get to the Free States. All persons are forbidden, under penalty of the law, to harbor or employ said slave. $150 will be given to whoever takes her in the state, and $300 if taken out of the state and delivered to me, or lodged in jail.

Dr. Flint.

XVIII. MONTHS OF PERIL

THE SEARCH FOR ME was kept up with more perseverance than I had anticipated. I began to think that escape was impossible. I was in great

---

1 Harriet Jacobs. *Incidents in the Life of a Slave Girl.* Mineola, New York: Dover Publications, 2001. [Chapter IX.] 46.

2 See the Appendix below for the text of the Fugitive Slave Act.

anxiety lest I should implicate the friend who harbored me. I knew the consequences would be frightful; and much as I dreaded being caught, even that seemed better than causing an innocent person to suffer for kindness to me. A week had passed in terrible suspense, when my pursuers came into such close vicinity that I concluded they had tracked me to my hiding-place. I flew out of the house, and concealed myself in a thicket of bushes. There I remained in an agony of fear for two hours. Suddenly, a reptile of some kind seized my leg. In my fright, I struck a blow which loosened its hold, but I could not tell whether I had killed it; it was so dark, I could not see what it was; I only knew it was something cold and slimy. The pain I felt soon indicated that the bite was poisonous. I was compelled to leave my place of concealment, and I groped my way back into the house. The pain had become intense, and my friend was startled by my look of anguish. I asked her to prepare a poultice of warm ashes and vinegar, and I applied it to my leg, which was already much swollen. The application gave me some relief, but the swelling did not abate. The dread of being disabled was greater than the physical pain I endured. My friend asked an old woman, who doctored among the slaves, what was good for the bite of a snake or a lizard. She told her to steep a dozen coppers in vinegar, over night, and apply the cankered vinegar to the inflamed part.[3]

I had succeeded in cautiously conveying some messages to my relatives. They were harshly threatened, and despairing of my having a chance to escape, they advised me to return to my master, ask his forgiveness, and let him make an example of me. But such counsel had no influence on me. When I started upon this hazardous undertaking, I had resolved that, come what would, there should be no turning back. "Give me liberty, or give me death," was my motto. When my friend contrived to make known to my relatives the painful situation I had been in for twenty-four hours, they said no more about my going back to my master. Something must be done, and that speedily; but where to turn for help, they knew not. God in his mercy raised up "a friend in need."

---

3 "The poison of a snake is a powerful acid, and is counteracted by powerful alkalies, such as potash, ammonia, &c. The Indians are accustomed to apply wet ashes, or plunge the limb into strong lye. White men, employed to lay out railroads in snaky places, often carry ammonia with them as an antidote." [Note by Jacobs's original editor.]

Among the ladies who were acquainted with my grandmother, was one who had known her from childhood, and always been very friendly to her. She had also known my mother and her children, and felt interested for them. At this crisis of affairs she called to see my grandmother, as she not unfrequently did. She observed the sad and troubled expression of her face, and asked if she knew where Linda was, and whether she was safe. My grandmother shook her head, without answering. "Come, Aunt Martha," said the kind lady, "tell me all about it. Perhaps I can do something to help you." The husband of this lady held many slaves, and bought and sold slaves. She also held a number in her own name; but she treated them kindly, and would never allow any of them to be sold. She was unlike the majority of slaveholders' wives. My grandmother looked earnestly at her. Something in the expression of her face said "Trust me!" and she did trust her. She listened attentively to the details of my story, and sat thinking for a while. At last she said, "Aunt Martha, I pity you both. If you think there is any chance of Linda's getting to the Free States, I will conceal her for a time. But first you must solemnly promise that my name shall never be mentioned. If such a thing should become known, it would ruin me and my family. No one in my house must know of it, except the cook. She is so faithful that I would trust my own life with her; and I know she likes Linda. It is a great risk; but I trust no harm will come of it. Get word to Linda to be ready as soon as it is dark, before the patrols are out. I will send the housemaids on errands, and Betty shall go to meet Linda." The place where we were to meet was designated and agreed upon. My grandmother was unable to thank the lady for this noble deed; overcome by her emotions, she sank on her knees and sobbed like a child.

I received a message to leave my friend's house at such an hour, and go to a certain place where a friend would be waiting for me. As a matter of prudence no names were mentioned. I had no means of conjecturing who I was to meet, or where I was going. I did not like to move thus blindfolded, but I had no choice. It would not do for me to remain where I was. I disguised myself, summoned up courage to meet the worst, and went to the appointed place. My friend Betty was there; she was the last person I expected to see. We hurried along in silence. The pain in my leg was so intense that it seemed as if I should drop; but fear gave me strength. We reached the house and entered unobserved. Her first words were: "Honey, now you is safe. Dem devils ain't coming to search *dis* house. When I get you into missis' safe place, I will bring some nice hot supper. I specs you need it after all dis skeering." Betty's vocation led her to think eating the most important thing in life. She did not realize that my heart was too full for me to care much about supper.

The mistress came to meet us, and led me up stairs to a small room over her own sleeping apartment. "You will be safe here, Linda," said she; "I keep this room to store away things that are out of use. The girls are not accustomed to be sent to it, and they will not suspect anything unless they hear some noise. I always keep it locked, and Betty shall take care of the key. But you must be very careful, for my sake as well as your own; and you must never tell my secret; for it would ruin me and my family. I will keep the girls busy in the morning, that Betty may have a chance to bring your breakfast; but it will not do for her to come to you again till night. I will come to see you sometimes. Keep up your courage. I hope this state of things will not last long." Betty came with the "nice hot supper," and the mistress hastened down stairs to keep things straight till she returned. How my heart overflowed with gratitude! Words choked in my throat; but I could have kissed the feet of my benefactress. For that deed of Christian womanhood may God forever bless her!

I went to sleep that night with the feeling that I was for the present the most fortunate slave in town. Morning came and filled my little cell with light. I thanked the heavenly Father for this safe retreat. Opposite my window was a pile of feather beds. On the top of these I could lie perfectly concealed, and command a view of the street through which Dr. Flint passed to his office. Anxious as I was, I felt a gleam of satisfaction when I saw him. Thus far I had outwitted him, and I triumphed over it. Who can blame slaves for being cunning? They are constantly compelled to resort to it. It is the only weapon of the weak and oppressed against the strength of their tyrants. ...

... As I sat very still in my retreat above stairs, cheerful visions floated through my mind. I thought Dr. Flint would soon get discouraged, and would be willing to sell my children, when he lost all hopes of making them the means of my discovery. I knew who was ready to buy them. Suddenly I heard a voice that chilled my blood. The sound was too familiar to me, it had been too dreadful, for me not to recognize at once my old master. He was in the house, and I at once concluded that he had come to seize me. I looked round in terror. There was no way of escape. The voice receded. I supposed the constable was with him, and they were searching the house. In my alarm I did not forget the trouble I was bringing on my generous benefactress. It seemed as if I were born to bring sorrow on all who befriended me, and that was the bitterest drop in the bitter cup of my life. After a while I heard approaching footsteps; the key was turned in my door. I braced myself against the wall to keep from falling. I ventured to look up, and there stood my kind benefactress. I was too much overcome to speak, and sunk down upon the floor.

"I thought you would hear your master's voice," she said; "and knowing you would be terrified, I came to tell you there is nothing to fear. You may even indulge in a laugh at the old gentleman's expense. He is so sure you are in New York, that he came to borrow five hundred dollars to go in pursuit of you. My sister had some money to loan on interest. He has obtained it, and proposes to start for New York to-night. So, for the present, you see you are safe. The doctor will merely lighten his pocket hunting after the bird he has left behind."

XX. NEW PERILS

THE DOCTOR, more exasperated than ever, again tried to revenge himself on my relatives. He arrested uncle Phillip on the charge of having aided my flight. He was carried before a court, and swore truly that he knew nothing of my intention to escape, and that he had not seen me since I left my master's plantation. The doctor then demanded that he should give bail for five hundred dollars that he would have nothing to do with me. Several gentlemen offered to be security for him; but Mr. Sands told him he had better go back to jail, and he would see that he came out without giving bail.

The news of his arrest was carried to my grandmother, who conveyed it to Betty. In the kindness of her heart, she again stowed me away under the floor; and as she walked back and forth, in the performance of her culinary duties, she talked apparently to herself, but with the intention that I should hear what was going on. I hoped that my uncle's imprisonment would last but few days; still I was anxious. I thought it likely that Dr. Flint would do his utmost to taunt and insult him, and I was afraid my uncle might lose control of himself, and retort in some way that would be construed into a punishable offence; and I was well aware that in court his word would not be taken against any white man's. The search for me was renewed. Something had excited suspicions that I was in the vicinity. They searched the house I was in. I heard their steps and their voices. At night, when all were asleep, Betty came to release me from my place of confinement. The fright I had undergone, the constrained posture, and the dampness of the ground, made me ill for several days. My uncle was soon after taken out of prison; but the movements of all my relatives, and of all our friends, were very closely watched.

We all saw that I could not remain where I was much longer. I had already staid longer than was intended, and I knew my presence must be a source of perpetual anxiety to my kind benefactress. During this time, my friends had laid many plans for my escape, but the extreme vigilance of my persecutors made it impossible to carry them into effect. …

I had not the slightest idea where I was going. Betty brought me a suit of sailor's clothes,—jacket, trousers, and tarpaulin hat. She gave me a small bundle, saying I might need it where I was going. In cheery tones, she exclaimed, "I'se *so* glad you is gwine to free parts! Don't forget ole Betty. P'raps I'll come 'long by and by."

I tried to tell her how grateful I felt for all her kindness, but she interrupted me. "I don't want no tanks, honey. I'se glad I could help you, and I hope de good Lord vill open de path for you. I'se gwine wid you to de lower gate. Put your hands in your pockets, and walk ricketty, like de sailors."

I performed to her satisfaction. At the gate I found Peter, a young colored man, waiting for me. I had known him for years. He had been an apprentice to my father, and had always borne a good character. I was not afraid to trust to him. Betty bade me a hurried good by, and we walked off. "Take courage, Linda," said my friend Peter. "I've got a dagger, and no man shall take you from me, unless he passes over my dead body."

It was a long time since I had taken a walk out of doors, and the fresh air revived me. It was also pleasant to hear a human voice speaking to me above a whisper. I passed several people whom I knew, but they did not recognize me in my disguise. I prayed internally that, for Peter's sake, as well as my own, nothing might occur to bring out his dagger. We walked on till we came to the wharf. My aunt Nancy's husband was a seafaring man, and it had been deemed necessary to let him into our secret. He took me into his boat, rowed out to a vessel not far distant, and hoisted me on board. We three were the only occupants of the vessel. I now ventured to ask what they proposed to do with me. They said I was to remain on board till near dawn, and then they would hide me in Snaky Swamp, till my uncle Phillip had prepared a place of concealment for me. If the vessel had been bound north, it would have been of no avail to me, for it would certainly have been searched. About four o'clock, we were again seated in the boat, and rowed three miles to the swamp. My fear of snakes had been increased by the venomous bite I had received, and I dreaded to enter this hiding-place. But I was in no situation to choose, and I gratefully accepted the best that my poor, persecuted friends could do for me.

Peter landed first, and with a large knife cut a path through bamboos and briers of all descriptions. He came back, took me in his arms, and carried me to a seat made among the bamboos. Before we reached it, we were covered with hundreds of mosquitos. In an hour's time they had so poisoned my flesh that I was a pitiful sight to behold. As the light increased, I saw snake after snake crawling round us. I had been accustomed to the sight of snakes all my life, but these were larger than any I had ever seen. To this day I shudder when I remember that morning. As evening approached, the number of snakes increased so much that we were continually obliged to thrash them with sticks to keep them from crawling over us. The bamboos were so high and so thick that it was impossible to see beyond a very short distance. Just before it became dark we procured a seat nearer to the entrance of the swamp, being fearful of losing our way back to the boat. It was not long before we heard the paddle of oars, and the low whistle, which had been agreed upon as a signal. We made haste to enter the boat, and were rowed back to the vessel. I passed a wretched night; for the heat of the swamp, the mosquitos, and the constant terror of snakes, had brought on a burning fever. I had just dropped asleep, when they came and told me it was time to go back to that horrid swamp. I could scarcely summon courage to rise. But even those large, venomous snakes were less dreadful to my imagination than the white men in that community called civilized. This time Peter took a quantity of tobacco to burn, to keep off the mosquitos. It produced the desired effect on them, but gave me nausea and severe headache. At dark we returned to the vessel. I had been so sick during the day, that Peter declared I should go home that night, if the devil himself was on patrol. They told me a place of concealment had been provided for me at my grandmother's. I could not imagine how it was possible to hide me in her house, every nook and corner of which was known to the Flint family. They told me to wait and see. We were rowed ashore, and went boldly through the streets, to my grandmother's. I wore my sailor's clothes, and had blackened my face with charcoal. I passed several people whom I knew. The father of my children came so near that I brushed against his arm; but he had no idea who it was.

"You must make the most of this walk," said my friend Peter, "for you may not have another very soon."

I thought his voice sounded sad. It was kind of him to conceal from me what a dismal hole was to be my home for a long, long time.

XXI. THE LOOPHOLE OF RETREAT

A SMALL SHED had been added to my grandmother's house years ago. Some boards were laid across the joists at the top, and between these boards and the roof was a very small garret, never occupied by any thing but rats and mice. It was a pent roof, covered with nothing but shingles, according to the southern custom for such buildings. The garret was only nine feet long, and seven wide. The highest part was three feet high, and sloped down abruptly to the loose board floor. There was no admission for either light or air. My uncle Philip, who was a carpenter, had very skillfully made a concealed trap door, which communicated with the storeroom. He had been doing this while I was waiting in the swamp. The storeroom opened upon a piazza. To this hole I was conveyed as soon as I entered the house. The air was stifling; the darkness total. A bed had been spread on the floor. I could sleep quite comfortably on one side; but the slope was so sudden that I could not turn on the other without hitting the roof. The rats and mice ran over my bed; but I was weary, and I slept such sleep as the wretched may, when a tempest has passed over them. Morning came. I knew it only by the noises I heard; for in my small den day and night were all the same. I suffered for air even more than for light. But I was not comfortless. I heard the voices of my children.

There was joy and there was sadness in the sound. It made my tears flow. How I longed to speak to them! I was eager to look on their faces; but there was no hole, no crack, through which I could peep. This continued darkness was oppressive. It seemed horrible to sit or lie in a cramped position day after day, without one gleam of light. Yet I would have chosen this, rather than my lot as a slave, though white people considered it an easy one; and it was so compared with the fate of others. I was never cruelly over-worked; I was never lacerated with the whip from head to foot; I was never so beaten and bruised that I could not turn from one side to the other; I never had my heel-strings cut to prevent my running away; I was never chained to a log and forced to drag it about, while I toiled in the fields from morning till night; I was never branded with hot iron, or torn by bloodhounds. On the contrary, I had always been kindly treated, and

tenderly cared for, until I came into the hands of Dr. Flint. I had
never wished for freedom till then. But though my life in slavery was
comparatively devoid of hardships, God pity the woman who is compelled to lead such a life!

My food was passed up to me through the trap-door my uncle had
contrived; and my grandmother, my uncle Phillip, and aunt Nancy
would seize such opportunities as they could, to mount up there and
chat with me at the opening. But of course this was not safe in the
daytime. It must all be done in darkness. It was impossible for me to
move in an erect position, but I crawled about my den for exercise.
One day I hit my head against something, and found it was a gimlet.
My uncle had left it sticking there when he made the trap-door. I was
as rejoiced as Robinson Crusoe could have been in finding such a
treasure. It put a lucky thought into my head. I said to myself, "Now
I will have some light. Now I will see my children." I did not dare
to begin my work during the daytime, for fear of attracting attention.
But I groped round; and having found the side next the street, where
I could frequently see my children, I stuck the gimlet in and waited
for evening. I bored three rows of holes, one above another; then I
bored out the interstices between. I thus succeeded in making one
hole about an inch long and an inch broad. I sat by it till late into the
night, to enjoy the little whiff of air that floated in. In the morning I
watched for my children. The first person I saw in the street was Dr.
Flint. I had a shuddering, superstitious feeling that it was a bad omen.
Several familiar faces passed by. At last I heard the merry laughing of
children, and presently two sweet little faces were looking up at me,
as though they knew I was there, and were conscious of the joy they
imparted. How I longed to *tell* them I was there!

My condition was now a little improved. But for weeks I was tormented by hundreds of little red insects, fine as a needle's point, that
pierced through my skin, and produced an intolerable burning. The
good grandmother gave me herb teas and cooling medicines, and finally I got rid of them. The heat of my den was intense, for nothing
but thin shingles protected me from the scorching summer's sun. But
I had my consolations. Through my peeping-hole I could watch the
children, and when they were near enough, I could hear their talk.
Aunt Nancy brought me all the news she could hear at Dr. Flint's.
From her I learned that the doctor had written to New York to a
colored woman, who had been born and raised in our neighborhood,
and had breathed his contaminating atmosphere. He offered her a
reward if she could find out any thing about me. I know not what

was the nature of her reply; but he soon after started for New York in haste, saying to his family that he had business of importance to transact. I peeped at him as he passed on his way to the steamboat. It was a satisfaction to have miles of land and water between us, even for a little while; and it was a still greater satisfaction to know that he believed me to be in the Free States. My little den seemed less dreary than it had done. He returned, as he did from his former journey to New York, without obtaining any satisfactory information. When he passed our house next morning, Benny was standing at the gate. He had heard them say that he had gone to find me, and he called out, "Dr. Flint, did you bring my mother home? I want to see her." The doctor stamped his foot at him in a rage, and exclaimed, "Get out of the way, you little damned rascal! If you don't, I'll cut off your head."

Benny ran terrified into the house, saying, "You can't put me in jail again. I don't belong to you now." It was well that the wind carried the words away from the doctor's ear. I told my grandmother of it, when we had our next conference at the trap-door; and begged of her not to allow the children to be impertinent to the irascible old man.

Autumn came, with a pleasant abatement of heat. My eyes had become accustomed to the dim light, and by holding my book or work in a certain position near the aperture I contrived to read and sew. That was a great relief to the tedious monotony of my life. But when winter came, the cold penetrated through the thin shingle roof, and I was dreadfully chilled. The winters there are not so long, or so severe, as in northern latitudes; but the houses are not built to shelter from cold, and my little den was peculiarly comfortless. The kind grandmother brought me bed-clothes and warm drinks. Often I was obliged to lie in bed all day to keep comfortable; but with all my precautions, my shoulders and feet were frostbitten. O, those long, gloomy days, with no object for my eye to rest upon, and no thoughts to occupy my mind, except the dreary past and the uncertain future! I was thankful when there came a day sufficiently mild for me to wrap myself up and sit at the loophole to watch the passers by. Southerners have the habit of stopping and talking in the streets, and I heard many conversations not intended to meet my ears. I heard slave-hunters planning how to catch some poor fugitive. Several times I heard allusions to Dr. Flint, myself, and the history of my children, who, perhaps, were playing near the gate. One would say, "I wouldn't move my little finger to catch her, as old Flint's property." Another would say, "I'll catch *any* nigger for the reward. A man ought to have what belongs to him, if he *is* a damned brute." The opinion was often expressed that I was in the Free States. Very rarely did any one suggest that I might be in the vicinity. Had the least suspicion rested on my grandmother's house, it would have been burned to the ground. But it was the last place they thought of. Yet there was no place, where slavery existed, that could have afforded me so good a place of concealment.

Dr. Flint and his family repeatedly tried to coax and bribe my children to tell something they had heard said about me. One day the doctor took them into a shop, and offered them some bright little silver pieces and gay handkerchiefs if they would tell where their mother was. Ellen shrank away from him, and would not speak; but Benny spoke up, and said, "Dr. Flint, I don't know where my mother is. I guess she's in New York; and when you go there again, I wish you'd ask her to come home, for I want to see her; but if you put her in jail, or tell her you'll cut her head off, I'll tell her to go right back."

XXIX. PREPARATIONS FOR ESCAPE

I HARDLY EXPECT that the reader will credit me, when I affirm that I lived in that little dismal hole, almost deprived of light and air, and with no space to move my limbs, for nearly seven years. But it is a fact; and to me a sad one, even now; for my body still suffers from the effects of that long imprisonment, to say nothing of my soul. Members of my family, now living in New York and Boston, can testify to the truth of what I say.

Countless were the nights that I sat late at the little loophole scarcely large enough to give me a glimpse of one twinkling star. There, I heard the patrols and slave-hunters conferring together about the capture of runaways, well knowing how rejoiced they would be to catch me.

Season after season, year after year, I peeped at my children's faces, and heard their sweet voices, with a heart yearning all the while to say, "Your mother is here." Sometimes it appeared to me as if ages had rolled away since I entered upon that gloomy, monotonous existence. At times, I was stupefied and listless; at other times I became very impatient to know when these dark years would end, and I should again be allowed to feel the sunshine, and breathe the pure air.

... I was likely to be drowned out of my den, if I remained much longer; for the slight roof was getting badly out of repair, and uncle Phillip was afraid to remove the shingles, lest some one should get a glimpse of me. When storms occurred in the night, they spread mats and bits of carpet, which in the morning appeared to have been laid out to dry; but to cover the roof in the daytime might have attracted attention. Consequently, my clothes and bedding were often drenched; a process by which the pains and aches in my cramped and stiffened limbs were greatly increased. I revolved various plans of escape in my mind, which I sometimes imparted to my grandmother, when she came to whisper with me at the trap-door. The kind-hearted old woman had an intense sympathy for runaways. She had known too much of the cruelties inflicted on those who were captured. Her memory always flew back at once to the sufferings of her bright and handsome son, Benjamin, the youngest and dearest of her flock. So, whenever I alluded to the subject, she would groan out, "O, don't think of it, child. You'll break my heart." I had no good old aunt Nancy now to encourage me; but my brother William and my children were continually beckoning me to the north. ...

I was to escape in a vessel; but I forbear to mention any further particulars. ...

I made all my arrangements to go on board as soon as it was dusk. The intervening time I resolved to spend with my son. I had not spoken to him for seven years, though I had been under the same roof, and seen him every day, when I was well enough to sit at the loophole. I did not dare to venture beyond the storeroom; so they brought him there, and locked us up together, in a place concealed from the piazza door. It was an agitating interview for both of us. After we had talked and wept together for a little while, he said, "Mother, I'm glad you're going away. I wish I could go with you. I knew you was here; and I have been *so* afraid they would come and catch you!"

I was greatly surprised, and asked him how he had found it out.

He replied, "I was standing under the eaves, one day, before Ellen went away, and I heard somebody cough up over the wood shed. I don't know what made me think it was you, but I did think so. I missed Ellen, the night before she went away; and grandmother brought her back into the room in the night; and I thought maybe she'd been to see *you*, before she went, for I heard grandmother whisper to her, 'Now go to sleep; and remember never to tell.'"

I asked him if he ever mentioned his suspicions to his sister. He said he never did; but after he heard the cough, if he saw her playing with other children on that side of the house, he always tried to coax her round to the other side, for fear they would hear me cough, too. He said he had kept a close lookout for Dr. Flint, and if he saw him speak to a constable, or a patrol, he always told grandmother. I now recollected that I had seen him manifest uneasiness, when people were on that side of the house, and I had at the time been puzzled to conjecture a motive for his actions. Such prudence may seem extraordinary in a boy of twelve years, but slaves, being surrounded by mysteries, deceptions, and dangers, early learn to be suspicious and watchful, and prematurely cautious and cunning. He had never asked a question of grandmother, or uncle Phillip, and I had often heard him chime in with other children, when they spoke of my being at the north.

I told him I was now really going to the Free States, and if he was a good, honest boy, and a loving child to his dear old grandmother, the Lord would bless him, and bring him to me, and we and Ellen would live together. He began to tell me that grandmother had not eaten any thing all day. While he was speaking, the door was unlocked, and she came in with a small bag of money, which she wanted me to take. I begged her to keep a part of it, at least, to pay for Benny's being sent to the north; but she insisted, while her tears were falling fast, that I should take the whole. "You may be sick among strangers," she said, "and they would send you to the poorhouse to die." Ah, that good grandmother!

For the last time I went up to my nook. Its desolate appearance no longer chilled me, for the light of hope had risen in my soul. Yet, even with the blessed prospect of freedom before me, I felt very sad at leaving forever that old homestead, where I had been sheltered so long by the dear old grandmother; where I had dreamed my first young dream of love; and where, after that had faded away, my children came to twine themselves so closely round my desolate heart. As the hour approached for me to leave, I again descended to the storeroom. My grandmother and Benny were there. She took me by the hand, and said, "Linda, let us pray." We knelt down together, with my child pressed to my heart, and my other arm round the faithful, loving old friend I was about to leave forever. On no other occasion has it ever been my lot to listen to so fervent a supplication for mercy and protection. It thrilled through my heart, and inspired me with trust in God.

Peter was waiting for me in the street. I was soon by his side, faint in body, but strong of purpose. I did not look back upon the old place, though I felt that I should never see it again.

XXX. NORTHWARD BOUND

I NEVER COULD TELL how we reached the wharf. My brain was all of a whirl, and my limbs tottered under me. At an appointed place we met my uncle Phillip, who had started before us on a different route, that he might reach the wharf first, and give us timely warning if there was any danger. A row-boat was in readiness. As I was about to step in, I felt something pull me gently, and turning round I saw Benny, looking pale and anxious. He whispered in my ear, "I've been peeping into the doctor's window, and he's at home. Don't cry; I'll come." He hastened away. I clasped the hand of my good uncle, to whom I owed so much, and of Peter, the brave, generous friend who had volunteered to run such terrible risks to secure my safety. To this day I remember how bright his face beamed with joy, when he told me he had discovered a safe method for me to escape. Yet that intelligent, enterprising, noble-hearted man was a chattel! liable, by the laws of a country that calls itself civilized, to be sold with horses and pigs! We parted in silence. Our hearts were all too full for words!

Swiftly the boat glided over the water. After a while, one of the sailors said, "Don't be down-hearted, madam. We will take you safely to your husband, in ——." At first I could not imagine what he meant; but I had presence of mind to think that it probably referred to something the captain had told him; so I thanked him, and said I hoped we should have pleasant weather.

When I entered the vessel the captain came forward to meet me. He was an elderly man, with a pleasant countenance. He showed me to a little box of a cabin, where sat my friend Fanny. She started as if she had seen a spectre. She gazed on me in utter astonishment, and exclaimed, "Linda, can this be *you*? or is it your ghost?" When we were locked in each other's arms, my overwrought feelings could no longer be restrained. My sobs reached the ears of the captain, who came and very kindly reminded us, that for his safety, as well as our own, it would be prudent for us not to attract any attention. He said that when there was a sail in sight he wished us to keep below; but at other times, he had no objection to our being on deck. He assured us that he would keep a good lookout, and if we acted prudently, he thought we should be in no danger. He had represented us as women going to meet our husbands in ——. We thanked him, and promised to observe carefully all the directions he gave us.

Fanny and I now talked by ourselves, low and quietly, in our little cabin. She told me of the sufferings she had gone through in making her escape, and of her terrors while she was concealed in her mother's house. Above all, she dwelt on the agony of separation from all her children on that dreadful auction day. She could scarcely credit me, when I told her of the place where I had passed nearly seven years. "We have the same sorrows," said I. "No," replied she, "you are going to see your children soon, and there is no hope that I shall ever even hear from mine."

The vessel was soon under way, but we made slow progress. The wind was against us. I should not have cared for this, if we had been out of sight of the town; but until there were miles of water between us and our enemies, we were filled with constant apprehension that the constables would come on board. Neither could I feel quite at ease with the captain and his men. I was an entire stranger to that class of people, and I had heard that sailors were rough, and sometimes cruel. We were so completely in their power, that if they were bad men, our situation would be dreadful. Now that the captain was paid for our passage, might he not be tempted to make more money by giving us up to those who claimed us as property? I was naturally of a confiding disposition, but slavery had made me suspicious of every body. Fanny did not share my distrust of the captain or his men. She said she was afraid at first, but she had been on board three days while the vessel lay in the dock, and nobody had betrayed her, or treated her otherwise than kindly.

The captain soon came to advise us to go on deck for fresh air. His friendly and respectful manner, combined with Fanny's testimony, reassured me, and we went with him. He placed us in a comfortable seat, and occasionally entered into conversations. He told us he was a Southerner by birth, and had spent the greater part of his life in the Slave States, and that he had recently lost a brother who traded in slaves. "But," said he, "it is a pitiable and degrading business, and I always felt ashamed to acknowledge my brother in connection with it." As we passed Snaky Swamp, he pointed to it, and said, "There is a slave territory that defies all the laws." I though of the terrible days I had spent there, and though it was not called Dismal Swamp, it made me feel very dismal as I looked at it.

I shall never forget that night. The balmy air of spring was so refreshing! And how shall I describe my sensations when we were fairly sailing on Chesapeake Bay? O, the beautiful sunshine! the exhilarating breeze! and I could enjoy them without fear or restraint. I had never realized what grand things air and sunlight are till I had been deprived of them.

Ten days after we left land we were approaching Philadelphia. The captain said we should arrive there in the night, but he thought we had better wait till morning, and go on shore in broad daylight, as the best way to avoid suspicion.

I replied, "You know best. But will you stay on board and protect us?"

He saw that I was suspicious, and he said he was sorry, now that he had brought us to the end of our voyage, to find I had so little confidence in him. Ah, if he had ever been a slave he would have known how difficult it was to trust a white man. He assured us that we might sleep through the night without fear; that he would take care we were not left unprotected. Be it said to the honor of this captain, Southerner as he was, that if Fanny and I had been white ladies, and our passage lawfully engaged, he could not have treated us more respectfully. My intelligent friend, Peter, had rightly estimated the character of the man to whose honor he had intrusted us.

The next morning I was on deck as soon as the day dawned. I called Fanny to see the sunrise, for the first time in our lives, on free soil; for such I *then* believed it to be. We watched the reddening sky, and saw the great orb come up slowly out of the water, as it seemed. Soon the waves began to sparkle, and every thing caught the beautiful glow. Before us lay the city of strangers. We looked at each other, and the eyes of both were moistened with tears. We had escaped from slavery, and we supposed ourselves to be safe from the hunters. But we were alone in the world, and we had left dear ties behind us; ties cruelly sundered by the demon Slavery.

XXXI. INCIDENTS IN PHILADELPHIA

I HAD HEARD that the poor slave had many friends at the north. I trusted we should find some of them. Meantime, we would take it for granted that all were friends, till they proved to the contrary. I sought out the kind captain, thanked him for his attentions, and told him I should never cease to be grateful for the service he had rendered us. I gave him a message to the friends I had left at home, and he promised to deliver it. We were placed in a row-boat, and in about fifteen minutes were landed on a wood wharf in Philadelphia. As I stood looking round, the friendly captain touched me on the shoulder, and said, "There is a respectable-looking colored man behind you. I will speak to him about the New York trains, and tell him you wish to go directly on." I thanked him, and asked him to direct me to some shops where I could buy gloves and veils. He did so, and said he would talk with the colored man till I returned. I made what haste I could. Constant exercise on board the vessel, and frequent rubbing with salt water, had nearly restored the use of my limbs. The noise of the great city confused me, but I found the shops, and bought some double veils and gloves for Fanny and myself. The shopman told me they were so many levies. I had never heard the word before, but I did not tell him so. I thought if he knew I was a stranger he might ask me where I came from. I gave him a gold piece, and when he returned the change, I counted it, and found out how much a levy was. I made my way back to the wharf, where the captain introduced me to the colored man, as the Rev. Jeremiah Durham, minister of Bethel church. He took me by the hand, as if I had been an old friend. He told us we were too late for the morning cars to New York, and must wait until the evening, or the next morning. He invited me to go home with him, assuring me that his wife would give me a cordial welcome; and for my friend he would provide a home with one of his neighbors. I thanked him for so much kindness to strangers, and told him if I must be detained, I should like to hunt up some people who formerly went from our part of the country. Mr. Durham insisted that I should dine with him, and then he would assist me in finding my friends. The sailors came to bid us good by. I shook their hardy hands, with tears in my eyes. They had all been kind to us, and they had rendered us a greater service than they could possibly conceive of.

I had never seen so large a city, or been in contact with so many people in the streets. It seemed as if those who passed looked at us with an expression of curiosity. My face was so blistered and peeled by sitting on deck, in wind and sunshine, that I thought they could not easily decide to what nation I belonged.

Mrs. Durham met me with a kindly welcome, without asking any questions. I was tired, and her friendly manner was a sweet refreshment. God bless her! I was sure that she had comforted other weary hearts, before I received her sympathy. She was surrounded by her husband and children, in a home made sacred by protecting laws. I thought of my own children and sighed.

… I went to my room, glad to shut out the world for a while. … In the midst of my meditations I was startled by a knock at the door. Mrs. Durham entered, her face all beaming with kindness, to say that there was an anti-slavery friend down stairs, who would like to see me. I overcame my dread of encountering strangers, and went with her. Many questions were asked concerning my experiences, and my escape from slavery; but I observed how careful they all were not to say any thing that might wound my feelings. How gratifying this was, can be fully understood only by those who have been accustomed to be treated as if they were not included within the pale of human beings. The anti-slavery friend had come to inquire into my plans, and to offer assistance, if needed. Fanny was comfortably established, for the present, with a friend of Mr. Durham. The Anti-Slavery Society agreed to pay her expenses to New York. The same was offered to me but I declined to accept it; telling them that my grandmother had given me sufficient [funds] to pay my expenses to the end of my journey. We were urged to remain in Philadelphia a few days, until some suitable escort could be found for us. I gladly accepted the proposition, for I had a dread of meeting slaveholders, and some dread also of railroads. I had never entered a railroad car in my life, and it seemed to me quite an important event.

That night I sought my pillow with feelings I had never carried to it before. I verily believed myself to be a free woman. ...

At the end of five days, one of Mrs. Durham's friends offered to accompany us to New York the following morning. ...

When Mr. Durham handed us our tickets, he said, "I am afraid you will have a disagreeable ride, but I could not procure tickets for the first class cars."

Supposing I had not given him money enough, I offered more. "O, no," said he, "they could not be had for any money. They don't allow colored people to go in the first-class cars."

This was the first chill to my enthusiasm about the Free States. Colored people were allowed to ride in a filthy box, behind white people, at the south, but there they were not required to pay for the privilege. It made me sad to find how the north aped the customs of slavery.

We were stowed away in a large, rough car, with windows on each side, too high for us to look out without standing up. It was crowded with people, apparently of all nations. There were plenty of beds and cradles, containing screaming and kicking babies. Every other man had a cigar or pipe in his mouth, and jugs of whiskey were handed round freely. The fumes of the whiskey and the dense tobacco smoke were sickening to my senses, and my mind was equally nauseated by the coarse jokes and ribald songs around me. It was a very disagreeable ride. Since that time there has been some improvement in these matters.

XL. THE FUGITIVE SLAVE LAW

... ABOUT THE TIME that I reentered the Bruce family, an event occurred of disastrous import to the colored people. The slave Hamlin,
the first fugitive that came under the new law, was given up by the
bloodhounds of the north to the bloodhounds of the south. It was
the beginning of a reign of terror to the colored population. The
great city rushed on in its whirl of excitement, taking no note of the
"short and simple annals of the poor." But while fashionables were
listening to the thrilling voice of Jenny Lind in Metropolitan Hall, the
thrilling voices of poor hunted colored people went up, in an agony
of supplication, to the Lord, from Zion's church. Many families, who
had lived in the city for twenty years, fled from it now. Many a poor
washerwoman, who, by hard labor, had made herself a comfortable
home, was obliged to sacrifice her furniture, bid a hurried farewell to
friends, and seek her fortune among strangers in Canada. Many a wife
discovered a secret she had never known before—that her husband
was a fugitive, and must leave her to insure his own safety. Worse
still, many a husband discovered that his wife had fled from slavery
years ago, and as "the child follows the condition of its mother," the
children of his love were liable to be seized and carried into slavery.
Every where, in those humble homes, there was consternation and
anguish. But what cared the legislators of the "dominant race" for the
blood they were crushing out of trampled hearts?

When my brother William spent his last evening with me, before he
went to California, we talked nearly all the time of the distress brought
on our oppressed people by the passage of this iniquitous law; and
never had I seen him manifest such bitterness of spirit, such stern
hostility to our oppressors. He was himself free from the operation of
the law; for he did not run from any Slaveholding State, being brought
into the Free States by his master. But I was subject to it; and so were
hundreds of intelligent and industrious people all around us. I seldom
ventured into the streets; and when it was necessary to do an errand for
Mrs. Bruce, or any of the family, I went as much as possible through
back streets and by-ways. What a disgrace to a city calling itself free,
that inhabitants, guiltless of offence, and seeking to perform their duties
conscientiously, should be condemned to live in such incessant fear,
and have nowhere to turn for protection! This state of things, of course,
gave rise to many impromptu vigilance committees. Every colored
person, and every friend of their persecuted race, kept their eyes wide
open. Every evening I examined the newspapers carefully, to see what

Southerners had put up at the hotels. I did this for my own sake, thinking my young mistress and her husband might be among the list; I wished also to give information to others, if necessary; for if many were "running to and fro," I resolved that "knowledge should be increased."

... All that winter I lived in a state of anxiety. When I took the children out to breathe the air, I closely observed the countenances of all I met. I dreaded the approach of summer, when snakes and slaveholders make their appearance. I was, in fact, a slave in New York, as subject to slave laws as I had been in a Slave State. Strange incongruity in a State called free!

SOURCE: Harriet Jacobs. *Incidents in the Life of a Slave Girl*. Mineola, New York: Dover Publications, 2001. [Originally published in Boston in 1861.]

JANE JOHNSON

Trial of the Emancipators of Col. J. H. Wheeler's Slaves, Jane Johnson and Her Two Little Boys

[William Still]

Still explains in this tale of hard-won legal freedom one of the roles of the Vigilance Committee in Philadelphia, for which organization he was collecting these narratives. As one of the actors in this case, Still also narrates much of it first-hand.

AMONG OTHER DUTIES devolving on the Vigilance Committee when hearing of slaves brought into the State by their owners, was immediately to inform such persons that as they were not fugitives, but were brought into the State by their masters, they were entitled to their freedom without another moment's service, and that they could have the assistance of the Committee and the advice of counsel without charge, by simply availing themselves of these proffered favors.

Many slave-holders fully understood the law in this particular, and were also equally posted with regard to the vigilance of abolitionists. Consequently they avoided bringing slaves beyond Mason and Dixon's Line in traveling North. But some slave-holders were not thus mindful of the laws, or were too arrogant to take heed, as may be seen in the case of Colonel John H. Wheeler, of North Carolina, the United States Minister to Nicaragua. In passing through Philadelphia from Washington, one very warm July day in 1855, accompanied by three of his slaves, his high official equilibrium, as well as his assumed rights under the Constitution, received a terrible shock at the hands of the Committee. Therefore, for the readers of these pages, and in order to completely illustrate the various phases of the work of the Committee in the days of Slavery, this case, selected from many others, is a fitting one. However, for more than a brief recital of some of the more prominent incidents, it will not be possible to find room in this volume. And, indeed, the necessity of so doing is precluded by the fact that Mr. Williamson in justice to himself and the cause of freedom, with great pains and singular ability, gathered the most important facts bearing on his memorable trial and imprisonment, and published them in a neat volume for historical reference.

In order to bring fully before the reader the beginning of this interesting and exciting case, it seems only necessary to publish the subjoined letter, written by one of the actors in the drama, and addressed to *The New York Tribune*, and an additional paragraph which may be requisite to throw light on a special point, which Judge Kane decided was concealed in the "obstinate" breast of Passmore Williamson, as said Williamson persistently refused before the said Judge's court, to own that he had a knowledge of the mystery in question. After which, a brief glance at some of the more important points of the case must suffice.

[Correspondence of *The N.Y. Tribune.*]

PHILADELPHIA, Monday, July 30, 1855.

AS THE PUBLIC have not been made acquainted with the facts and particulars respecting the agency of Mr. Passmore Williamson and others, in relation to the slave case now agitating this city, and especially as the poor slave mother and her two sons have been so grossly misrepresented, I deem it my duty to lay the facts before you, for publication or otherwise, as you may think proper.

On Wednesday afternoon, week, at 4½ o'clock, the following note was placed in my hands by a colored boy whom I had never before seen, to my recollection:

"Mr. Still—Sir: Will you come down to Bloodgood's Hotel as soon as possible—as there are three fugitive slaves here and they want liberty. Their master is here with them, on his way to New York."

The note was without date, and the signature so indistinctly written as not to be understood by me, having evidently been penned in a moment of haste.

Without delay I ran with the note to Mr. P. Williamson's office, Seventh and Arch, found him at his desk, and gave it to him, and after reading it, he remarked that he could not go down, as he had to go to Harrisburg that night on business but he advised me to go, and to get the names of the slave-holder and the slaves, in order to telegraph to New York to have them arrested there, as no time remained to procure a writ of habeas corpus here.

I could not have been two minutes in Mr. W.'s office before starting in haste for the wharf. To my surprise, however, when I reached the wharf, there I found Mr. W., his mind having undergone a sudden change; he was soon on the spot.

I saw three or four colored persons in the hall at Bloodgood's, none of whom I recognized except the boy who brought me the note. Before having time for making inquiry some one said they had gone on board the boat. "Get their description," said Mr. W. I instantly inquired of one of the colored persons for the desired description, and was told that she was "a tall, dark woman, with two little boys."

Mr. W. and myself ran on board of the boat, looked among the passengers on the first deck, but saw them not. "They are up on the second deck," an unknown voice uttered. In a second we were in their presence. We approached the anxious-looking slave-mother with her two boys on her left-hand; close on her right sat an ill-favored white man having a cane in his hand which I took to be a sword-cane. (As to its being a sword-cane, however, I might have been mistaken.)

The first words to the mother were: "Are you traveling?" "Yes," was the prompt answer. "With whom?" She nodded her head toward the ill-favored man, signifying with him. Fidgeting on his seat, he said something, exactly what I do not now recollect. In reply I remarked: "Do they belong to you, Sir?" "Yes, they are in my charge," was his answer. Turning from him to the mother and her sons, in substance, and word for word, as near as I can remember, the following remarks were earnestly though calmly addressed by the individuals who rejoiced to meet them on free soil, and who felt unmistakably assured that they were justified by the laws of Pennsylvania as well as the Law of God, in informing them of their rights:

"You are entitled to your freedom according to the laws of Pennsylvania, having been brought into the State by your owner. If you prefer freedom to slavery, as we suppose everybody does, you have the chance to accept it now. Act calmly—don't be frightened by your master—you are as much entitled to your freedom as we are, or as he is—be determined and you need have no fears but that you will be protected by the law. Judges have time and again decided cases in this city and State similar to yours in favor of freedom! Of course, if you want to remain a slave with your master, we cannot force you to leave; we only want to make you sensible of your rights. *Remember, if you lose this chance you may never get such another,*" etc.

This advice to the woman was made in the hearing of a number of persons present, white and colored; and one elderly white gentleman of genteel address, who seemed to take much interest in what was going on, remarked that they would have the same chance for their freedom in New Jersey and New York as they then had—seeming to sympathize with the woman, etc.

During the few moments in which the above remarks were made, the slaveholder frequently interrupted—said she understood all about the laws making her free, and her right to leave if she wanted to; but contended that she did not want to leave—that she was on a visit to New York to see her friends—afterward *wished to return to her three children whom she left in Virginia, from whom it would be HARD to separate her*. Furthermore, he diligently tried to constrain her to say that she did not want to be interfered with—that she wanted to go with him—that she was on a visit to New York—had children in the South, etc.; but the woman's desire to be free was altogether too strong to allow her to make a single acknowledgment favorable to his wishes in the matter. On the contrary, she repeatedly said, distinctly and firmly, *"I am not free, but I want my freedom—ALWAYS wanted to be free! but he holds me."*

While the slaveholder claimed that she belonged to him, he said *that she was free!* Again he said that he was *going to give her her freedom,* etc. When his eyes would be off of hers, such eagerness as her looks expressed, indicative of her entreaty that we would not forsake her and her little ones in their weakness, it had never been my lot to witness before, under any circumstances.

The last bell tolled! The last moment for further delay passed! The arm of the woman being slightly touched, accompanied with the word, "Come!" she instantly arose. "Go along—go along!" said some, who sympathized, to the boys, at the same time taking hold of their arms. By this time the parties were fairly moving toward the stairway leading to the deck below. Instantly on their starting, the slave-holder rushed at the woman and her children, to prevent their leaving; and, if I am not mistaken, he simultaneously took hold of the woman and Mr. Williamson, which resistance on his part caused Mr. W. to take hold of him and set him aside quickly.

The passengers were looking on all around, but none interfered in behalf of the slaveholder except one man, whom I took to be another slaveholder. He said harshly, "Let them alone; they are his *property!*" The youngest boy, about 7 years of age—too young to know what these things meant—cried "Massa John! Massa John!" The elder boy, 11 years of age, took the matter more dispassionately, and the mother *quite calmly*. The mother and her sympathizers all moved down the stairs together in the presence of quite a number of spectators on the first deck and on the wharf, all of whom, as far as I was able to discern, seemed to look upon the whole affair with the greatest indifference. The woman and children were assisted, but not forced to leave. Nor were there any violence or threatenings as I saw or heard. The only words that I heard from any one of an objectionable character, were: "Knock him down; knock him down!" but who uttered it or who was meant I knew not, nor have I since been informed. However, if it was uttered by a colored man, I regret it, as there was not the slightest cause for such language, especially as the sympathies of the spectators and citizens seemed to justify the course pursued.

While passing off of the wharf and down Delaware-avenue to Dock st., and up Dock to Front, where a carriage was procured, the slaveholder and one police officer were of the party, if no more.

The youngest boy on being put in the carriage was told that he was "a fool for crying so after 'Massa John,' who would sell him if he ever caught him." Not another whine was heard on the subject.

The carriage drove down town slowly, the horses being fatigued and the weather intensely hot; the inmates were put out on Tenth street not at any house after which they soon found hospitable friends and quietude. The excitement of the moment having passed by, the mother *seemed very cheerful, and rejoiced greatly that herself and boys had* been, as she thought, so *"providentially delivered from the house of bondage!"* For the first time in her life she could look upon herself and children and feel free!

Having felt the iron in her heart for the best half of her days—having been sold with her children on the auction block—having had one of her children sold far away from her without hope of her seeing him again—she very naturally and wisely concluded to go to Canada, fearing if she remained in this city—as some assured her she could do with entire safety—that she might again find herself in the clutches of the tyrant from whom she had fled. A few items of what she related concerning the character of her master may be interesting to the reader—

Within the last two years he had sold all his slaves—between thirty and forty in number—having purchased the present ones in that space of time. She said that before leaving Washington, coming on the cars, and at his father-in-law's in this city, a number of persons had told him that in bringing his slaves into Pennsylvania they would be free. When told at his father-in-law's, as she overheard it, that he "could not have done a worse thing," &c., he replied that "Jane would not leave him."

As much, however, as he affected to have such implicit confidence in Jane, he scarcely allowed her to be out of his presence a moment while in this city. To use Jane's own language, he was "on her heels every minute," fearing that some one might get to her ears the sweet music of freedom. By the way, Jane had it deep in her heart before leaving the South, and was bent on succeeding in New York, if disappointed in Philadelphia.

At Bloodgood's, after having been belated and left by the 2 o'clock train, while waiting for the 5 o'clock line, his appetite tempted her "master" to take a hasty dinner. So after placing Jane where bethought she would be pretty secure from "evil communications" from the colored waiters, and after giving her a double counselling, he made his way to the table; remained but a little while, however, before leaving to look after Jane; finding her composed, looking over a banister near where he left her, he returned to the table again and finished his meal.

But, alas, for the slave-holder! Jane had her "top eye open," and in that brief space had appealed to the sympathies of a person whom she ventured to trust, saying, "I and my children are slaves, and we want liberty!" I am not certain, but suppose that person, in the goodness of his heart, was the cause of the note being sent to the Anti-Slavery office, and hence the result.

As to her going on to New York to see her friends, and wishing to return to her three children in the South, and his going to free her, &c., Jane declared repeatedly and very positively, that there was not a particle of truth in what her master said on these points. The truth is she had not the slightest hope of freedom through any act of his. She had only left one boy in the South, who had been sold far away, where she scarcely ever heard from him, indeed never expected to see him any more.

In appearance Jane is tall and well formed, high and large forehead, of genteel manners, chestnut color, and seems to possess, naturally, uncommon good sense, though of course she has never been allowed to read. Thus I have given as truthful a report as I am capable of doing, of Jane and the circumstances connected with her deliverance.

W. Still.

P. S.—Of the five colored porters who promptly appeared, with warm hearts throbbing in sympathy with the mother and her children, too much cannot be said in commendation. In the present case they acted nobly, whatever may be said of their general character, of which I know nothing. How human beings, who have ever tasted oppression, could have acted differently under the circumstances I cannot conceive.

The mystery alluded to, which the above letter did not contain, and which the court failed to make Mr. Williamson reveal, might have been truthfully explained in these words. The carriage was procured at the wharf, while Col. Wheeler and Mr. Williamson were debating the question relative to the action of the Committee, and at that instant, Jane and her two boys were invited into it and accompanied by the writer, who procured it, were driven down town, and on Tenth Street, below Lombard, the inmates were invited out of it, and the said conductor paid the driver and discharged him. For prudential reasons he took them to a temporary resting-place, where they could tarry until after dark; then they were invited to his own residence, where they were made welcome, and in due time forwarded East. Now, what disposition was made of them after they had left the wharf, while Williamson and Wheeler were discussing matters—(as was clearly sworn to by Passmore, in his answer to the writ of Habeas Corpus)—he Williamson did not know. That evening, before seeing the member of the Committee, with whom he acted in concert on the boat, and who had entire charge of Jane and her boys, he left for

Harrisburg, to fulfill business engagements. The next morning his father (Thomas Williamson) brought the writ of Habeas Corpus (which had been served at Passmore's office after he left) to the Anti-Slavery Office. In his calm manner he handed it to the writer, at the same time remarking that "Passmore had gone to Harrisburg," and added, "thee had better attend to it" (the writ). Edward Hopper, Esq., was applied to with the writ, and in the absence of Mr. Williamson, appeared before the court, and stated "that the writ had not been served, as Mr. W. was out of town," etc.

After this statement, the Judge postponed further action until the next day. In the meanwhile, Mr. Williamson returned and found the writ awaiting him, and an agitated state of feeling throughout the city besides. Now it is very certain, that he did not seek to know from those in the secret, where Jane Johnson and her boys were taken after they left the wharf, or as to what disposition had been made of them, in any way; except to ask simply, "are they safe?" (and when told "yes," he smiled) consequently, he might have been examined for a week, by the most skillful lawyer, at the Philadelphia bar, but he could not have answered other than he did in making his return to the writ, before Judge Kane, namely: *"That the persons named in the writ, nor either of them, are now nor was at the time of issuing of the writ, or the original writ, or at any other time in the custody, power, or possession of the respondent, nor by him confined or restrained; wherefore he cannot have the bodies,"* etc.

Thus, while Mr. W. was subjected to the severest trial of his devotion to Freedom, his noble bearing throughout, won for him the admiration and sympathy of the friends of humanity and liberty throughout the entire land, and in proof of his fidelity, he most cheerfully submitted to imprisonment rather than desert his principles. But the truth was not wanted in this instance by the enemies of Freedom; obedience to Slavery was demanded to satisfy the South. The opportunity seemed favorable for teaching abolitionists and negroes, that they had no right to interfere with a "chivalrous southern gentleman," while passing through Philadelphia with his slaves. Thus, to make an effective blow, all the pro-slavery elements of Philadelphia were brought into action, and matters looked for a time as though Slavery in this instance would have everything its own way. Passmore was locked up in prison on the flimsy pretext of contempt of court, and true bills were found against him and half a dozen colored men, charging them with "riot," "forcible abduction," and "assault and battery," and there was no lack of hard swearing on the part of Col.

Wheeler and his pro-slavery sympathizers in substantiation of these grave charges. But the pro-slaveryites had counted without their host—Passmore would not yield an inch, but stood as firmly by his principles in prison, as he did on the boat. Indeed, it was soon evident, that his resolute course was bringing floods of sympathy from the ablest and best minds throughout the North. On the other hand, the occasion was rapidly awakening thousands daily, who had hitherto manifested little or no interest at all on the subject, to the wrongs of the slave.

It was soon discovered by the "chivalry" that keeping Mr. Williamson in prison would indirectly greatly aid the cause of Freedom that every day he remained would make numerous converts to the cause of liberty; that Mr. Williamson was doing ten-fold more in prison for the cause of universal liberty than he could possibly do while pursuing his ordinary vocation.

With regard to the colored men under bonds, Col. Wheeler and his satellites felt very confident that there was no room for them to escape. They must have had reason so to think, judging from the hard swearing they did, before the committing magistrate. Consequently, in the order of events, while Passmore was still in prison, receiving visits from hosts of friends, and letters of sympathy from all parts of the North, William Still, William Curtis, James P. Braddock, John Ballard, James Martin and Isaiah Moore, were brought into court for trial. The first name on the list in the proceedings of the court was called up first.

Against this individual, it was pretty well understood by the friends of the slave, that no lack of pains and false swearing would be resorted to on the part of Wheeler and his witnesses, to gain a verdict.

Mr. McKim and other noted abolitionists managing the defense, were equally alive to the importance of overwhelming the enemy in this particular issue. The Hon. Charles Gibbons, was engaged to defend William Still, and William S. Pierce, Esq., and William B. Birney, Esq., the other five colored defendants.

In order to make the victory complete, the anti-slavery friends deemed it of the highest importance to have Jane Johnson in court, to face her master, and under oath to sweep away his "refuge of lies," with regard to her being "abducted," and her unwillingness to "leave her master," etc. So Mr. McKim and the friends very privately arranged to have Jane Johnson on hand at the opening of the defense.

Mrs. Lucretia Mott, Mrs. McKim, Miss Sarah Pugh and Mrs. Plumly, volunteered to accompany this poor slave mother to the court-house and to occupy seats by her side, while she should face her master, and boldly, on oath, contradict all his hard swearing. A better subject for the occasion than Jane, could not have been desired. She entered the court room veiled, and of course was not known by the crowd, as pains had been taken to keep the public in ignorance of the fact, that she was to be brought on to bear witness. So that, at the conclusion of the second witness on the part of the defense, "Jane Johnson" was called for, in a shrill voice. Deliberately, Jane arose and answered, in a lady-like manner to her name, and was then the observed of all observers. Never before had such a scene been witnessed in Philadelphia. It was indescribable. Substantially, her testimony on this occasion, was in keeping with the subjoined affidavit, which was as follows—

STATE OF NEW YORK, CITY AND COUNTY OF NEW YORK.

JANE JOHNSON being sworn, makes oath and says—

"My name is Jane—Jane Johnson; I was the slave of Mr. Wheeler of Washington; he bought me and my two children, about two years ago, of Mr. Cornelius Crew, of Richmond, Va.; my youngest child is between six and seven years old, the other between ten and eleven; I have one other child only, and he is in Richmond; I have not seen him for about two years; never expect to see him again; Mr. Wheeler brought me and my two children to Philadelphia, on the way to Nicaragua, to wait on his wife; I didn't want to go without my two children, and he consented to take them; we came to Philadelphia by the cars; stopped at Mr. Sully's, Mr. Wheeler's father-in-law, a few moments; then went to the steamboat for New York at 2 o'clock, but were too late; we went into Bloodgood's Hotel; Mr. Wheeler went to dinner; Mr. Wheeler had told me in Washington to have nothing to say to colored persons, and if any of them spoke to me, to say I was a free woman traveling with a minister; we staid at Bloodgood's till 5 o'clock; Mr. Wheeler kept his eye on me all the time except when he was at dinner; he left his dinner to come and see if I was safe, and then went back again; while he was at dinner, I saw a colored woman and told her I was a slave woman, that my master had told me not to speak to colored people, and that if any of them spoke to me to say that I was free; but I am not free; but I want to be free; she said: 'poor thing, I pity you;' after that I saw a colored man and said the same thing to him, he said he would telegraph to New York, and two men would meet me at 9 o'clock and take me with them; after that we went on board the boat, Mr. Wheeler sat beside me on the deck; I saw a colored gentleman come on board, he beckoned to me; I nodded my head, and could not go; Mr. Wheeler was beside me and I was afraid; a white gentleman then came and said to Mr. Wheeler, 'I want to speak to your servant, and tell her of her rights;' Mr. Wheeler rose and said, 'If you have anything to say, say it to me—she knows her rights;' the white gentleman asked me if I wanted to be free; I said 'I do, but I belong to this gentleman and I can't have it;' he replied, 'Yes, you can, come with us, you are as free as your master, if you want your freedom come now; if you go back to Washington you may never get it;' I rose to go, Mr. Wheeler spoke, and said, 'I will give you your freedom,' but he had never promised it before, and I knew he would never give it to me; the white gentleman held out his hand and I went toward him; I was ready for the word before it was given me; I took the children by the hands, who both cried, for they were frightened, but both stopped when they got on shore; a colored man carried the little one, I led the other by the hand. We walked down the street till we got to a hack; nobody forced me away; nobody pulled me, and nobody led me; I went away of my own free will; I always wished to be free and meant to be free when I came North; I hardly expected it in Philadelphia, but I thought I should get free in New York; I have been comfortable and happy since I left Mr. Wheeler, and so are the children; I don't want to go back; I could have gone in Philadelphia if I had wanted to; I could go now; but I had rather die than go back. I wish to make this statement before a magistrate, because I understand that Mr. Williamson is in prison on my account, and I hope the truth may be of benefit to him."

her
JANE X JOHNSON.
mark.

It might have been supposed that her honest and straightforward testimony would have been sufficient to cause even the most relentless slaveholder to abandon at once a pursuit so monstrous and utterly hopeless as Wheeler's was. But although he was sadly confused and put to shame, he hung on to the "lost cause" tenaciously. And his counsel, David Webster, Esq., and the United States District Attorney, Vandyke, completely imbued with the pro-slavery spirit, were equally as unyielding. And thus, with a zeal befitting the most

worthy object imaginable, they labored with untiring effort to con-
vict the colored men.

By this policy, however, the counsel for the defense was doubly
aroused. Mr. Gibbons, in the most eloquent and indignant strains,
perfectly annihilated the "distinguished Colonel John H. Wheeler,
United States Minister Plenipotentiary near the Island of Nicaragua,"
taking special pains to ring the changes repeatedly on his long appel-
lations. Mr. Gibbons appeared to be precisely in the right mood to
make himself surpassingly forcible and eloquent, on whatever point
of law he chose to touch bearing on the case; or in whatever direction
he chose to glance at the injustice and cruelty of the South. Most
vividly did he draw the contrast between the States of "Georgia" and
"Pennsylvania," with regard to the atrocious laws of Georgia. Scarcely
less vivid is the impression after a lapse of sixteen years, than when
this eloquent speech was made. With the District Attorney, Wm. B.
Mann, Esq., and his Honor, Judge Kelley, the defendants had no
cause to complain. Throughout the entire proceedings, they had reason to feel, that neither of these officials sympathized in the least with
Wheeler or Slavery. Indeed in the Judge's charge and also in the
District Attorney's closing speech the ring of freedom could be distinctly heard much more so than was agreeable to Wheeler and his
Pro-Slavery sympathizers. The case of Wm. Still ended in his acquit-
tal; the other five colored men were taken up in order. And it is
scarcely necessary to say that Messrs. Peirce and Birney did full justice
to all concerned. Mr. Peirce, especially, was one of the oldest, ablest
and most faithful lawyers to the slave of the Philadelphia Bar. He
never was known, it may safely be said, to hesitate in the darkest days
of Slavery to give his time and talents to the fugitive, even in the most
hopeless cases, and when, from the unpopularity of such a course,
serious sacrifices would be likely to result. Consequently he was but
at home in this case, and most nobly did he defend his clients, with
the same earnestness that a man would defend his fireside against the
approach of burglars. At the conclusion of the trial, the jury returned
a verdict of "not guilty," as to all the persons in the first count, charging them with riot. In the second count, charging them with "Assault
and Battery" (on Col. Wheeler) Ballard and Curtis were found
"guilty," the rest "not guilty." The guilty were given about a week
in jail. Thus ended this act in the Wheeler drama. …

SOURCE: William Still, 1872 (see the Bibliography on p. 203 for complete
information).

LEW JONES, OSCAR PAYNE, MOSE WOOD, DAVE DIGGS, JACK, HEN, AND BILL DADE, AND JOE BALL

Arrival from the Old Dominion: Nine Very Fine "Articles"

[William Still]

The nine fugitives (eight men and one woman) who arrived from Virginia, "the Old Dominion," had tired of being deceived, disrespected, defrauded, and defined as chattel. Becoming passengers on the Underground Railroad enabled them to sever all ties to "those who had been enjoying the fruits of their unpaid labor."

THE COMING of this interesting party was as gratifying, as their departure must have been disagreeable to those who had been enjoying the fruits of their unpaid labor. Stockholders of the Underground Rail Road, conductors, etc., about this time were well pleased with the wonderful success of the road, especially as business was daily increasing.

Upon inquiry of these passengers individually, the following results were obtained:

Lewis was about fifty-two years of age, a man of superior stature, six feet high, with prominent features, and about one third of Anglo-Saxon blood in his veins. The apparent solidity of the man both with respect to body and mind was calculated to inspire the idea that he would be a first-rate man to manage a farm in Canada.

Of his bondage and escape the following statement was obtained from him: "I was owned by a man named Thomas Sydan, a Catholic, and a farmer. He was not a very hard man, but was very much opposed to black folks having their liberty. He owned six young slaves not grown up. It was owing to Sydan's mother's estate that I came into his hands; before her death I had hoped to be free for a long time as soon as she died. My old mistress' name was Nancy Sydan; she was lame for twenty years, and couldn't walk a step without crutches, and I was her main support. I was foreman on the farm; sometimes nobody but me would work, and I was looked up to for support. A good deal of the time I would have to attend to her. If she was going to ride, I would have to pick her up in my arms and put her in the carriage, and many times I would have to lift her in her sick room. Nobody couldn't wait upon her but me. She had a husband, and he had a master, and that was rum; he drank very hard, he killed himself drinking. He was poor support. When he died, fifteen years ago, he left three sons, Thomas, James, and Stephen, they were all together then, only common livers. After his death about six years mistress died. I felt sure then I would be free, but was very badly disappointed. I went to my young masters and asked them about my freedom; they laughed at me and said, no such thought had entered their heads, that I was to be free. The neighbors said it was a shame that they should keep me out of my freedom, after I had been the making of the family, and had behaved myself so faithful. One gentleman asked master John what he would take for me, and offered a thousand dollars; that was three months before I ran away, and massa John said a thousand dollars wouldn't buy one leg. I hadn't anything to hope for from them. I served them all my life, and they didn't thank me for it. A short time before I come away my aunt died, all the kin I had, and they wouldn't let me go to the funeral. They said 'the time couldn't be spared.' This was the last straw on the camel's back."

In Lewis' grief and disappointment he decided that he would run away the first chance that he could get, and seek a home in Canada. He held counsel with others in whom he could confide, and they fixed on a time to start, and resolved that they would suffer anything else but Slavery. Lewis was delighted that he had managed so cunningly to leave master Tom and mistress Margaret, and their six children to work for their own living. He had an idea that they would want Lew for many things; the only regret he felt was that he had served them so long, that they had received his substance and strength for half a century. Fortunately Lewis' wife escaped three days in advance of him, in accordance with a mutual understanding. They had no children. The suffering on the road cost Lewis a little less than death, but the joy of success came soon to chase away the effects of the pain and hardship which had been endured.

Oscar, the next passenger, was advertised as follows:

$200 REWARD.—Ran away from the service of the Rev. J. P. McGuire, Episcopal High School, Fairfax county, Va., on Saturday, 10th inst., Negro Man, Oscar Payne, aged 30 years, 5 feet 4 inches in height, square built, mulatto color, thick, bushy suit of hair, round, full face, and when spoken to has a pleasant manner—clothes not recollected.

I will give $200 for his recovery if taken out of the State, or $150 if taken in the State, and secured that I can get him. T. D. FENDALL. *jγ17-6t.*

Such announcements never frightened the Underground Rail Road Committee; indeed, the Committee rather preferred seeing the names of their passengers in the papers, as, in that case, they could all the more cautiously provide against Messrs. slave-hunters. Oscar was a "prime, first-class article," worth $1,800. The above description of him is endorsed. His story ran thus:

"I have served under Miss Mary Dade, of Alexandria—Miss Dade was a very clever mistress, she hired me out. When I left I was hired at the Episcopal school High School of Virginia. With me times had been very well. No privilege was allowed me to study books. I cannot say that I left for any other cause than to get my freedom, as I believe I have been used as well as any slave in the District. I left no relatives but two cousins; my two brothers ran away, Brooks and Lawrence, but where they went I can't tell, but would be pleased to know. Three brothers and one sister have been sold South, can't tell where they are." Such was Oscar's brief narrative; that he was truthful there was no room to doubt.

The next passenger was MOSES or "Mose," who looked as though he had been exceedingly well-cared for, being plump, fat, and extrasmart. He declared that General Briscoe, of Georgetown, D.C., had been defrauding him out of thirteen dollars per month, this being the amount for which he was hired, and, instead of being allowed to draw it for himself, the general pocketed it. For this "kind treatment" he summed up what seemed to be a true bill for ten years against the general. But he made another charge of a still graver character: he said that the general professed to own him. But as he (Moses) was thoroughly tired, and believed that Slavery was no more justifiable than murder, he made up his mind to leave and join the union party for Canada. He stated that the general owned a large number of slaves, which he hired out principally. Moses had no special fault to find with his master, except such as have been alluded to, but as to mistress Briscoe, he said, that she was pretty rough. Moses left four sisters in bondage.

David, the next member of this freedom-loving band, was an intelligent man; his manners and movements were decidedly prepossessing. He was about thirty-seven years of age, dark, tall, and rather of a slender stature, possessing very large hopes. He charged Dr. Josiah Harding of Rockville, Montgomery county, with having enslaved him contrary to his wish or will.

As a slave, David had been required at one time to work on a farm, and at another time to drive carriage, of course, without pay. Again he had been bound as a waiter on the no pay system, and again he had been called into the kitchen to cook, all for the benefit of the Doctor—the hire going into the Dr.'s pocket. This business David protested against in secret, but when on the Underground Rail Road his protestations were "over and above board."

Of the Doctor, David said, that "he was clever, but a Catholic;" he also said, that he thought his wife was "tolerable clever," although he had never been placed under her where he would have had an opportunity of learning her bad traits if she had any.

The Doctor had generously bargained with David, that he could have himself by paying $1,000; he had likewise figured up how the money might be paid, and intimated what a nice thing it would be for "Dave" to wake up some morning and find himself his own man. This was how it was to be accomplished: Dave was to pay eighty-five dollars annually, and in about twelve years he would have the thousand, and a little over, all made up. On this principle and suggestion Dave had been digging faithfully and hard, and with the aid of friends he had nearly succeeded. Just when he was within sight of the grand prize, and just as the last payment was about to be made, to Dave's utter surprise the Doctor got very angry one day about some trifling matter (all pretension) and in his pretended rage he said there were too many "free niggers" going about, and he thought that Dave would do better as a slave, etc.

After that, all the satisfaction that he was able to get out of the Doctor, was simply to the effect, that he had hired him to Mr. Morrison for one hundred and fifty dollars a year. After his "lying and cheating" in this way, David resolved that he would take his chances on the Underground Rail Road. Not a spark of faith did he have in the Doctor. For a time, however, before the opportunity to escape offered, he went to Mr. Morrison as a waiter, where it was his province to wait on six of the Judges of the Supreme Court of the United States. In the meantime his party matured arrangements for their trip, so Dave "took out" and left the Judges without a waiter. The more he reflected over the nature of the wrongs he had suffered under, the less he thought of the Doctor.

Joe, who also came with this band, was half Anglo-Saxon; an able-bodied man, thirty-four years of age. He said, that "Miss Elizabeth Gordon, a white woman living in Alexandria," claimed him. He did not find much fault with her. She permitted him to hire his time, find his own clothing, etc., by which regulation Joe got along smoothly. Nevertheless he declared, that he was tired of wearing the yoke, and felt constrained to throw it off as soon as possible. Miss Gordon was getting old, and Joe noticed that the young tribe of nephews and nieces was multiplying in large numbers. This he regarded as a very bad sign; he therefore, gave the matter of the Underground Rail Road his serious attention, and it was not long ere he was fully persuaded that it would be wisdom for him to tarry no longer in the prison-house. Joe had a wife and four children, which were as heavy weights to hold him in Virginia, but the spirit of liberty prevailed. Joe, also, left two sisters, one free, the other a slave. His wife belonged to the widow Irwin. She had assured her slaves, that she had "provided for them in her will," and that at her death all would be freed. They were daily living on the faith thus created, and obviously thought the sooner the Lord relieved the old mistress of her earthly troubles the better.

Although Joe left his wife and children, he did not forget them, but had strong faith they would be reunited. After going to Canada, he addressed several letters to the Secretary of the Committee concerning his family, and as will be seen by the following, he looked with ardent hopes for their arrival:

TORONTO, Nov. 7th, 1857.

DEAR MR. STILL:—As I must again send you a letter fealing myself oblidge to you for all you have done and your kindness. Dear Sir my wife will be on to Philadelphia on the 8th 7th, and I would [like] you to look out for her and get her an ticket and send her to me Toronto. Her name are May Ball with five children. Please send her as soon as you can.

Yours very truly,   JOSEPH BALL.

Will you please to telegraph to me, No. 31 Dummer st.

Jake, another member of the company of nine, was twenty-two years of age, of dark hue, round-made, keen eyes, and apparently a man of superior intelligence. Unfortunately his lot had been of such a nature that no helping opportunity had been afforded for the cultivation of his mind.

He condemned in very strong terms a man by the name of Benjamin B. Chambers, who lived near Elkton, but did not there require the services of Jake, hiring Jake out just as he would have hired a horse, and likewise keeping his pay. Jake thought that if justice could have been awarded him, Chambers would either have had to restore that of which he had wronged him, or expiate the wrong in prison.

Jake, however, stood more in awe of a young master, who was soon likely to come into power, than he did of the old master. This son had already given Jake to understand that once in his hands it "wouldn't be long before he would have him jingling in his pocket," signifying, that he would sell him as soon as his father was gone.

The manner of the son stirred Jake's very blood to boiling heat it seemed. His suffering, and the suffering of his fellow-bondsmen had never before appeared so hard. The idea that he must work, and be sold at the pleasure of another, made him decide to "pull up stakes," and seek refuge elsewhere. Such a spirit as he possessed could not rest in servitude.

Mary Ann, the wife of Jake, who accompanied him, was a pleasant-looking bride. She said that she was owned by "Elias Rhoads, a farmer, and a pretty fair kind of a man." She had been treated very well.

John and Henry Dade, ages twenty and twenty-five years, were from Washington. They belonged to the class of well-cared for slaves; at least they said that their mistress had not dealt severely with them, and they never would have consented to pass through the severe sufferings encountered on their journey, but for the strong desire they had to be free. From Canada John wrote back as follows:

St. Catherines, Canada.

Mr. Still, Sir:—I ar rivd on Friday evenen bot I had rite smart treble for my mony gave out at the bridge and I had to fot et to St. Catherin tho I went rite to worke at the willard house for 8 dolor month bargend for to stae all the wentor bot I havent eny clouse nor money please send my tronke if et has come. Derate et to St. Catharines to the willard house to John Dade and if et ant come plice rite for et soon as posable deract your letter to Rosenen Dade Washington send your deraction please tend to this rite a way for I haf made a good start I think that I can gate a longe en this plase. If my brother as well send him on for I haf a plase for him ef he ant well please dont send him for this as no plase for a sik possan. The way I got this plase I went to see a fran of myen from Washington. Dan al well and he gave me werke. Pleas ancer this as soon as you gat et you must excues this bad riting for my chance wars bot small to line this mouch,

JOHN H. DADE

If yon haf to send for my tronke to Washington send the name of John Trowharte. Sir please rite as soon as you gat this for et as enporten. JOHN H. DADE.

SOURCE: William Still, 1872 (see the Bibliography on p. 203 for complete information).

REVEREND J. W. LOGUEN

Letter from His Old Mistress and His Reply

[*The Liberator*]

J. W. Loguen ("Jarm") was the former slave of the Logue family. After his escape, Loguen received a letter from Mrs. Logue. She requested that he send her $1,000 in exchange for his "bill of sale" and threatened to have him seized by slave-hunters if he did not comply. Loguen responded that he would neither send $1,000 nor allow himself to be re-enslaved. He was outraged by her proposition and informed Mrs. Logue that he valued his freedom more than her, more than his own life, and "more than all the lives of all the slaveholders and tyrants under heaven."

The Liberator said on April 27, 1860:

The following letter was received a day or two since by Rev. Mr. Loguen, of this city, from his old mistress 'way down in Tennessee.

The old lady is evidently "hard up," financially, and attempts to frighten her former servant into the payment of $1,000 as "hush money." We imagine she sent to the wrong man, as Mr. Loguen needs no "bill of sale" to secure himself from capture in this section of the State. Besides his own stalwart arm, he has hosts of friends who would make this region too hot to hold the man-hunters who would venture on such an errand as the old lady hints at in her somewhat singular epistle. Her lamentations about the old mare are decidedly funny (we may add womanly) and all the misfortunes of the family are traced directly to the escape of "Jarm." But here is her letter:

MAURY COUNTY, STATE OF TENNESSEE, Feb. 20, 1860.

TO JARM:—I now take my pen to write you a few lines, to let you know how we all are. I am a cripple, but I am still able to get about. The rest of the family are all well. Cherry is as well as common. I write you these lines to let you know the situation we are in, —partly in consequence of your running away and stealing Old Rock, our fine mare. Though we got the mare back, she never was worth much after you took her;—and, as I now stand in need of some funds, I have determined to sell you, and I have had an offer for you, but did not see fit to take it. If you will send me one thousand dollars, and pay for the old mare, I will give up all claim I have to you. Write to me as soon as you get these lines, and let me know if you will accept my proposition. In consequence of your running away, we had to sell Abe and Ann and twelve acres of land; and I want you to send me the money, that I may be able to redeem the land that you was the cause of our selling, and on receipt of the above-named sum of money, I will send you your bill of sale. If you do not comply with my request, I will send you to some one else, and you may rest assured that the time is not far distant when things will be changed with you. Write to me as soon as you get these lines. Direct your letter to Bigbyville, Maury County, Tennessee. You had better comply with my request.

I understand that you are a preacher. As the Southern people are so bad, you had better come and preach to your old acquaintances. I would like to know if you read your Bible. If so, can you tell what will become of the thief if he does not repent? I deem it unnecessary to say much more at present. A word to the wise is sufficient. You know where the liar has his part. You know that we reared you as we reared our own children; that you was never abused, and that shortly before you ran away, when your master asked if you would like to be sold, you said you would not leave him to go with any body.

—SARAH LOGUE

* * *

Mr. Loguen's Reply

SYRACUSE (N.Y.) March 28, 1860

MRS. SARAH LOGUE: Yours of the 20th of February is duly received, and I thank you for it. It is a long time since I heard from my poor old mother, and I am glad to know that she is yet alive, and, as you say, "as well as common." What that means, I don't know. I wish you had said more about her.

You are a woman; but, had you a woman's heart, you never could have insulted a brother by telling him you sold his only remaining brother and sister, because he put himself beyond your power to convert him into money.

You sold my brother and sister, Abe and Ann, and twelve acres of land, you say, because I ran away. Now you have the unutterable meanness to ask me to return and be your miserable chattel, or, in lieu thereof, send you $1000 to enable you to redeem the *land*, but not to redeem my poor brother and sister! If I were to send you money, it would be to get my brother and sister, and not that you should get land. You say you are a *cripple*, and doubtless you say it to stir my pity, for you knew I was susceptible in that direction. I do pity you from the bottom of my heart. Nevertheless, I am indignant beyond the power of words to express, that you should be so sunken and cruel as to tear the hearts I love so much all in pieces; that you should be willing to impale and crucify us all, out of compassion for your poor *foot* or *leg*. Wretched woman! Be it known to you that I value my freedom, to say nothing of my mother, brothers and sisters, more than your whole body; more, indeed, than my own life; more than all the lives of all the slaveholders and tyrants under heaven.

You say you have offers to buy me, and that you shall sell me if I do not send you a $1000, and in the same breath and almost in the same sentence, you say, "You know we raised you as we did our own children." Woman, did you raise your *own children* for the market? Did you raise them for the whipping-post? Did you raise them to be driven off, bound to a coffle in chains? Where are my poor bleeding brothers and sisters? Can you tell? Who was it that sent them off into sugar and cotton fields, to be kicked and cuffed, and whipped, and to groan and die; and where no kin can hear their groans, or attend and sympathize at their dying bed, or follow in their funeral? Wretched woman! Do you say *you* did not do it? Then I reply, your husband did, and *you* approved the deed—and the very letter you sent me shows that your heart approves it all. Shame on you!

But, by the way, where is your husband? You don't speak of him. I infer, therefore, that he is dead; that he has gone to his great account, with all his sins against my poor family upon his head. Poor man! gone to meet the spirits of my poor, outraged and murdered people, in a world where Liberty and Justice are *Masters*.

But you say I am a thief, because I took the old mare along with me. Have you got to learn that I had a better right to the old mare, as you call her, than Mannasseth Logue had to me? Is it a greater sin for me to steal his horse, than it was for him to rob my mother's cradle, and steal me? If he and you infer that I forfeit all my rights to you, shall not I infer that you forfeit all your rights to me? Have you got to learn that human rights are mutual and reciprocal, and if you take my liberty and life, you forfeit your own liberty and life? Before God and high heaven, is there a law for one man which is not a law for every other man?

If you or any other speculator on my body and rights, wish to know how I regard my rights, they need but come here, and lay their hands on me to enslave me. Did you think to terrify me by presenting the alternative to give my money to you, or give my body to slavery? Then let me say to you, that I meet the proposition with unutterable scorn and contempt. The proposition is an outrage and an insult. I will not budge one hair's breadth. I will not breathe a shorter breath, even to save me from your persecutions. I stand among a free people, who, I thank God, sympathize with my rights, and the rights of mankind; and if your emissaries and vendors come here to re-enslave me, and escape the unshrinking vigor of my own right arm, I trust my strong and brave friends, in this city and State, will be my rescuers and avengers.

Yours, &c.,   J. W. LOGUEN

SOURCE: Carter G. Woodson. *The Mind of the Negro: As Reflected in Letters During the Crisis 1800–1860*. Mineola, New York: Dover Publications, 2013.

MATILDA MAHONEY AND DR. J. W. PENNINGTON'S BROTHER AND SONS

Arrivals from Different Places: Captured and Carried Back

[William Still]

William Still tells two tales, back to back: the happy brief narrative of Matilda Mahoney and then the terrible setback of a family from Maryland that escaped but was ensnared by 1850's Fugitive Slave Law in New York City.

WHILE MANY SYMPATHIZED with the slave in his chains, and freely wept over his destiny, or gave money to help buy his freedom, but few could be found who were willing to take the risk of going into the South, and standing face to face with Slavery, in order to conduct a panting slave to freedom. The undertaking was too fearful to think of in most cases. But there were instances when men and women too, moved by the love of freedom, would take their lives in their hands, beard the lion in his den, and nobly rescue the oppressed. Such an instance is found in the case of Matilda Mahoney, in Baltimore.

The story of Matilda must be very brief, although it is full of thrilling interest. She was twenty-one years of age in 1854, when she escaped and came to Philadelphia, a handsome young woman, of a light complexion, quite refined in her manners, and in short, possessing great personal attractions. But her situation as a slave was critical, as will be seen.

Her claimant was Wm. Rigard, of Frederick, Md., who hired her to a Mr. Reese, in Baltimore; in this situation her duties were general housework and nursing. With these labors, she was not, however, so much dissatisfied as she was with other circumstances of a more alarming nature: her old master was tottering on the verge of the grave, and his son, a trader in New Orleans. These facts kept Matilda in extreme anxiety. For two years prior to her escape, the young trader had been trying to influence his father to let him have her for the Southern market; but the old man had not consented. Of course the trader knew quite well, that an "article" of her appearance would command readily a very high price in the New Orleans market. But Matilda's attractions had won the heart of a young man in the North, one who had known her in Baltimore in earlier days, and this lover was willing to make desperate efforts to rescue her from her perilous situation. Whether or not he had nerve enough to venture down to Baltimore to accompany his intended away on the Underground Rail Road, his presence would not have aided in the case. He had, however, a friend who consented to go to Baltimore on this desperate mission. The friend was James Jefferson, of Providence, R. I. With the strategy of a skilled soldier, Mr. Jefferson hurried to the Monumental City, and almost under the eyes of the slave-holders and slave-catchers, despite of pro-slavery breastworks, seized his prize and speeded her away on the Underground Railway, before her owner was made acquainted with the fact of her intended escape. On Matilda's arrival at the station in Philadelphia, several other passengers from different points, happened to come to hand just at that time, and gave great solicitude and anxiety to the Committee. Among these were a man and his wife and their four children, (noticed elsewhere), from Maryland. Likewise an interesting and intelligent young girl who had been almost miraculously rescued from the prison-house at Norfolk, and in addition to these, the brother of J. W. Pennington, D. D., with his two sons.

While it was a great gratification to have travelers coming along so fast, and especially to observe in every countenance, determination, rare manly and womanly bearing, with remarkable intelligence, it must be admitted, that the acting committee felt at the same time, a very lively dread of the slave-hunters, and were on their guard. Arrangements were made to send the fugitives on by different trains, and in various directions.

Matilda and all the others with the exception of the father and two sons (relatives of Dr. Pennington) successfully escaped and reached their longed-for haven in a free land. The Penningtons, however, although pains had been taken to apprize the Doctor of the good news of the coming of his kin, whom he had not seen for many, many years, were captured after being in New York some twenty-four hours. In answer to an advisory letter from the secretary of the Committee the following from the Doctor is explicit, relative to his wishes and feelings with regard to their being sent on to New York.

29 6TH AVENUE, NEW YORK, MAY 24TH, 1854.

MY DEAR MR. STILL:—Your kind letter of the 22d inst has come to hand and I have to thank you for your offices of benevolence to my bone and my flesh, I have had the pleasure of doing a little for your brother Peter, but I do not think it an offset. My burden has been great about these brethren. I hope they have started on to me. Many thanks, my good friend. Yours Truly,

J. W. C. PENNINGTON.

This letter only served to intensify the deep interest which had already been awakened for the safety of all concerned. At the same time also it made the duty of the Committee clear with regard to forwarding them to N.Y. Immediately, therefore, the Doctor's brother and sons were furnished with free tickets and were as carefully cautioned as possible with regard to slave hunters, if encountered on the road. In company with several other Underground Rail Road passengers, under the care of an intelligent guide, all were sent off in due order, looking quite as well as the most respectable of their race, from any part of the country. The Committee in New York, with the Doctor, were on the look out of course; thus without difficulty all arrived safely in the Empire City.

It would seem that the coming of his brother and sons so over-powered the Doctor that he forgot how imminent their danger was. The meeting and interview was doubtless very joyous. Few perhaps could realize, even in imagination, the feelings that filled their hearts, as the Doctor and his brother reverted to their boyhood, when they were both slaves together in Maryland; the separation—the escape of the former many years previous—the contrast, one elevated to the dignity of a Doctor of Divinity, a scholar and noted clergyman, and as such well known in the United States, and Great Britain, whilst, at the same time, his brother and kin were held in chains, compelled to do unrequited labor, to come and go at the bidding of another. Were not these reflections enough to incapacitate the Doctor for the time being, for cool thought as to how he should best guard against the enemy? Indeed, in view of Slavery and its horrid features, the wonder is, not that more was not done, but that any thing was done, that the victims were not driven almost out of their senses. But time rolled on until nearly twenty-four hours had passed, and while re-posing their fatigued and weary limbs in bed, just before day-break, hyena-like the slave-hunters pounced upon all three of them, and soon had them hand-cuffed and hurried off to a United States' Commissioner's office. Armed with the Fugitive Law, and a strong guard of officers to carry it out, resistance would have been simply useless. Ere the morning sun arose the sad news was borne by the telegraph wires to all parts of the country of this awful calamity on the Underground Rail Road.

Scarcely less painful to the Committee was the news of this accident, than the news of a disaster, resulting in the loss of several lives, on the Camden and Amboy Road, would have been to its managers. This was the first accident that had ever taken place on the road after passengers had reached the Philadelphia Committee, although, in various instances, slave-hunters had been within a hair's breadth of their prey.

All that was reported respecting the arrest and return of the Doctor's kin, so disgraceful to Christianity and civilization, is taken from *The Liberator*, as follows:

THREE FUGITIVE SLAVES ARRESTED IN NEW YORK, AND GIVEN UP TO THEIR OWNERS.

New York, May 25th.

About three o'clock this morning, three colored men, father and two sons, known as Jake, Bob, and Stephen Pennington, were arrested at the instance of David Smith and Jacob Grove, of Washington Co., Md., who claimed them as their slaves. They were taken before Commissioner Morton, of the United States Court, and it was understood that they would be examined at 11 o'clock; instead of that, however, the case was heard at once, no persons being present, when the claimants testified that they were the owners of said slaves and that they escaped from their service at Baltimore, on Sunday last.

From what we can gather of the proceedings, the fugitives acknowledged themselves to be slaves of Smith and Grove. The commissioner considering the testimony sufficient, ordered their surrender, and they were accordingly given up to their claimants, who hurried them off at once, and they are now on their way to Baltimore. A telegraph despatch has been sent to Philadelphia, as it is understood an attempt will be made to rescue the parties, when the cars arrive. There was no excitement around the commissioner's office, owing to a misunderstanding as to the time of examination. The men were traced to this city by the claimants, who made application to the United States Court, when officers Horton and De Angeles were deputed by the marshal to effect their arrest, and those officers, with deputy Marshal Thompson scoured the city, and finally found them secreted in a house in Broome St. They were brought before Commissioner Morton this morning. No counsel appeared for the fugitives. The case being made out, the usual affidavits of fear of rescue were made, and the warrants thereupon issued, and the three fugitives were delivered over to the U.S. Marshal, and hurried off to Maryland. They were a father and his two sons, father about forty-five and sons eighteen or nineteen. The evidence shows them to have recently escaped. The father is the brother of the Rev. Dr. Pennington, a highly respected colored preacher of this city.

NEW YORK, May 28.

LAST EVENING THE CHURCH at the corner of Prince and Marion streets was filled with an intelligent audience of white and colored people, to hear Dr. Pennington relate the circumstance connected with the arrest of his brother and nephews. He showed that he attempted to afford his brother the assistance of counsel, but was unable to do so, the officers at the Marshal's office having deceived him in relation to the time the trial was to take place before the Commissioners. Hon. E. F. Culver next addressed the audience, showing, that a great injustice had been done to the brother of Dr. Pennington, and though he, up to that time, had advocated peace, he now had the spirit to tear down the building over the Marshal's head. Intense interest was manifested during the proceedings, and much sympathy in behalf of Dr. Pennington.

THE FUGITIVE SLAVES IN BALTIMORE.

THE U.S. MARSHAL, A. T. HILLYER, ESQ., received a dispatch this morning from officers Horton and Dellugelis, at Baltimore, stating, that they had arrived there with the three slaves, arrested here yesterday (the Penningtons), the owners accompanying them. The officers will return to New York, this evening.—*N. Y. Express, 27th.*

NEW YORK, May 30.

THE REV. DR. PENNINGTON has received a letter from Mr. Grove, the claimant of his brother, who was recently taken back from this city, offering to sell him to Dr. Pennington, should he wish to buy him, and stating, that he would await a reply, before "selling him to the slave-drivers." Mr. Groce, who accompanied his "sweet heart," Matilda, in the same train which conveyed the Penningtons to New York, had reason to apprehend danger to all the Underground Rail Road passengers, as will appear from his subjoined letter:

ELMIRA, May 28th.

Dear LUKE:—I arrived home safe with my precious charge, and found all well. I have just learned, that the Penningtons are taken. Had he done as I wished him he would never have been taken. Last night our tall friend from Baltimore came, and caused great excitement here by his information. The lady is perfectly safe now in Canada. I will write you and Mr. Still as soon as I get over the excitement. This letter was first intended for Mr. Gains, but I now send it to you. Please let me hear their movements. Yours truly,

C. L. GROCE.

But sadly as this blow was felt by the Vigilance Committee, it did not cause them to relax their efforts in the least. Indeed it only served to stir them up to renewed diligence and watchfulness, although for a length of time afterwards the Committee felt disposed, when sending, to avoid New York as much as possible, and in lieu thereof, to send *via* Elmira, where there was a depot under the agency of John W. Jones. Mr. Jones was a true and prompt friend of the fugitive, and wide awake with regard to Slavery and slave-holders, and slave hunters, for he had known from sad experience in Virginia every trait of character belonging to these classes.

In the midst of the Doctor's grief, friends of the slave soon raised money to purchase his brother, about $1,000; but the unfortunate sons were doomed to the auction block and the far South, where, the writer has never exactly learned.

SOURCE: William Still, 1872 (see the Bibliography on p. 203 for complete information).

MARGARET

Born on a Slave Ship

[Eber M. Pettit]

The importation of slaves was outlawed in 1808, though illegal shipments inter-mittently continued. Margaret (last name not given) was among the last slaves who were "legally" brought into the country. When she grew up and married, her husband was sold off and she decided to run away with her infant—during which escape she was, as Pettit introduced it in his book, "hunted with blood-hounds and rescued by a mastiff."

ON THE EASTERN SHORE of the Chesapeake, in the State of Maryland, there lived, about forty years ago, a remarkable woman by the name of Margaret. She was born on a slave ship on its way from Africa to Baltimore, just before the importation of slaves was prohibited. She, with her mother, fell into the hands of a family who gave them religious instruction, and Margaret, while young, exhibited traits of character that were regarded as remarkable for one of her race. Of a proud, indomitable spirit, yet having acute moral sense, a disposition naturally amiable, of cheerful temperament, and crushed with a sense of her degraded condition, she was unusually capable in all kinds of housework, and especially active and competent as nurse when any of the family were sick. By observation she learned the polite manners and graceful deportment of ladies of the family and those who visited there. Her obedience to every command, her kindness to any one who was in trouble, and polite deportment toward all, seemed to be the result of a conscientious desire to imitate her Saviour whom she had early learned to love.

At sixteen years of age she went to live with her young mistress, who was married to a planter in that fertile country known as the "Eastern Shore." At eighteen Margaret was a large woman, tall and well formed, her complexion black as jet, her countenance always pleasant, though she seldom laughed. She talked but little, even to those of her own race. At twenty years of age she became the wife of a worthy young man to whom she had given her best affections.

Not long after, her young master became very angry with her for what he called stubbornness and resistance to his will, and threatened to chastise her by whipping—a degradation that she had always felt that she could not submit to, and yet to obey her master in the thing he demanded would be still worse. She therefore told him that she would not be whipped, she would rather die, and gave him warning that any attempt to execute his threat would surely result in the death of one of them. He knew her too well to risk the experiment, and decided to punish her in another way. He sold her husband, and she saw him bound in chains and driven off with a large drove of men and women for the New Orleans market. He then put her in the hands of a brutal overseer, with directions to work her to the extent of her ability on a tobacco plantation, which command was enforced up to the day of the birth of her child. At the end of one week she was driven again to the field and compelled to perform a full task, having at no time any abatement of her work on account of her situation, with the exception of one week. It was the custom on the plantations to establish nurseries, presided over by old, broken down slaves, where mothers might leave their infants during the work hours, but this privilege was denied to Margaret. She was obliged to leave her child under the shade of a bush in the field, returning to it but twice during the long day. On returning to the child one evening she found it apparently senseless, exhausted with crying, and a large serpent lying across it. Although she felt that it would be better for both herself and child if it were dead, yet a mother's heart impelled her to make an effort to save it, and by caressing and careful handling she resuscitated it.

As soon as she heard its feeble, wailing cry, she made a vow to deliver her boy from the cruel power of slavery or die in the attempt, and falling prostrate, she prayed for strength to perform her vow, and for grace and patience to sustain her in her suffering, toil and hunger; then pressing her child to her bosom, she fled with all the speed of which she was capable toward the North Star. Having gone a mile or two, she heard something pursuing her; on looking round she saw Watch, the old house dog. Watch was a large mastiff, somewhat old, and with him Margaret had ever been a favorite, and since she had been driven to the field, Watch often visited her at her cabin in the evening. She feared it would not be safe to allow Watch to go with her, but she could not induce him to go back, so she resumed her flight, accompanied by her faithful escort. At break of day she hid herself on the border of a plantation and soon fell asleep.

Toward evening she was aroused by the noise made by the slaves returning to their quarters, and seeing an old woman lingering behind all the others, she called her, told her troubles and asked for food. The old woman returned about midnight with a pretty good supply of food, which Margaret divided with Watch, and then started on taking the north star for her guide. The second day after she left, the Overseer employed a hunter with his dogs to find her. He started with an old slut and three whelps, thinking, no doubt, that as the game was only a woman and her infant child, it would be a good time to train his pups.

Margaret had been missed at roll call the morning after her flight, but the Overseer supposed she was hiding near the place for a day or two, and that hunger would soon drive her up; therefore, when the hunter started, he led the old dog, expecting to find her in an hour or two, but not overtaking her the first day, on the next morning he let his hounds loose, intending to follow on horseback, guided by their voices. About noon, the old dog struck the track at the place where Margaret had made her little camp the day before, and she bounded off with fresh vigor, leaving the man and the younger dogs beyond sight and hearing. The young dogs soon lost the track where Margaret forded the streams, and the old dog was miles away, leaving the hunter without a guide to direct him.

Margaret had been lying in the woods on the bank of a river, intend-ing to start again as soon as it was dark, when she was startled by the whining and nervous motions of old Watch, and listening, she heard the hoarse ringing bay of a blood-hound. Although she had expected that she would be hunted with dogs, and recalled over and over again the shocking accounts related by Overseers to the slaves, of fugitives over-taken and torn in pieces by the savage Spanish blood-hounds, she had not, until now, realized the horrors of her situation. She expected to have to witness the destruction of her child by the savage brute, and then be torn in pieces herself. She did not, however, lose her presence of mind. The river or inlet near her camp was too wide and too deep to be forded at that place, but she fastened her child to her shoulders and waded in as far as she could, taking a club to defend herself. Meanwhile, old Watch lay with his nose between his feet, facing the coming foe. The hound, rendered more fierce by the freshness of the track, came rushing headlong with nose to the ground, scenting her prey, and seemed not to see old Watch, until, leaping to pass over him, she found her wind-pipe suddenly collapsed in the massive jaws of the old mastiff. The struggle was not very noisy, for Watch would not even growl, and the hound could not, but it was terribly energetic. The hound made rapid and persuasive gestures with her paws and tail, but it was of no use, the jaws of old Watch relaxed not until all signs of life in his enemy had ceased. Margaret came back from the river, and would have embraced her faithful friend, but fearing that a stronger pack was following, she hastily threw the dead hound into the river and pursued her journey.

It would make this sketch too long to relate all Margaret's adventures before she reached New York City, where she lived many years. Within a few hours after her providential escape by the aid of her faithful friend, old Watch, from the fangs of the slave hunter's hound, she fell into the hands of friends, who kept her secreted until she could be sent into a free State; while there, she learned about the pursuit by the hunter, and that he never knew what became of his best hound. After the chase was abandoned, she, through a regular line, similar to our U. G. R. R., was sent to Philadelphia and then to New York, where she became a celebrated nurse, and always befriended the poor of all colors and all nationalities. She rented a good house which was a home for herself and boy, and also for old Watch while he lived. When her boy, whom she called Samuel, was old enough to go to school, she found a place for him in Westchester Co., where he obtained the rudiments of an education, and afterwards in the family of a gentleman in Central New York, he enjoyed the advantages of a thorough education, and became a devoted minister of the gospel in the Congregational Church. I often met him during the early history of the U. G. R. R., of which he was an efficient agent. Samuel was one of the most eloquent men I have ever heard speak. He was a fine looking man, though he was so black it was sometimes said that it grew dark when he entered a room; but it grew light when he began to speak. ...

SOURCE: Eber M. Pettit. *Sketches in the History of the Underground Railroad Comprising Many Thrilling Incidents of the Escape of Fugitives from Slavery, and the Perils of Those Who Aided Them*. Fredonia, New York: W. McKinstry and Son, 1879.

MARY FRANCES MELVIN, ELIZA HENDERSON, AND NANCY GRANTHAM

Arrival from Virginia, 1858

[William Still]

Mary Frances Melvin, Eliza Henderson, and Nancy Grantham fled dissimilar situations in Virginia: Melvin, a dress-maker and house servant, called her owner "kind" but did not want to be her property; Henderson was incensed that her

owner thought punching her in the face was warranted or acceptable; and
Grantham was repulsed by the sexual aggression and demands of her "chivalric"
owner. Although their experiences differed, they had the same desire for freedom
and the same determination to escape.

MARY FRANCES hailed from Norfolk; she had been in servitude under
Mrs. Chapman, a widow lady, against whom she had no complaint
to make; indeed, she testified that her mistress was very kind, although fully allied to slavery. She said that she left, not on account of
bad treatment, but simply because she wanted her freedom. Her calling as a slave had been that of a dress-maker and house servant. Mary
Frances was about twenty-three years of age, of mixed blood, refined
in her manners and somewhat cultivated.

Eliza Henderson, who happened at the station at the same time that
Frances was on hand, escaped from Richmond. She was twenty-eight
years of age, medium size, quite dark color, and of pleasant countenance. Eliza alleged that one William Waverton had been wronging
her by keeping her down-trodden and withholding her hire. Also,
that this same Waverton had, on a late occasion, brought his heavy
fist violently against her "jaws," which visitation, however "kindly"
intended by her chivalrous master, produced such an unfavorable
impression on the mind of Eliza that she at once determined not to
yield submission to him a day longer than she could find an
Underground Rail Road conductor who would take her North.

The blow that she had thus received made her almost frantic; she
had however thought seriously on the question of her rights before
this outrage.

In Waverton's household Eliza had become a fixture as it were,
especially with regard to his children; she had won their affections
completely, and she was under the impression that in some instances
their influence had saved her from severe punishment; and for them
she manifested kindly feelings. In speaking of her mistress she said that
she was "only tolerable."

It would be useless to attempt a description of the great satisfaction
and delight evinced by Eliza on reaching the Committee in
Philadelphia.

Nancy Grantham also fled from near Richmond, and was fortunate
in that she escaped from the prison-house at the age of nineteen. She
possessed a countenance peculiarly mild, and was good-looking and
interesting, and although evidently a slave her father belonged strictly

to the white man's party, for she was fully half white. She was moved to escape simply to shun her master's evil designs; his brutal purposes were only frustrated by the utmost resolution. This chivalric gentleman was a husband, the father of nine children, and the owner of three hundred slaves. He belonged to a family bearing the name of Christian, and was said to be an M. D. "He was an old man, but very cruel to all his slaves." It was said that Nancy's sister was the object of his lust, but she resisted, and the result was that she was sold to New Orleans. The auction-block was not the only punishment she was called upon to endure for her fidelity to her womanhood, for resistance to her master, but before being sold she was cruelly scourged.

Nancy's sorrows first commenced in Alabama. Five years previous to her escape she was brought from a cotton plantation in Alabama, where she had been accustomed to toil in the cotton-field. In comparing and contrasting the usages of slave-holders in the two States in which she had served, she said she had "seen more flogging under old Christian" than she had been accustomed to see in Alabama; yet she concluded, that she could hardly tell which State was the worst; her cup had been full and very bitter in both States.

Nancy said, "the very day before I escaped, I was required to go to his (her master's) bed-chamber to keep the flies off of him as he lay sick, or pretended to be so. Notwithstanding, in talking with me, he said that he was coming to my pallet that night, and with an oath he declared if I made a noise he would cut my throat. I told him I would not be there. Accordingly he did go to my room, but I had gone for shelter to another room. At this his wrath waxed terrible. Next morning I was called to account for getting out of his way, and I was beaten awfully." This outrage moved Nancy to a death-struggle for her freedom, and she succeeded by dressing herself in male attire.

After her harrowing story was told with so much earnestness and intelligence, she was asked as to the treatment she had received at the hand of Mrs. Christian (her mistress). In relation to her, Nancy said, "Mrs. Christian was afraid of him (master); if it hadn't been for that I think she would have been clever; but I was often threatened by her, and once she undertook to beat me, but I could not stand it. I had to resist, and she got the worst of it that time."

All that may now be added, is, that the number of young slave girls shamefully exposed to the base lusts of their masters, as Nancy was—truly was legion. Nancy was but one of the number who resisted influences apparently overpowering. All honor is due her name and memory!

She was brought away secreted on a boat, but the record is silent as to which one of the two or three Underground Rail Road captains (who at that time occasionally brought passengers), helped her to escape. It was hard to be definite concerning minor matters while absorbed in the painful reflections that her tale of suffering had naturally awakened. If one had arisen from the dead the horrors of Slavery could scarcely have been more vividly pictured! But in the multitude of travelers coming under the notice of the Committee, Nancy's story was soon forgotten, and new and marvellous narratives were told of others who had shared the same bitter cup, who had escaped from the same hell of Slavery, who had panted for the same freedom and won the same prize.

SOURCE: William Still, 1872 (see the Bibliography on p. 203 for complete information).

AUNT HANNAH MOORE

"Seeing a Ray of Hope She Availed Herself of the Opportunity to Secure Her Freedom"

[William Still]

In Philadelphia, Hannah Moore took advantage of the Pennsylvania law enacted in 1847 that gave freedom to any slave who entered the state with his or her slaveholder. William Still was charmed by Hannah Moore and took down most of her woeful story of fifty-seven years of enslavement in her own words.

IN 1854 in company with her so-called Mistress (Mary Moore) Aunt Hannah arrived in Philadelphia, from Missouri, being en route to California, where she with her mistress was to join her master, who had gone there years before to seek his fortune. The mistress having relatives in this city tarried here a short time, not doubting that she had sufficient control over Aunt Hannah to keep her from contact with either abolitionists or those of her own color, and that she would have no difficulty in taking her with her to her journey's end. If such were her calculations she was greatly mistaken. For although Aunt Hannah was destitute of book-learning she was nevertheless a woman of thought and natural ability, and while she wisely kept her counsel from her mistress she took care to make her wants known to an abolitionist. She had passed many years under the yoke, under different owners, and now seeing a ray of hope she availed herself of the opportunity to secure her freedom. She had occasion to go to a store in the neighborhood where she was stopping, and to her unspeakable joy she found the proprietor an abolitionist and a friend who inquired into her condition and proffered her assistance. The store-keeper quickly made known her condition at the Anti-slavery Office, and in double-quick time J. M. McKim and Charles Wise as abolitionists and members of the Vigilance Committee repaired to the stopping-place of the mistress and her slave to demand in the name of humanity and the laws of Pennsylvania that Aunt Hannah should be no longer held in fetters but that she should be immediately proclaimed free. In the eyes of the mistress this procedure was so extraordinary that she became very much excited and for a moment threatened them with the "broomstick," but her raving had no effect on Messrs. McKim and Wise, who did not rest contented until Aunt Hannah was safely in their hands. She had lived a slave in Moore's family in the State of Missouri about ten years and said she was treated very well, had plenty to eat, plenty to wear, and a plenty of work. It was prior to her coming into the possession of Moore that Aunt Hannah had been made to drink the bitter waters of oppression. From this point, therefore, we shall present some of the incidents of her life, from infancy, and very nearly word for word as she related them:

"Moore bought me from a man named McCaully, who owned me about a year. I fared dreadful bad under McCaully. One day in a rage he undertook to beat me with the limb of a cherry-tree; he began at me and tried in the first place to snatch my clothes off, but he did not succeed. After that he beat the cherry-tree limb all to pieces over me. The first blow struck me on the back of my neck and knocked me down; his wife was looking on, sitting on the side of the bed crying to him to lay on. After the limb was worn out he then went out to the yard and got a lath, and he come at me again and beat me with that until he broke it all to pieces. He was not satisfied then; he next went to the fence and tore off a paling, and with that he took both hands, 'cursing' me all the time as hard as he could. With an oath he would say, 'now don't you love me?' 'Oh master, I will pray for you,'

I would cry, then he would 'cuss' harder than ever. He beat me until he was tired and quit. I crept out of doors and throwed up blood; some days I was hardly able to creep. With this beating I was laid up several weeks. Another time Mistress McCaully got very angry. One day she beat me as bad as he did. She was a woman who would get very mad in a minute. One day she began scolding and said the kitchen wasn't kept clean. I told her the kitchen was kept as clean as any kitchen in the place; she spoke very angry, and said she didn't go by other folks but she had rules of her own. She soon ordered me to come in to her. I went in as she ordered me; she met me with a mule-rope, and ordered me to cross my hands. I crossed my hands and she tied me to the bedstead. Here her husband said, 'My dear, now let me do the fighting.' In her mad fit she said he shouldn't do it, and told him to stand back and keep out of the way or I will give you the cowhide she said to him. He then 'sot' down in a 'cheer' and looked like a man condemned to be hung; then she whipped me with the cowhide until I sunk to the floor. He then begged her to quit. He said to his wife she has begged and begged and you have whipped her enough. She only raged 'wus;' she turned the butt end of the cowhide and struck me five or six blows over my head as hard as she could; she then throwed the cowhide down and told a little girl to untie me. The little girl was not able to do it; Mr. McCaully then untied me himself. Both times that I was beat the blood run down from my head to my feet.

"They wouldn't give you anything to eat hardly. McCaully bore the name of coming by free colored children without buying them, and selling them afterwards. One boy on the place always said that he was free but had been kidnapped from Arkansas. He could tell all about how he was kidnapped, but could not find anybody to do anything for him, so he had to content himself.

"McCaully bought me from a man by the name of Landers. While in Landers' hands I had the rheumatism and was not able to work. He was afraid I was going to die, or he would lose me, and I would not be of any service to him, so he took and traded me off for a wagon. I was something better when he traded me off; well enough to be about. My health remained bad for about four years, and I never got my health until Moore bought me. Moore took me for a debt. McCaully owed Moore for wagons. I was not born in Missouri but was born in Virginia. From my earliest memory I was owned by Conrad Hackler; he lived in Grason County. He was a very poor man, and had no other slave but me. He bought me before I was quite four years old, for one hundred dollars. Hackler bought me from a man named William Scott. I must go back by good rights to the beginning and tell all: Scott bought me first from a young man he met one day in the road, with a bundle in his arms. Scott, wishing to know of the young man what he had in his bundle, was told that he had a baby. 'What are you going to do with it?' said Scott. The young man said that he was going to take it to his sister; that its mother was dead, and it had nobody to take care of it. Scott offered the young man a horse for it, and the young man took him up. This is the way I was told that Scott came by me. I never knowed anything about my mother or father, but I have always believed that my mother was a white woman, and that I was put away to save her character; I have always thought this. Under Hackler I was treated more like a brute than a human being. I was fed like the dogs; had a trough dug out of a piece of wood for a plate. After I growed up to ten years old they made me sleep out in an old house standing off some distance from the main house where my master and mistress lived. A bed of straw and old rags was made for me in a big trough called the tan trough (a trough having been used for tanning purposes). The cats about the place came and slept with me, and was all the company I had. I had to work with the hoe in the field and help do everything in doors and out in all weathers. The place was so poor that some seasons he would not raise twenty bushels of corn and hardly three bushels of wheat. As for shoes I never knowed what it was to have a pair of shoes until I was grown up. After I growed up to be a woman my master thought nothing of taking my clothes off, and would whip me until the blood would run down to the ground. After I was twenty-five years old they did not treat me so bad; they both professed to get religion about that time; and my master said he would never lay the weight of his finger on me again. Once after that mistress wanted him to whip me, but he didn't do it, nor never whipped me any more. After awhile my master died; if they had gone according to law I would have been hired out or sold, but my mistress wanted to keep me to carry on the place for her support. So I was kept for seven or eight years after his death. It was understood between my mistress, and her children, and her friends, who all met after master died, that I was to take care of mistress, and after mistress died I should not serve anybody else. I done my best to keep my mistress from suffering. After a few years they all became dissatisfied, and moved to Missouri. They scattered, and took up government land. Without means they lived as poor people commonly live, on small farms in the woods. I still lived with my mistress. Some of the heirs got dissatisfied, and sued for their rights or a settlement; then I was sold with my child, a boy."

Thus Aunt Hannah reviewed her slave-life, showing that she had been in the hands of six different owners, and had seen great tribulation under each of them, except the last; that she had never known a mother's or a father's care; that Slavery had given her one child, but no husband as a protector or a father. The half of what she passed through in the way of suffering has scarcely been hinted at in this sketch. Fifty-seven years were passed in bondage before she reached Philadelphia. Under the good Providence through which she came in possession of her freedom, she found a kind home with a family of Abolitionists, (Mrs. Gillingham's), whose hearts had been in deep sympathy with the slave for many years. In this situation Aunt Hannah remained several years, honest, faithful, and obliging, taking care of her earnings, which were put out at interest for her by her friends. Her mind was deeply imbued with religious feeling, and an unshaken confidence in God as her only trust; she connected herself with the A. M. E. Bethel Church, of Philadelphia, where she has walked, blameless and exemplary up to this day. Probably there is not a member in that large congregation whose simple faith and whose walk and conversation are more commendable than Aunt Hannah's. Although she has passed through so many hardships she is a woman of good judgment and more than average intellect; enjoys good health, vigor, and peace of mind in her old days, with a small income just sufficient to meet her humble wants without having to live at service. After living in Philadelphia for several years, she was married to a man of about her own age, possessing all her good qualities; had served a life-time in a highly respectable Quaker family of this city, and had so won the esteem of his kind employer that at his death he left him a comfortable house for life, so that he was not under the necessity of serving another. The name of the recipient of the good Quaker friend's bounty and Aunt Hannah's companion, was Thomas Todd. After a few years of wedded life, Aunt Hannah was called upon to be left alone again in the world by the death of her husband, whose loss was mourned by many friends, both colored and white, who knew and respected him.

SOURCE: William Still, 1872 (see the Bibliography on p. 203 for complete information).

ALFRED S. THORNTON

Arrival from Virginia, 1858

[William Still]

Alfred Thornton considered himself a "contented" slave until he learned that his owner had sold him to a trader instead of a trusted neighbor. Fearing "a fate in the far South more horrid than death," Thornton fled immediately, narrowly avoiding the trader, separating himself from his parents, and heading North.

THE SUBJECT OF THIS SKETCH was a young man about twenty-two years of age, of dark color, but bright intellectually. Alfred found no fault with the ordinary treatment received at the hands of his master; he had evidently been on unusually intimate terms with him. Nor was any fault found with his mistress, so far as her treatment of him was concerned; thus, comparatively, he was "happy and contented," little dreaming of trader or a change of owners. One day, to his utter surprise, he saw a trader with a constable approaching him. As they drew nearer and nearer he began to grow nervous. What further took place will be given, as nearly as possible, in Alfred's own words as follows:

"William Noland (a constable), and the trader was making right up to me almost on my heels, and grabbed at me, they were so near. I flew, I took off my hat and run, took off my jacket and run harder, took off my vest and doubled my pace, the constable and the trader both on the chase hot foot. The trader fired two barrels of his revolver after me, and cried out as loud as he could call, 'G-d d——n, etc.,' but I never stopped running, but run for my master. Coming up to him, I cried out, 'Lord, master, have you sold me?' 'Yes,' was his answer. 'To the trader?' I said. 'Yes,' he answered. 'Why couldn't you sold me to some of the neighbors?' I said. 'I don't know,' he said, in a dry way. With my arms around my master's neck, I begged and prayed him to tell me why he had sold me. The trader and constable was again pretty near. I let go my master and took to my heels to save me. I run about a mile off and run into a mill dam up to my head in water. I kept my head just above and hid the rest part of my body for more than two hours. I had not made up my mind to escape until I had got into the water. I run only to have little more time to breathe before going to Georgia or New Orleans; but I pretty soon made up my mind in the water to try and get to a free State, and go to Canada and make the trial anyhow, but I didn't know which way to travel."

Such great changes in Alfred's prospects having been wrought in so short a while, together with such a fearful looking-for of a fate in the far South more horrid than death, suddenly, as by a miracle, he turns his face in the direction of the North. But the North star, as it were, hid its face from him. For a week he was trying to reach free soil, the rain scarcely ceasing for an hour. The entire journey was extremely discouraging, and many steps had to be taken in vain, hungry and weary. But having the faith of those spoken of in the Scriptures, who wandered about in dens and caves of the earth, being destitute, afflicted and tormented, he endured to the end and arrived safely to the Committee.

He left his father and mother, both slaves, living near Middleburg, in Virginia, not far from where he said his master lived, who went by the name of C. E. Shinn, and followed farming. His master and mistress were said to be members of the "South Baptist Church," and both had borne good characters until within a year or so previous to Alfred's departure. Since then a very serious disagreement had taken place between them, resulting in their separation, a heavy lawsuit, and consequently large outlays. It was this domestic trouble, in Alfred's opinion, that rendered his sale indispensable. Of the merits of the grave charges made by his master against his mistress, Alfred professed to have formed no opinion; he knew, however, that his master blamed a school-master, by the name of Conway, for the sad state of things in his household. Time would fail to tell of the abundant joy Alfred derived from the fact, that his "heels" had saved him from a Southern market. Equally difficult would it be to express the interest felt by the Committee in this passenger and his wonderful hair-breadth escape.

Source: William Still, 1872 (see the Bibliography on p. 203 for complete information).

SOJOURNER TRUTH

Narrative of Sojourner Truth (1850)
(excerpts)

[Olive Gilbert]

Sojourner Truth (born Isabella Baumfree) walked away from her owner when he broke his promise to free her one year before the New York State Emancipation Act took effect. She was directed by Levi Rowe, a Quaker she trusted, to the home of Isaac and Maria Van Wagener, a married couple who "never turned the needy away." When Isabella's former owner arrived to reclaim her, Isaac Van Wagener purchased her services for the rest of the year and paid an extra amount so that she could keep her infant daughter. Isabella's religious life intensified during the year she lived with the Van Wageners, which led her to adopt the name Sojourner Truth, to become an itinerant preacher, and to fight for the abolition of slavery, the achievement of women's rights, and the realization of other social changes.

SLAVEHOLDER'S PROMISES

AFTER EMANCIPATION had been decreed by the State, some years before the time fixed for its consummation, Isabella's master told her if she would do well, and be faithful, he would give her "free papers," one year before she was legally free by statute. In the year 1826, she had a badly diseased hand, which greatly diminished her usefulness; but on the arrival of July 4, 1827, the time specified for her receiving her "free papers," she claimed the fulfilment of her master's promise; but he refused granting it, on account (as he alleged) of the loss he had sustained by her hand. She plead that she had worked all the time, and done many things she was not wholly able to do, although she knew she had been less useful than formerly; but her master remained inflexible. Her very faithfulness probably operated against her now, and he found it less easy than he thought to give up the profits of his faithful Bell, who had so long done him efficient service.

But Isabella inwardly determined that she would remain quietly with him only until she had spun his wool—about one hundred pounds—and then she would leave him, taking the rest of the time to herself. "Ah!" she says, with emphasis that cannot be written, "the slaveholders are TERRIBLE for promising to give you this or that, or such and such a privilege, if you will do thus and so; and when the time of fulfilment comes, and one claims the promise, they, forsooth, recollect nothing of the kind: and you are, like as not, taunted with being a LIAR; or, at best, the slave is accused of not having performed *his* part or condition of the contract.

"Oh!" said she, "I have felt as if I could not live through the *operation* sometimes. Just think of us! *so* eager for our pleasures, and just foolish enough to keep feeding and feeding ourselves up with the idea that we should get what had been thus fairly promised; and when we think it is almost in our hands, find ourselves flatly denied! Just think! how *could* we bear it? Why, there was Charles Brodhead promised his slave Ned, that when harvesting was over, he might go and see his wife, who lived some twenty or thirty miles off. So Ned worked early and late, and as soon as the harvest was all in, he claimed the promised boon. His master said, he had merely told him he 'would *see* if he could go, when the harvest was over; but now he saw that he *could not* go.' But Ned, who still claimed a positive promise, on which he had fully depended, went on cleaning his shoes. His master asked him if he intended going, and on his replying 'yes,' took up a sled-stick that lay near him, and gave him such a blow on the head as broke his skull, killing him dead on the spot. The poor colored people all felt struck down by the blow." Ah! and well they might. Yet it was but one of a long series of bloody, and other most effectual blows, struck against their liberty and their lives.[1] But to return from our digression.

The subject of this narrative was to have been free July 4, 1827, but she continued with her master till the wool was spun, and the heaviest of the "fall's work" closed up, when she concluded to take her freedom into her own hands, and seek her fortune in some other place.

HER ESCAPE

THE QUESTION in her mind, and one not easily solved, now was, "How can I get away?" So, as was her usual custom, she "told God she was afraid to go in the night, and in the day every body would

---

1 Yet no official notice was taken of his more than brutal murder. [Note by Olive Gilbert.]

see her." At length, the thought came to her that she could leave just before the day dawned, and get out of the neighborhood where she was known before the people were much astir. "Yes," said she, fervently, "that's a good thought! Thank you, God, for *that* thought!" So, receiving it as coming direct from God, she acted upon it, and one fine morning, a little before day-break, she might have been seen stepping stealthily away from the rear of Master Dumont's house, her infant on one arm and her wardrobe on the other; the bulk and weight of which, probably, she never found so convenient as on the present occasion, a cotton handkerchief containing both her clothes and her provisions.

As she gained the summit of a high hill, a considerable distance from her master's, the sun offended her by coming forth in all his pristine splendor. She thought it never was so light before; indeed, she thought it much too light. She stopped to look about her, and ascertain if her pursuers were yet in sight. No one appeared, and, for the first time, the question came up for settlement, "Where, and to whom, shall I go?" In all her thoughts of getting away, she had not once asked herself whither she should direct her steps. She sat down, fed her infant, and again turning her thoughts to God, her only help, she prayed him to direct her to some safe asylum. And soon it occurred to her, that there was a man living somewhere in the direction she had been pursuing, by the name of Levi Rowe, whom she had known, and who, she thought, would be likely to befriend her. She accordingly pursued her way to his house, where she found him ready to entertain and assist her, though he was then on his death-bed. He bade her partake of the hospitalities of his house, said he knew of two good places where she might get in, and requested his wife to show her where they were to be found. As soon as she came in sight of the first house, she recollected having seen it and its inhabitants before, and instantly exclaimed, "That's the place for me; I shall stop there." She went there, and found the good people of the house, Mr. and Mrs. Van Wagener, absent, but was kindly received and hospitably entertained by their excellent mother, till the return of her children. When they arrived, she made her case known to them. They listened to her story, assuring her they never turned the needy away, and willingly gave her employment.

She had not been there long before her old master, Dumont, appeared, as she had anticipated; for when she took French leave of him, she resolved not to go too far from him, and not put him to as much trouble in looking her up—for the latter he was sure to do—as

Tom and Jack had done when they ran away from him, a short time before. This was very considerate in her, to say the least, and a proof that "like begets like." He had often considered *her* feelings, though not always, and she was equally considerate.

When her master saw her, he said, "Well, Bell, so you've run away from me." "No, I did not *run away*; I walked away by day-light, and all because you had promised me a year of my time." His reply was, "You must go back with me." Her decisive answer was, "No, I *won't* go back with you." He said, "Well, I shall take the *child*." *This* also was as stoutly negatived.

Mr. Isaac S. Van Wagener then interposed, saying, he had never been in the practice of buying and selling slaves; he did not believe in slavery; but, rather than have Isabella taken back by force, he would buy her services for the balance of the year—for which her master charged twenty dollars, and five in addition for the child. The sum was paid, and her master Dumont departed; but not till he had heard Mr. Van Wagener tell her not to call him master—adding, "there is but *one* master; and he who is *your* master is *my* master." Isabella inquired what she *should* call him? He answered, "call me Isaac Van Wagener, and my wife is Maria Van Wagener." Isabella could not understand this, and thought it a *mighty change*, as it most truly was from a master whose word was law, to simple Isaac S. Van Wagener, who was master to *no* one. With these noble people, who, though they could not be the masters of slaves, were undoubtedly a portion of God's nobility, she resided one year, and from them she derived the name of Van Wagener; he being her last master in the eye of the law, and a slave's surname is ever the same as his master; that is, if he is allowed to have any other name than Tom, Jack, or Guffin. Slaves have sometimes been severely punished for adding their master's name to their own. But when they have no particular title to it, it is no particular offence.

SOURCE: Olive Gilbert. *Narrative of Sojourner Truth*. Mineola, New York: Dover Publications, 1997. [Originally published in 1850.]

HARRIET TUBMAN

Harriet Tubman: The Moses of Her People
(excerpts)

[Sarah Bradford]

Harriet Tubman, the well-known runaway slave from Maryland, repeatedly risked her life to deliver fellow slaves to freedom in the North. Always successful, she became known as "Moses," a reference to the Old Testament prophet who led the Hebrews to freedom from Egypt. Tubman's thoughts about slavery and freedom are revealed by her words to interviewer Benjamin Drew: "I grew up like a neglected weed,—ignorant of liberty, having no experience of it. Then I was not happy or contented: every time I saw a white man I was afraid of being carried away. I had two sisters carried away in a chain-gang,—one of them left two children. We were always uneasy. Now I've been free, I know what a dreadful condition slavery is. I have seen hundreds of escaped slaves, but I never saw one who was willing to go back and be a slave. I have no opportunity to see my friends in my native land. We would rather stay in our native land, if we could be as free there as we are here. I think slavery is the next thing to hell. If a person would send another into bondage, he would, it appears to me, be bad enough to send him into hell, if he could."[1] The following narratives describe Tubman's own escape and her subsequent work as one of the most resolute conductors of the Underground Railroad.

WHAT WAS TO BECOME of the slaves on this plantation now that the master was dead? Were they all to be scattered and sent to different parts of the country? Harriet had many brothers and sisters, all of whom with the exception of the two, who had gone South with the chain-gang, were living on this plantation, or were hired out to planters not far away. The word passed through the cabins that another owner was coming in, and that none of the slaves were to be sold out of the State. This assurance satisfied the others, but it did not satisfy

---

1 Benjamin Drew. *A North-Side View of Slavery. The Refugee: or the Narratives of Fugitive Slaves in Canada. Related by Themselves, with an Account of the History and Condition of the Colored Population of Upper Canada.* Boston: J. P. Jewett and Company, 1856. 30.

Harriet. Already the inward monitor was whispering to her, "Arise, flee for your life!" and in the visions of the night she saw the horse-men coming, and heard the shrieks of women and children, as they were being torn from each other, and hurried off no one knew whither.

And beckoning hands were ever motioning her to come, and she seemed to see a line dividing the land of slavery from the land of freedom, and on the other side of that line she saw lovely white ladies waiting to welcome her, and to care for her. Already in her mind her people were the Israelites in the land of Egypt, while far away to the north somewhere, was the land of Canaan; but had she as yet any prevision that she was to be the Moses who was to be their leader, through clouds of darkness and fear, and fires of tribulation to that promised land? This she never said.

One day there were scared faces seen in the negro quarter, and hurried whispers passed from one to another. No one knew how it had come out, but some one had heard that Harriet and two of her brothers were very soon, perhaps to-day, perhaps to-morrow, to be sent far South with a gang, bought up for plantation work. Harriet was about twenty or twenty-five years old at this time, and the con-stantly recurring idea of escape at sometime, took sudden form that day, and with her usual promptitude of action she was ready to start at once.

She held a hurried consultation with her brothers, in which she so wrought upon their fears, that they expressed themselves as willing to start with her that very night, for that far North, where, could they reach it in safety, freedom awaited them. But she must first give some intimation of her purpose to the friends she was to leave be-hind, so that even if not understood at the time, it might be remem-bered afterward as her intended farewell. Slaves must not be seen talking together, and so it came about that their communication was often made by singing, and the words of their familiar hymns, telling of the heavenly journey, and the land of Canaan, while they did not attract the attention of the masters, conveyed to their brethren and sisters in bondage something more than met the ear. And so she sang, accompanying the words, when for a moment unwatched, with a meaning look to one and another:

> "When dat ar ole chariot comes,
> I'm gwine to lebe you,

> *I'm boun' for de promised land,*
> *Frien's, I'm gwine to lebe you."*

Again, as she passed the doors of the different cabins, she lifted up her well-known voice; and many a dusky face appeared at door or window, with a wondering or scared expression; and thus she continued:

> *"I'm sorry, frien's, to lebe you,*
> *Farewell! oh, farewell!*
> *But I'll meet you in de mornin',*
> *Farewell! oh, farewell!*
>
> *"I'll meet you in de mornin',*
> *When you reach de promised land;*
> *On de oder side of Jordan,*
> *For I'm boun' for de promised land."*

The brothers started with her, but the way was strange, the north was far away, and all unknown, the masters would pursue and recapture them, and their fate would be worse than ever before; and so they broke away from her, and bidding her goodbye, they hastened back to the known horrors of slavery, and the dread of that which was worse.

Harriet was now left alone, but after watching the retreating forms of her brothers, she turned her face toward the north, and fixing her eyes on the guiding star, and committing her way unto the Lord, she started again upon her long, lonely journey. Her farewell song was long remembered in the cabins, and the old mother sat and wept for her lost child. No intimation had been given her of Harriet's intention, for the old woman was of a most impulsive disposition, and her cries and lamentations would have made known to all within hearing Harriet's intended escape. And so, with only the North Star for her guide, our heroine started on the way to liberty. "For," said she, "I had reasoned dis out in my mind; there was one of two things I had a right to, liberty, or death; if I could not have one, I would have de oder; for no man should take me alive; I should fight for my liberty as long as my strength lasted, and when de time came for me to go, de Lord would let dem take me."

And so without money, and without friends, she started on through unknown regions; walking by night, hiding by day, but always conscious of an invisible pillar of cloud by day, and of fire by night, under the guidance of which she journeyed or rested. Without knowing whom to trust, or how near the pursuers might be, she carefully felt her way, and by her native cunning, or by God given wisdom, she managed to apply to the right people for food, and sometimes for shelter; though often her bed was only the cold ground, and her watchers the stars of night.

After many long and weary days of travel, she found that she had passed the magic line, which then divided the land of bondage from the land of freedom. But where were the lovely white ladies whom in her visions she had seen, who, with arms outstretched, welcomed her to their hearts and homes. All these visions proved deceitful: she was more alone than ever; but she had crossed the line; no one could take her now, and she would never call any man "Master" more.

"I looked at my hands," she said, "to see if I was de same person now I was free. Dere was such a glory ober eberything, de sun came like gold trou de trees, and ober de fields, and I felt like I was in heaven." But then came the bitter drop in the cup of joy. She was alone, and her kindred were in slavery, and not one of them had the courage to dare what she had dared. Unless she made the effort to liberate them she would never see them more, or even know their fate.

"I knew of a man," she said, "who was sent to the State Prison for twenty-five years. All these years he was always thinking of his home, and counting by years, months, and days, the time till he should be free, and see his family and friends once more. The years roll on, the time of imprisonment is over, the man is free. He leaves the prison gates, he makes his way to his old home, but his old home is not there. The house in which he had dwelt in his childhood had been torn down, and a new one had been put up in its place; his family were gone, their very name was forgotten, there was no one to take him by the hand to welcome him back to life."

"So it was wid me," said Harriet, "I had crossed de line of which I had so long been dreaming. I was free; but dere was no one to welcome me to de land of freedom, I was a stranger in a strange land, and my home after all was down in de old cabin quarter, wid de ole folks, and my brudders and sisters. But to dis solemn resolution I came; I was free, and dey should be free also; I would make a home for dem in de North, and de Lord helping me, I would bring dem all dere.

Oh, how I prayed den, lying all alone on de cold, damp ground; 'Oh, dear Lord,' I said, 'I haint got no friend but you. Come to my help, Lord, for I'm in trouble!'"

It would be impossible here to give a detailed account of the journeys and labors of this intrepid woman for the redemption of her kindred and friends, during the years that followed. Those years were spent in work, almost by night and day, with the one object of the rescue of her people from slavery. All her wages were laid away with this sole purpose, and as soon as a sufficient amount was secured, she disappeared from her Northern home, and as suddenly and mysteriously she appeared some dark night at the door of one of the cabins on a plantation, where a trembling band of fugitives, forewarned as to time and place, were anxiously awaiting their deliverer. Then she piloted them North, traveling by night, hiding by day, scaling the mountains, fording the rivers, threading the forests, lying concealed as the pursuers passed them. She, carrying the babies, drugged with paregoric, in a basket on her arm. So she went nineteen times, and so she brought away over three hundred pieces of living and breathing "property," with God given souls.

The way was so toilsome over the rugged mountain passes, that often the men who followed her would give out, and foot-sore, and bleeding, they would drop on the ground, groaning that they could not take another step. They would lie there and die, or if strength came back, they would return on their steps, and seek their old homes again. Then the revolver carried by this bold and daring pioneer, would come out, while pointing it at their heads she would say, "Dead niggers tell no tales; you go on or die!" And by this heroic treatment she compelled them to drag their weary limbs along on their northward journey.

But the pursuers were after them. A reward of $40,000 was offered by the slave-holders of the region from whence so many slaves had been spirited away, for the head of the woman who appeared so mysteriously, and enticed away their property, from under the very eyes of its owners. Our sagacious heroine has been in the car, having sent her frightened party round by some so-called "Under-ground Railway," and has heard this advertisement, which was posted over her head, read by others of the passengers. She never could read or write herself, but knowing that suspicion would be likely to fall upon any black woman traveling North, she would turn at the next station, and journey towards the South. Who would suspect a fugitive with such a price set upon her head, of rushing at railway speed into the jaws of destruction? With a daring almost heedless, she went even to the very village where she would be most likely to meet one of the masters to whom she had been hired; and having stopped at the Market and bought a pair of live fowls, she went along the street with her sun-bonnet well over her face, and with the bent and decrepit air of an aged woman. Suddenly on turning a corner, she spied her old master coming towards her. She pulled the string which tied the legs of the chickens; they began to flutter and scream, and as her master passed, she was stooping and busily engaged in attending to the fluttering fowls. And he went on his way, little thinking that he was brushing the very garments of the woman who had dared to steal herself, and others of his belongings.

SOURCE: Sarah Bradford. *Harriet Tubman: The Moses of Her People*. Mineola, New York: Dover Publications, 2004. [Originally published in 1869; these excerpts are from the second edition published in 1886.]

HARRIET TUBMAN (CONTINUED)

"Moses" Arrives with Six Passengers

[William Still]

... HARRIET TUBMAN had been their "Moses," but not in the sense that Andrew Johnson was the "Moses of the colored people." She had faithfully gone down into Egypt, and had delivered these six bondmen by her own heroism. Harriet was a woman of no pretensions, indeed, a more ordinary specimen of humanity could hardly be found among the most unfortunate-looking farm hands of the South. Yet, in point of courage, shrewdness and disinterested exertions to rescue her fellow-men, by making personal visits to Maryland among the slaves, she was without her equal.

Her success was wonderful. Time and again she made successful visits to Maryland on the Underground Rail Road, and would be absent for weeks, at a time, running daily risks while making preparations for herself and passengers. Great fears were entertained for her safety, but she seemed wholly devoid of personal fear. The idea of being captured by slave-hunters or slave-holders, seemed never to enter her mind. She was apparently proof against all adversaries. While she thus manifested such utter personal indifference, she was much more watchful with regard to those she was piloting. Half of her time, she had the appearance of one asleep, and would actually sit down by the road-side and go first asleep when on her errands of mercy through the South, yet, she would not suffer one of her party to whimper once, about "giving out and going back," however wearied they might be from hard travel day and night. She had a very short and pointed rule or law of her own, which implied death to any who talked of giving out and going back. Thus, in an emergency she would give all to understand that "times were very critical and therefore no foolishness would be indulged in on the road." That several who were rather weak-kneed and faint-hearted were greatly invigorated by Harriet's blunt and positive manner and threat of extreme measures, there could be no doubt.

After having once enlisted, "they had to go through or die." Of course Harriet was supreme, and her followers generally had full faith in her, and would back up any word she might utter. So when she said to them that "a live runaway could do great harm by going back, but that a dead one could tell no secrets," she was sure to have obedience. Therefore, none had to die as traitors on the "middle passage." It is obvious enough, however, that her success in going into Maryland as she did, was attributable to her adventurous spirit and utter disregard of consequences. Her like it is probable was never known before or since. On examining the six passengers who came by this arrival they were thus recorded:

DECEMBER 29TH, 1854—John is twenty years of age, chestnut color, of spare build and smart. He fled from a farmer, by the name of John Campbell Henry, who resided at Cambridge, Dorchester Co., Maryland. On being interrogated relative to the character of his master, John gave no very amiable account of him. He testified that he was a "hard man" and that he "owned about one hundred and forty slaves and sometimes he would sell," etc. John was one of the slaves who were "hired out." He "desired to have the privilege of hunting his own master." His desire was not granted. Instead of meekly submitting, John felt wronged, and made this his reason for running away. This looked pretty spirited on the part of one so young as John. The Committee's respect for him was not a little increased, when they heard him express himself.

Benjamin was twenty-eight years of age, chestnut color, medium size, and shrewd. He was the so-called property of Eliza Ann Brodins, who lived near Buckstown, in Maryland. Ben did not hesitate to say, in unqualified terms, that his mistress was "very devilish." He considered his charges, proved by the fact that three slaves (himself one of them) were required to work hard and fare meagerly, to support his mistress' family in idleness and luxury. The Committee paid due attention to his ex parte statement, and was obliged to conclude that his argument, clothed in common and homely language, was forcible, if not eloquent, and that he was well worthy of aid. Benjamin left his parents besides one sister, Mary Ann Williamson, who wanted to come away on the Underground Rail Road.

Henry left his wife, Harriet Ann, to be known in future by the name of "Sophia Brown." He was a fellow-servant of Ben's, and one of the supports of Eliza A. Brodins.

Henry was only twenty-two, but had quite an insight into matters and things going on among slaves and slave-holders generally, in country life. He was the father of two small children, whom he had to leave behind.

Peter was owned by George Wenthrop, a farmer, living near Cambridge, Md. In answer to the question, how he had been used, he said "hard." Not a pleasant thought did he entertain respecting his master, save that he was no longer to demand the sweat of Peter's brow. Peter left parents, who were free; he was born before they were emancipated, consequently, he was retained in bondage.

Jane, aged twenty-two, instead of regretting that she had unadvisedly left a kind mistress and indulgent master, who had afforded her necessary comforts, affirmed that her master, "Rash Jones, was the worst man in the country." The Committee were at first disposed to doubt her sweeping statement, but when they heard particularly how she had been treated, they thought Catharine had good ground for all that she said. Personal abuse and hard usage, were the common lot of poor slave girls.

Robert was thirty-five years of age, of a chestnut color, and well made. His report was similar to that of many others. He had been provided with plenty of hard drudgery—hewing of wood and drawing of water, and had hardly been treated as well as a gentleman would treat a dumb brute. His feelings, therefore, on leaving his old master and home, were those of an individual who had been unjustly in prison for a dozen years and had at last regained his liberty.

The civilization, religion, and customs under which Robert and his companions had been raised, were, he thought, "very wicked." Although these travelers were all of the field-hand order, they were, nevertheless, very promising, and they anticipated better days in Canada. Good advice was proffered them on the subject of temperance, industry, education, etc. Clothing, food and money were also given them to meet their wants, and they were sent on their way rejoicing.

SOURCE: William Still, 1872 (see the Bibliography on p. 203 for complete information).

PHILIP YOUNGER

"Escape from Alabama Is Almost Impossible"

[Benjamin Drew]

Younger explains that his escape from Alabama was by the skin of his teeth. Yet his "freedom" in the Northern states was precarious and, especially after the Fugitive Slave Law of 1850, dangerous, so he fled to Ontario: "I had rather starve to death here, being a free man, than to have plenty in slavery." The abolitionist Drew (born in Boston in 1812) collected and in 1856 published, with money donated by the Canadian Anti-Slavery Society, hundreds of his interviews of refugee slaves in Canada.

I SERVED IN SLAVERY fifty-five years, and am now nearly seventy-two years old. I was born in Virginia, went, at ten, to Tennessee; at twelve, to Alabama: was, all the time, body servant of a military man. My treatment was various,—sometimes rough,—sometimes good. Many awful scenes I have seen while moving about. I have had to put chains on men, myself, to go into a chain gang: I have seen men whipped to death,—have seen them die. I have ridden hundreds of miles in Alabama, and have heard the whip going, all along from farm to farm, while they were weighing out cotton.

In Alabama, the patrols go out in companies at about dark, and ride nearly all night. If they meet a colored man without a pass, it is thirty-nine lashes; but they don't stop for the law, and if they tie a man up, he is very well off if he gets only two hundred. If there is a party assembled at the quarters, they rush in half drunk, and thrash round with their sticks, perhaps before they look at a pass,—all must be whipped unless they rush out: I can't paint it so bad as 'tis. Sometimes a stout man will fight his way through.

As a general thing the treatment on the plantations in Alabama is very hard. Once in a while a man is kind, as kindness is out there, and then he is hated by all the other masters. They say "his niggers spoil our niggers." These servants are not allowed on the other plantations at all,—if caught there, they will put as much on them as they can bear. I have as good a chance to know as any man there,—I have travelled there on the plantations,—I was there before the country was opened,—at the war,—and have seen it grow up by the colored man's labor. I have seen miles of fences around plantations, where I had been through woods with the surveyors. Escape from Alabama is almost impossible,—if a man escapes, it is by the skin of his teeth.

There was a free man in Huntsville—a barber,—whose wife—a free woman—was taken by a patrol, as she was walking out at dark, and put in jail, just to disgrace her,—as she was in a little better standing than the patrol was. Her husband grumbled about it,—a rumpus was made, and people collected. It was in front of a tavern door. The folks then called out, "Shoot the d—d nigger! shoot him!" The patrol stabbed him with a bowie-knife, and he fell in the street. He was carried in, and a doctor dressed the wound, but he was never a sound man afterwards.

I hired my time, and made some money. I bought my wife's freedom first, and sent her away. I got off by skill. I have children and grandchildren in slavery.

I had rather starve to death here, being a free man, than to have plenty in slavery. I cannot be a slave any more,—nobody could hold me as a slave now, except in irons. Old as I am, I would rather face the Russian fire, or die at the point of the sword, than go into slavery.

We are placed in different circumstances here—some drag along, without doing much,—some are doing well. I have a house; I have taken up fifty acres of land, and have made the payments as required; I have other property besides. Here is Henry Blue, worth twelve thousand dollars; Syddles, worth a fortune; Lucky, worth a very handsome fortune; Ramsay, a great deal of land and other property, at least twelve thousand dollars; all these were slaves at some time. And there are many others wealthy, through their own skill and industry.

Before I came here, I resided in the free States. I came here in consequence of the passage of the Fugitive Slave Bill. It was a hardship at first; but I feel better here—more like a man—I know I am—than in the States. I suffer from want of education. I manage by skill and experience and industry—but it is as if feeling my way in the dark.

SOURCE: Benjamin Drew. *A North-Side View of Slavery. The Refugee: or the Narratives of Fugitive Slaves in Canada. Related by Themselves, with an Account of the History and Condition of the Colored Population of Upper Canada.* Boston: J. P. Jewett and Company, 1856.

THE FUGITIVE SLAVE ACT OF 1850

"An Act Respecting Fugitives from Justice, and Persons Escaping from the Service of Their Masters"

The Fugitive Slave Act of 1850 was embraced by slave-owners and their sympathizers but despised by slaves, abolitionists and lovers of freedom. The act required the capture and return of escaped slaves, regardless of where in the United States they were found, and made it illegal to "aid, abet, or assist" them. This law was regularly broken by abolitionists, caused fugitive slaves to live in constant fear of recapture and led to the abduction of free Blacks, who were often sold into slavery in the South. It was repealed by Congress in 1864.

SECTION 1

Be it enacted by the Senate and House of Representatives of the United States of America in Congress assembled, That the persons who have been, or may hereafter be, appointed commissioners, in virtue of any act of Congress, by the Circuit Courts of the United States, and Who, in consequence of such appointment, are authorized to exercise the powers that any justice of the peace, or other magistrate of any of the United States, may exercise in respect to offenders for any crime or offense against the United States, by arresting, imprisoning, or bailing the same under and by the virtue of the thirty-third section of the act of the twenty-fourth of September seventeen hundred and eighty-nine, entitled "An Act to establish the judicial courts of the United States" shall be, and are hereby, authorized and required to exercise and discharge all the powers and duties conferred by this act.

SECTION 2

And be it further enacted, That the Superior Court of each organized Territory of the United States shall have the same power to appoint commissioners to take acknowledgments of bail and affidavits, and to take depositions of witnesses in civil causes, which is now possessed by the Circuit Court of the United States; and all commissioners who shall hereafter be appointed for such purposes by the Superior Court of any organized Territory of the United States, shall possess all the powers, and exercise all the duties, conferred by law upon the commissioners appointed by the Circuit Courts of the United States for similar purposes, and shall moreover exercise and discharge all the powers and duties conferred by this act.

SECTION 3

And be it further enacted, That the Circuit Courts of the United States shall from time to time enlarge the number of the commissioners, with a view to afford reasonable facilities to reclaim fugitives from labor, and to the prompt discharge of the duties imposed by this act.

SECTION 4

And be it further enacted, That the commissioners above named shall have concurrent jurisdiction with the judges of the Circuit and District Courts of the United States, in their respective circuits and districts within the several States, and the judges of the Superior Courts of the Territories, severally and collectively, in term-time and vacation; shall grant certificates to such claimants, upon satisfactory proof being made, with authority to take and remove such fugitives from service or labor, under the restrictions herein contained, to the State or Territory from which such persons may have escaped or fled.

SECTION 5

And be it further enacted, That it shall be the duty of all marshals and deputy marshals to obey and execute all warrants and precepts issued under the provisions of this act, when to them directed; and should any marshal or deputy marshal refuse to receive such warrant, or other process, when tendered, or to use all proper means diligently to execute the same, he shall, on conviction thereof, be fined in the sum of one thousand dollars, to the use of such claimant, on the motion of such claimant, by the Circuit or District Court for the district of such marshal; and after arrest of such fugitive, by such marshal or his deputy, or whilst at any time in his custody under the provisions of this act, should such fugitive escape, whether with or without the assent of such marshal or his deputy, such marshal shall be liable, on his official bond, to be prosecuted for the benefit of such claimant, for the full value of the service or labor of said fugitive in the State, Territory, or District whence he escaped: and the better to enable the said commissioners, when thus appointed, to execute their duties faithfully and efficiently, in conformity with the requirements of the Constitution of the United States and of this act, they are hereby authorized and empowered, within their counties respectively, to appoint, in writing under their hands, any one or more suitable persons, from time to time, to execute all such warrants and other process as may be issued by them in the lawful performance of their respective duties; with authority to such commissioners, or the persons to be appointed by them, to execute process as aforesaid, to summon and call to their aid the bystanders, or posse comitatus of the proper county, when necessary to ensure a faithful observance of the clause of the Constitution referred to, in conformity with the provisions of this act; and all good citizens are hereby commanded to aid and assist in the prompt and efficient execution of this law, whenever their services may be required, as aforesaid, for that purpose; and said warrants shall run, and be executed by said officers, any where in the State within which they are issued.

SECTION 6

And be it further enacted, That when a person held to service or labor in any State or Territory of the United States, has heretofore or shall hereafter escape into another State or Territory of the United States, the person or persons to whom such service or labor may be due, or his, her, or their agent or attorney, duly authorized, by power of attorney, in writing, acknowledged and certified under the seal of some legal officer or court of the State or Territory in which the same may be executed, may pursue and reclaim such fugitive person, either by procuring a warrant from some one of the courts, judges, or commissioners aforesaid, of the proper circuit, district, or county, for the apprehension of such fugitive from service or labor, or by seizing and arresting such fugitive, where the same can be done without process, and by taking, or causing such person to be taken, forthwith before such court, judge, or commissioner, whose duty it shall be to hear and determine the case of such claimant in a summary manner; and upon satisfactory proof being made, by deposition or affidavit, in writing, to be taken and certified by such court, judge, or commissioner, or by other satisfactory testimony, duly taken and certified by some court, magistrate, justice of the peace, or other legal officer authorized to administer an oath and take depositions under the laws of the State or Territory from which such person owing service or labor may have escaped, with a certificate of such magistracy or other authority, as aforesaid, with the seal of the proper court or officer thereto attached, which seal shall be sufficient to establish the competency of the proof, and with proof, also by affidavit, of the identity of the person whose service or labor is claimed to be due as aforesaid, that the person so arrested does in fact owe service or labor to the person or persons claiming him or her, in the State or Territory from which such fugitive may have escaped as aforesaid, and that said person escaped, to make out and deliver to such claimant, his or her agent or attorney, a certificate setting forth the substantial facts as to the service or labor due from such fugitive to the claimant, and of his or her escape from the State or Territory in which he or she was arrested, with authority to such claimant, or his or her agent or attorney, to use such reasonable force and restraint as may be necessary, under the circumstances of the case, to take and remove such fugitive person back to the State or Territory whence he or she may have escaped as aforesaid. In no trial or hearing under this act shall the testimony of such alleged fugitive be admitted in evidence; and the certificates in this and the first [fourth] section mentioned, shall be conclusive of the right of the person or persons in whose favor granted, to remove such fugitive to the State or Territory from which he escaped, and shall prevent all molestation of such person or persons by any process issued by any court, judge, magistrate, or other person whomsoever.

SECTION 7

And be it further enacted, That any person who shall knowingly and willingly obstruct, hinder, or prevent such claimant, his agent or attorney, or any person or persons lawfully assisting him, her, or them, from arresting such a fugitive from service or labor, either with or without process as aforesaid, or shall rescue, or attempt to rescue, such fugitive from service or labor, from the custody of such claimant, his or her agent or attorney, or other person or persons lawfully assisting as aforesaid, when so arrested, pursuant to the authority herein given and declared; or shall aid, abet, or assist such person so owing service or labor as aforesaid, directly or indirectly, to escape from such claimant, his agent or attorney, or other person or persons legally authorized as aforesaid; or shall harbor or conceal such fugitive, so as to prevent the discovery and arrest of such person, after notice or knowledge of the fact that such person was a fugitive from service or labor as aforesaid, shall, for either of said offences, be subject to a fine not exceeding one thousand dollars, and imprisonment not exceeding six months, by indictment and conviction before the District Court of the United States for the district in which such offence may have been committed, or before the proper court of criminal jurisdiction, if committed within any one of the organized Territories of the United States; and shall moreover forfeit and pay, by way of civil damages to the party injured by such illegal conduct, the sum of one thousand dollars for each fugitive so lost as aforesaid, to be recovered by action of debt, in any of the District or Territorial Courts aforesaid, within whose jurisdiction the said offence may have been committed.

SECTION 8

And be it further enacted, That the marshals, their deputies, and the clerks of the said District and Territorial Courts, shall be paid, for their services, the like fees as may be allowed for similar services in other cases; and where such services are rendered exclusively in the arrest, custody, and delivery of the fugitive to the claimant, his or her agent or attorney, or where such supposed fugitive may be discharged out of custody for the want of sufficient proof as aforesaid, then such fees are to be paid in whole by such claimant, his or her agent or attorney; and in all cases where the proceedings are before a commissioner, he shall be entitled to a fee of ten dollars in full for his services in each case, upon the delivery of the said certificate to the claimant, his agent or attorney; or a fee of five dollars in cases where the proof shall not, in the opinion of such commissioner, warrant such certificate and delivery, inclusive of all services incident to such arrest and examination, to be paid, in either case, by the claimant, his or her agent or attorney. The person or persons authorized to execute the process to be issued by such commissioner for the arrest and detention of fugitives from service or labor as aforesaid, shall also be entitled to a fee of five dollars each for each person he or they may arrest, and take before any commissioner as aforesaid, at the instance and request of such claimant, with such other fees as may be deemed reasonable by such commissioner for such other additional services as may be necessarily performed by him or them; such as attending at the examination, keeping the fugitive in custody, and providing him with food and lodging during his detention, and until the final determination of such commissioners; and, in general, for performing such other duties as may be required by such claimant, his or her attorney or agent, or commissioner in the premises, such fees to be made up in conformity with the fees usually charged by the officers of the courts of justice within the proper district or county, as near as may be practicable, and paid by such claimants, their agents or attorneys, whether such supposed fugitives from service or labor be ordered to be delivered to such claimant by the final determination of such commissioner or not.

SECTION 9

And be it further enacted, That, upon affidavit made by the claimant of such fugitive, his agent or attorney, after such certificate has been issued, that he has reason to apprehend that such fugitive will he rescued by force from his or their possession before he can be taken beyond the limits of the State in which the arrest is made, it shall be the duty of the officer making the arrest to retain such fugitive in his custody, and to remove him to the State whence he fled, and there to deliver him to said claimant, his agent, or attorney. And to this end, the officer aforesaid is hereby authorized and required to employ so many persons as he may deem necessary to overcome such force, and to retain them in his service so long as circumstances may require. The said officer and his assistants, while so employed, to receive the same compensation, and to be allowed the same expenses, as are now allowed by law for transportation of criminals, to be certified by the judge of the district within which the arrest is made, and paid out of the treasury of the United States.

SECTION 10

And be it further enacted, That when any person held to service or labor in any State or Territory, or in the District of Columbia, shall escape therefrom, the party to whom such service or labor shall be due, his, her, or their agent or attorney, may apply to any court of record therein, or judge thereof in vacation, and make satisfactory proof to such court, or judge in vacation, of the escape aforesaid, and that the person escaping owed service or labor to such party. Whereupon the court shall cause a record to be made of the matters so proved, and also a general description of the person so escaping, with such convenient certainty as may be; and a transcript of such record, authenticated by the attestation of the clerk and of the seal of the said court, being produced in any other State, Territory, or district in which the person so escaping may be found, and being exhibited to any judge, commissioner, or other office, authorized by the law of the United States to cause persons escaping from service or labor to be delivered up, shall be held and taken to be full and conclusive evidence of the fact of escape, and that the service or labor of the person escaping is due to the party in such record mentioned. And upon the production by the said party of other and further evidence if necessary, either oral or by affidavit, in addition to what is contained in the said record of the identity of the person escaping, he or she shall be delivered up to the claimant. And the said court, commissioner, judge, or other person authorized by this act to grant certificates to claimants or fugitives, shall, upon the production of the record and other evidences aforesaid, grant to such claimant a certificate of his right to take any such person identified and proved to be owing service or labor as aforesaid, which certificate shall authorize such claimant to seize or arrest and transport such person to the State or Territory from which he escaped: Provided, That nothing herein contained shall be construed as requiring the production of a transcript of such record as evidence as aforesaid. But in its absence the claim shall be heard and determined upon other satisfactory proofs, competent in law.

APPROVED, SEPTEMBER 18, 1850.

SOURCE: United States Statutes at Large.

BIBLIOGRAPHY

David W. Blight, editor. *Passages to Freedom: The Underground Railroad in History and Memory*. Washington, D.C.: Smithsonian Books, 2004.

Charles L. Blockson, editor. *The Underground Railroad: First-Person Narratives of Escapes to Freedom in the North*. New York: Prentice Hall Press, 1987.

Fergus M. Bordewich. *Bound for Canaan: The Underground Railroad and the War for the Soul of America*. New York: HarperCollins, 2005.

Sarah Bradford. *Harriet Tubman: The Moses of Her People*. Introduction by Butler A. Jones. Mineola, New York: Dover Publications, 2004. (Originally published as *Scenes in the Life of Harriet Tubman* in Auburn, New York, in 1869.)

William Wells Brown. *Narrative of William Wells Brown, a Fugitive Slave*. Boston: The Anti-Slavery Office, 1847.

Levi Coffin. *Reminiscences of Levi Coffin, the Reputed President of the Underground Railroad; Being a Brief History of the Labors of a Lifetime in Behalf of the Slave, with the Stories of Numerous Fugitives, Who Gained Their Freedom Through His Instrumentality, and Many Other Incidents*. Second edition. Cincinnati: Robert Clarke and Company, 1880.

Documenting the American South. Primary Resources for the Study of Southern History, Literature and Culture. The University Library of the University of North Carolina at Chapel Hill. http://docsouth.unc.edu/index.html

Frederick Douglass. *Narrative of the Life of Frederick Douglass*. Mineola, New York: Dover Publications, 1995. (Original edition published in Boston by the Anti-Slavery Office, 1845.)

Benjamin Drew. *A North-Side View of Slavery. The Refugee: or the Narratives of Fugitive Slaves in Canada. Related by Themselves, with an Account of the History and Condition of the Colored Population of Upper Canada*. Boston: J. P. Jewett and Company, 1856.

Federal Writers' Project American Guide (Negro Writers' Unit). Pearl Randolph, Field Worker. Jacksonville, Florida, December 18, 1936. [Library of Congress website: "*Born in Slavery: Slave Narratives from the Federal Writers' Project, 1936–1938* contains more than 2,300 first-person accounts of slavery and 500 black-and-white photographs of former slaves. These narratives were collected in the 1930s as part of the Federal Writers' Project of the Works Progress Administration (WPA) and assembled and microfilmed in 1941 as the seventeen-volume *Slave Narratives: A Folk History of Slavery in the United States from Interviews with Former Slaves.*"]

Josiah Henson. *The Life of Josiah Henson, Formerly a Slave, Now an Inhabitant of Canada, as Narrated by Himself.* Boston: Arthur D. Phelps, 1849.

Harriet Jacobs. *Incidents in the Life of a Slave Girl.* Mineola, New York: Dover Publications, 2001. (Original edition published in Boston in 1861.)

Eber M. Pettit. *Sketches in the History of the Underground Railroad Comprising Many Thrilling Incidents of the Escape of Fugitives from Slavery, and the Perils of Those Who Aided Them.* Fredonia, New York: W. McKinstry and Son, 1879.

Wilbur H. Siebert. *The Underground Railroad from Slavery to Freedom: A Comprehensive History.* Mineola, New York: Dover Publications. 2006. Originally published by the Macmillan Company, New York, 1898.

William Still. *The Underground Rail Road: A Record of Facts, Authentic Narratives, Letters &c., Narrating the Hardships, Hair-breadth Escapes and Death Struggles of the Slaves in Their Efforts for Freedom, as Related by Themselves and Others, or Witnessed by the Author; Together with Sketches of Some of the Largest Stockholders, and Most Liberal Aiders and Advisers of the Road.* Philadelphia: Porter and Coates, 1872.

William Still. *The Underground Railroad: Authentic Narratives and First-Hand Accounts.* Edited by Ian Frederick Finseth. Mineola, New York: Dover Publications, 2007.

Jesse Torrey. *A Portraiture of Domestic Slavery, in the United States: With Reflections on the Practicability of Restoring the Moral Rights of the Slave, without Impairing the Legal Privileges of the Possessor; and a Project of a Colonial Asylum for Free Persons of Colour: Including Memoirs of Facts on the Interior Traffic in Slaves, and on Kidnapping.* Philadelphia, 1817.

Carter G. Woodson. *The Mind of the Negro: As Reflected in Letters During the Crisis, 1800–1860.* Introduction by Bob Blaisdell. Mineola, New York: Dover Publications, 2013.